making love

PATRICIA E. RALEY

making love

AVON
PUBLISHERS OF BARD, CAMELOT, DISCUS AND FLARE BOOKS

Grateful acknowledgment is made for permission to use the following material:

Excerpt from Breakfast of Champions: Or Goodbye Blue Monday: Copyright © 1973 by Kurt Vonnegut, Jr. A Seymour Lawrence Book/Delacorte Press. Used by permission.

Photograph on page forty-eight courtesy of Susan Gilbert.

Excerpt from Portnoy's Complaint: Copyright © 1968 by Philip Roth. Used by permission of the publisher, Random House, Inc.

Photograph on page fifty-one reproduced by permission.

Excerpt from Advertisements for Myself: Copyright © 1959 by Norman Mailer. Reprinted by permission of the publisher, G.P. Putnam's Sons.

Excerpt from Fear of Flying by Erica Jong: Copyright © 1973 by Erica Mann Jong. Reprinted by permission of Holt, Rinehart and Winston, Publishers.

"Le Sommeil" by Gustave Courbet used through the courtesy of Musée de Petit Palais, Paris. Photograph reproduced by permission of ETS J. E. Bulloz, Paris.

"3 Men and 3 Women Convicted of Rape": Copyright © 1975 Los Angeles Times. Reprinted by permission.

Excerpt from Sexus: Copyright © 1962, 1965 by Henry Miller, vol. 1. Reprinted by permission of the publisher, Grove Press, Inc.

"Black Children" by Gerald Gooch: Courtesy of the artist.

Excerpt from Ideal Marriage, Its Physiology and Technique by Theodor Henrik van de Velde: Copyright © 1965 by Stella Brown, translator. Revised Edition. Reprinted by permission of the publisher, Random House, Inc.

Illustration on page forty-nine from Thérèse Philosophe, courtesy of Donald Lunde, M.D.

"Simon and Vera" by Rupfer: from Die Weiberherrschaft in der geschichte der menshhert (1930, 1931) by Alfred King, vol. 2. Published by Verlag fur Kulturforschung, Vienna. Every effort has been made to locate the proprietor of this material. If the proprietor will write to the publisher, formal arrangements will be made.

Excerpt from Psychopathia Sexualis by Richard von Krafft-Ebing: Translated by Franklin W. Klaf. Reprinted by permission of the publisher, Crosby Lockwood Staples, Granada Publishing.

Illustration by Franz von Bayros: Fleurettens Purpurschnecke, Vienna, privately printed.

Excerpt from "The Truth about Gore Vidal—Right from Gore Vidal" by Curtis Bill Pepper: Reprinted by permission of Julian Bach Literary Agency, Inc. Copyright © 1974 by Conde Nast Publications, Inc.

Woodcut from Count Alexis, his memoirs, 1932. Privately printed.

Cover design by Casado Design

AVON BOOKS
A division of
The Hearst Corporation
105 Madison Avenue
New York, New York 10016

Text Copyright © 1976 by Patricia E. Raley
Photographs Copyright © 1976 by The Dial Press
Published by arrangement with The Dial Press
Library of Congress Catalog Card Number: 76-22765
ISBN: 0-380-48819-1

First Avon Printing: March 1980

AVON TRADEMARK REG. U.S. PAT. OFF. AND IN OTHER COUNTRIES.
MARCA REGISTRADA, HECHO EN U.S.A.

Printed in the U.S.A.

10 9 8 7 6 5

First I want to thank Charlotte Sheedy for her steady
enthusiasm about this book and her unflagging trust in me.
I am also indebted to Sally Bowie, Lilla Weinberger and Lawrence Zempel for
their generous suggestions on the manuscript; to Joyce Engelson, Warren Wallerstein
and Jack Ribik for their conviction and sensitivity in producing and
designing this book; and most of all to Ronald without whom this
book would have been possible but not much fun.

Contents

ACKNOWLEDGMENTS   (vi)

FOREWORD TO TEXT by David E. Scharff, M.D.   (viii)

INTRODUCTION   (2)

What Is Sex Therapy?
Who Needs This Book?
Why Not Go to a Sex Therapist?
How Do You Use This Book?

Fantasy   (8)

What Is a Fantasy?
What Is a Sex Fantasy?
  Fantasy-Completion Exercises
What Can You Learn from Sex Fantasy?
To Fantasize or Not to Fantasize?

A Sex History   (22)

Your Earliest Memories
Midchildhood, When You Were Five to Ten
Puberty and Early Adolescence
Your First "Sexual" Encounter
Your First Long Affair or Marriage
Now a Review of Your Twenties
Now You Are in Your Early Thirties
Put Yourself in Your Late Thirties
Now You Are in Your Forties
From About Fifty to Around Sixty
Now You Are Past Sixty-Five
Eighty and Beyond

An Attitude Survey   (46)

Measuring Up
Toujours Gai
Autoeroticism
The First Step
The Tie That Binds
Up Yours
The Monthlies
Some of My Best Friends . . .
Rape
Naked Lunch
Child's Play
Carnal Knowledge
Mother's Milk
A Close-Knit Family
Porno
Open and Closed
The Birds and the Bees

Love
Togetherness

Your Body   (70)

The Everyperson Gallery
Everyperson vs. The Real You
More Everyperson
Where Do Feelings About Body Image Come From?
Body Image and Self-Image

Sexual Anatomy and Physiology   (84)

The Externals
  Start with Your Anus
  On to Labia and Scrotum
  Inside the Scrotal Sac
  Inside the Labia
  Inside the Vagina
  The Clitoris
  The Penis
  The Breasts
The Internals
  The Female
  The Male
The Sex Hormones
Quickie Quiz
Control of Birth—Conception and Contraception
  Conception
  Contraception

Arousal   (110)

Barriers to Arousal
Turning On
Turning Off
Turning On to Yourself
A Guide to a Guide
Guide for Women
Guide for Men

Orgasm   (124)

Expectations
  Orgasm for You
  Analyzing Your Orgasms
The Aftermath
The Myths

Nonorgasmic Women   (138)

Sexual Troubles
  Never Orgasmic
  Unpredictably Orgasmic

Nonorgasmic Coitally
Sexual Aversion
Medical Troubles
 Pain
 Worn Out
 Pregnancy
 Vaginismus
 Anatomy
Psychological Troubles
 Impinging Past Experience
 Feminine Mystique
 Doomsaying
 Self-consciousness

Impotent Men (160)

Some Practical Suggestions for the Impotent Man
 A Daily Regimen
Psychological Issues
 Alcohol and Fear of Failure
 Premature Ejaculation and
  Fear of Failure
 Impinging Past Experience
 Relationship with Partner
 Bad Advice
Physical Problems
 Aging
 Medication
 Infection
 Pain
 Run-Down

Being Together Without Falling Apart (181)

Beyond the Big O
 Sensate Focus Exercises, First Week
 Sensate Focus Exercises, Second Week
Falling Apart
 Faking
 Testing Your Faking
Coming Too Fast—Men
Coming Too Fast—Women
Not Coming Fast Enough—Women
Not Coming Fast Enough—Men
Coming Together
Coming Apart

Words, Words, Words (208)

Finding a Sexual Vocabulary
 A Sexual Lexicon
Starting a Sexual Conversation
Practicing Sexual Communication

Some Refinements of Sexual Communication
Some Extensions of Sexual Communication
A Test of What Has Been Communicated

Connective Bargaining (220)

Case History A: In Which Frequency Is an Issue
Case History B: In Which the Problem Is Oral Sex
Case History C: In Which One Partner Mastur-
 bates to the Consternation of the Other
Case History D: Another Look at Oral Sex
Case History E: A Petty Problem?
Case History F: In Which Anal Sex Is Aired
Case History G: Melissa and Theresa and Melaney

Running Battles (241)

Power Plays
Scapegoating
Warfare
Sexual Surrogates
To the Rescue

An Erotic Life (252)

The Erotic Life
 Voyeurism
 Gamesmanship
 Consumption
 Contact Sports
 Inanimate Eros

CONCLUSION (266)
INDEX (270)

Foreword to Text

Since the ground-breaking work on sexuality by Masters and Johnson there has been no scarcity of literature on sex and sex therapy. Although their own works are mainly technical, there has been a wellspring of books on sexuality which summarize their work or report on the experience of patients in therapy. Other material urges people to join in or reports on how many of us have done so and with what results.

What then, does this book offer? In my view it fills an important niche. It combines a liberal, sympathetic attitude about sex and its role in human relationships with a number of new techniques in sex education and sex therapy. The result of this synthesis is a tool for those who would like to examine themselves, take stock, and use the book as a kind of personal companion in exploring new worlds—inner worlds, sexual worlds, and interpersonal worlds. It presents a therapeutic attitude to the self and to relationships, lending support and encouragement to the task of critically examining the delicate area of personal and sexual limitations.

Sex therapists and educators perform a similar function when they act as sympathetic, experienced and objective guides, and thereby provide a supportive environment for questioning sexual attitudes and practices. Their aim is to provide a climate which encourages sexual, emotional, and interpersonal growth.

Patricia Raley's book goes a long way to providing much of what we ask of an experienced therapist and educator. It supports, questions, guides. It gently probes. To the degree a book can substitute for a live helping person, I believe it does so. It seems to come alive as a companion on a journey—a journey which may at some times be arduous, at others joyful. The book reflects the author's warmth, humor, patience, tolerance and experience in the areas of sexuality and human relationships.

Making Love also offers a fresh view of sex, and a new window on life with another. Many of us get stuck in sexual development early on—bound by cultural attitudes from our growing up, by lack of information, even by misinformation. Bad habits cover the original minor difficulties; partners in love grow apart in sex and risk embitterment; and simple problems grow, over years, into major stumbling blocks coming to threaten marriages and long-standing relationships.

For many people, this book should provide the help necessary to make sex better. For others, it will not be enough. They will need to consult professionally trained therapists. For them, this book will have served as a "screening" experience, perhaps identifying specific areas of difficulty, telling them that more help is needed and most important, perhaps, letting them know that more help is available. They do not have to keep suffering from sexual dysfunctions, painful marriages, or even from a longing for relationships. The "screening" aspect of Making Love is one of its most important facets. No one yet knows how many people really can improve their own sexual lives by themselves, if provided both information and help with their own attitudes. I share with Patricia Raley the opinion that many people can help and even "cure" themselves, especially such groups as young adults not locked into life-long patterns, and those who are both motivated and committed to caring relationships. So I would join her in urging you to try a new kind of "experiment" in being therapeutic to yourself, to your marriage, and to your spouse or partner. But I would also urge you not to give up if the going gets rough. Either (1) keep trying (since practice helps); or (2) turn to a professional for help. At the very least you will know you have tried yourself and you will be that much readier to work with someone else. And, furthermore, you will have a better idea of where and why you are at an impasse.

Sex is, after all and above all, the physical aspect of human relationships. In sex, the body becomes a vehicle for emotional attachment between people who care about each other. Since reproduction of our species is only furthered in a small percent of sexual encounters, it seems clear that the sexual bonding of humans primarily serves a crucial emotional function. It is the integrity of human relationships, the bonds of families, and the ability of adults to enjoy life that are at stake in every sexual act and whim.

DAVID E. SCHARFF, M.D.
Director of Counseling and Sex Education
Preterm, A Center for Reproductive Health,
Washington, D.C.

making love

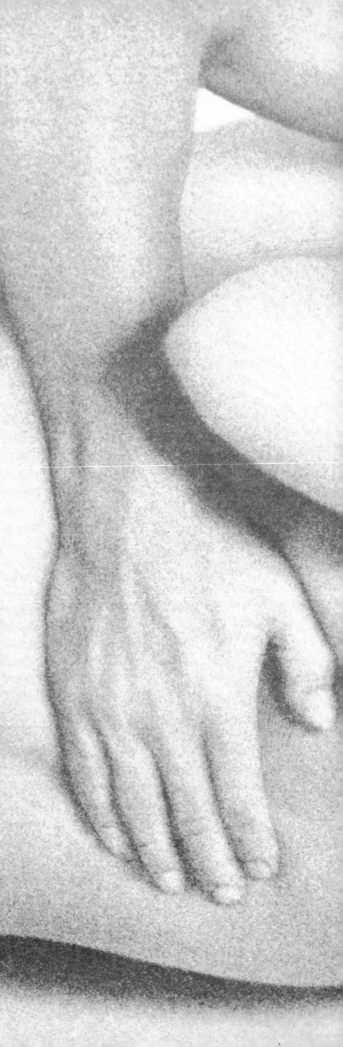

Introduction

We are all so bombarded by sex daily that it is hard to separate what sex is from what it is supposed to be. Is making love a drive, a duty, a sin, a job? Is the sex that sells cars, books, and hair pieces the sex to live by? Sex may be the sex of the stodgy clinician, the exotic erotic, the beautiful people, the politicians, or the people next door. With all the publicity, hopes, and expectations attending sex, we are bound to be anxious, disappointed, or downright mystified about it.

Here is an opportunity to find out what making love is for you. With this book you can think more clearly and worry more constructively about your own personal sexual concerns. Through a process of reflection, self-examination, and action, you can be your own sex therapist.

What is sex therapy?

"Sex therapy" usually refers to the behavior modification program for sexual dysfunctions pioneered by Masters and Johnson. It does not mean nude marathons, men in white coats watching you make love, or touchy-feely sessions. The therapy you'll find here combines conventional "sex therapy" with contributions from psychotherapy and sex education to form an accessible and comprehensive approach to sex.

Traditionally, the responsibility for telling people about sex has fallen upon parents, teachers, doctors, and nurses. They try to teach sexual anatomy, reproduction, birth control, and occasionally a little about sexual behavior. But they are often hampered by being the victims of poor sex education themselves. And, until recently, the facts about sex were hard to isolate from the emotional feelings they aroused. Thus, sex education for most of us comes from a hodgepodge of myths, half-truths, innuendoes, and media distortions, abetted by limited and often fumbling experience.

With the advent of research into sexual response and physiology, mainly by Masters and Johnson at the Reproductive Biology Research Foundation in St. Louis, amazing new material became available. William H. Masters, a gynecologist, and his assistant, Virginia E. Johnson, not only documented what really happens during sexual arousal and orgasm, they also were able to separate some facts from myths. They published their findings in Human Sexual Response in 1966.

Using this research and the techniques of behavior modification, Masters and Johnson found a way to help people with specific sexual problems. They described the problems and their treatment in Human Sexual Inadequacy, published in 1970. Dysfunctional sex therapy, as it is called, has proven extremely effective. However, it is designed for couples and is not suited to vague or nonspecific problems. These remain the province of psychiatrists, social workers, psychologists, marriage counselors, and ministers.

These professionals are not always willing or able to provide the sexual information their clients sometimes need. Sex education has only recently become a part of required professional training. In the past, professional schools taught that sexual symptoms could only be relieved by attention to such underlying psychic forces as dependency and oedipal conflicts. Unresolved underlying problems would just cause more problems. Although many professionals are now combin-

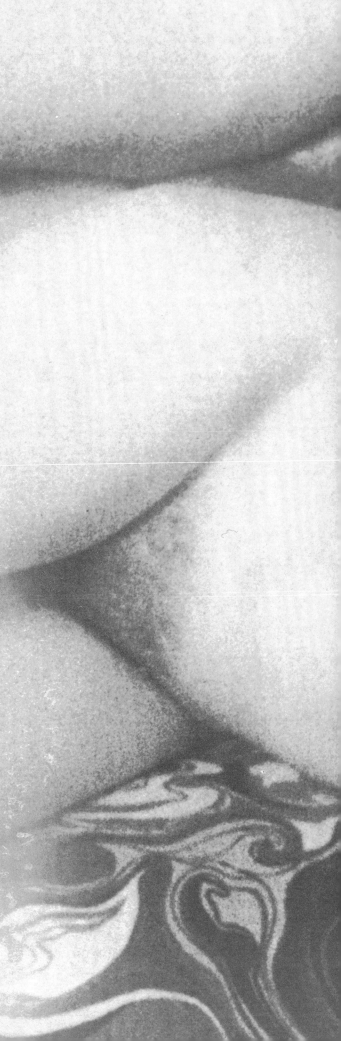

ing psychotherapy with sex therapy, it will be some time before the public can count on straightforward help for sex problems from them.

Sex therapy at its best combines sex education, psychotherapy, and behavior modification to provide accurate information, thoughtful analysis of feelings, and specific remedies for change. It can then address a broad range of sexual concerns from the most particular to the most diffuse.

Who needs this book?

Anyone who is interested in sex. If you want to know what experiences shaped your attitudes about sex and making love, this is for you. If you find sex thrilling, revolting, boring, or mysterious, there is something here for you. And it doesn't matter whether you are gay or straight, old or young, married or single.

What does matter is that you want to know more about yourself sexually. You could be curious about what is normal in sexual behavior, from the initiation and rejection of sex to sexual roles and fantasies. You could want help with a problem such as impotence, being nonorgasmic, coming too fast or not fast enough. This book can help you identify and confront your own sexual concerns, whatever they are.

One common concern among those who need this book is fear of failure. Some people are afraid of what will happen to them if they try to improve their sex lives and fail. Such fear can make you unable to ever seek help. Rather than giving up, you can take a risk in this low-risk way. If you can't go it alone with the help of this book, there are people out there to help you. (See Chapter 13.)

Why not go to a sex therapist?

Sex therapists have training, facts, and techniques that are valuable, but they do not have secret formulas for potency or happiness. Sometimes people don't realize how much they can do on their own. Although you may wish to consult a therapist later, you can start learning about your own sexuality now. Your self-knowledge, common sense, and willingness to explore can make you your own best therapist. And you may be more comfortable working on this very private matter by yourself.

If you aren't able, through a sustained and concentrated effort, to change and grow the way you'd like, don't despair. You will have done what you could without assistance and this book will have informed and prepared you for further help.

How do you use this book?

This book can help you be the lover you'd love to be, but just reading it won't catapult you into sexual ecstasy. You have to live it. Start by following the suggestions, answering the questions, and learning the facts. Try to be accepting of yourself and your limitations. You don't have to do everything by the book, but give it a chance to help you help yourself.

Set a realistic pace for yourself. If you keep peeking ahead, why don't you just sit down and read the whole book through? Then go back and do the exercises slowly. You'll have to determine the right pace for yourself, but you might want to consider working on more than one chapter at a time. If you find something hard going, go back to a part you found easy, entertaining, or useful. It's all right to get stuck, to feel awkward or dismayed. Keep trying.

Since you may feel hesitant to write in the book, consider the possibility of buying yourself a journal to keep notes of this experience. You'll then be able to leave this book lying around without worrying about what others might find in it. It doesn't really matter whether you make notes here or elsewhere as long as you keep track of yourself.

Recording your reactions and activities is therapeutic in itself. It is also therapeutic to talk to someone else about many of the issues raised here. You may prefer, at least in the beginning, to go it alone. Later, if you have an opportunity to talk over some chapters or sections with another person, you may find that the process of examination and reflection aloud aids your therapeutic progress, too. This person does not have to be a sexual partner; anyone you feel comfortable with will do.

A strong therapeutic technique used in this book is the listing of questions you are urged to ask yourself. Not all the questions will seem applicable to you, but try to answer as many as possible. That will help you discover your own concerns and show you the concerns of others. The suggestions that follow the questions won't all be popular with you and you shouldn't expect them to be. There is nothing spontaneous or natural about following directions in a book. But be daring and try new things, even if you feel inhibited or uneasy. Try to go past the point of being uncomfortable. Some people give up when they meet an unpleasant feeling. They decide it's abnormal and they lose hope. It's actually a common experience worth going beyond just to see what other feelings you have.

Remember, sex therapy is supposed to be challenging. It is also exciting, thought-provoking, and fun.

Fantasy

INTRODUCTION

If you are in a bookstore or library and have just taken this book off the shelf, several things could be flashing through your mind right now. You could be wondering what Making Love means, to you, to the author. You are probably also critical, hopeful, anxious, or amused by the idea of such a book.

Furthermore, you could be wondering if you're being watched. The person next to you might think that you need sex therapy, or that you would be easy to pick up, or that you have a professional interest in this book. If the book was a gift, you might think that the giver wanted to embarrass or enlighten you, mock or delight you. All such speculations and ruminations are fantasies.

Projections about what might happen to you if you read the book are fantasies too. For instance, maybe you imagine yourself in an orgy or a carefully controlled experiment as a result of this reading. Perhaps you like the idea of yourself as the therapist. You could be longing to substantiate your belief that all books like this turn out to be Mickey Mouse stuff. You could have wild hopes for fulfilling your erotic potential or milder curiosities about a particular sexual concern of yours.

Vaguer, less defined thoughts, such as a mental picture of a past lover or a memory of a particular sexual experience, are also fantasies. You might have an untraceable feeling of excitement or apprehension, accompanied by montages of erotic images. You may recall a sexual encounter in which you were suave or not so suave. You could be remembering other sex books you've read, good and not so good.

Fantasies can be elaborate, well-worked-out stories or they can be just fragments, drifting images with no particular direction or resolution. They can be about perfectly mundane, everyday events or about exotic things you'll never do or see. You may be unaware of fantasizing at all. If you feel there is something wrong with fantasizing, you could be all too aware of it.

The classic response to the person who has problems with sex is, "It's all in your mind." That always sounds as if there aren't any real sexual concerns—just imaginary ones—which isn't true at all. What goes on in your mind or imagination sometimes gives clues to what your needs, attitudes, and feelings are. In this chapter we'll look at sexual fantasies for hints about sexual concerns. But first let's look at some general fantasies.

WHAT IS A FANTASY?

Below are some examples of common fantasies. After each one is space for you to write down a fantasy along the same lines that you have had or that you are having now. As we go along in this book, you'll be asked to question yourself and write out your thoughts on the various subjects that come up. You don't have to do any of it. But often pausing to be honest with yourself, to think through your feelings with a pencil (or pen if you feel bold), can help you arrange and possibly change both attitudes and behavior. Such change may only be the acceptance of yourself, but that can make a momentous difference in your behavior. Just knowing your own fantasies and what they might

mean, for instance, can bring you closer to an understanding of yourself. Use your journal if you'd rather not write in the book.

A heroic fantasy Those people who just got on the bus look very suspicious to me. I wonder if that guy has a gun. Maybe they're going to rob us. . . . I guess I'm the only one here who could take charge. I'd be so cool and collected. At first, I'd pretend to be on their side and then . . .

Fantasy _____

_____

_____

_____

A death fantasy What if John is killed on his job? I'd get all his insurance, of course. I'd be very brave and comforting of others. Just like Ethel Kennedy. They'd all say how amazing I was. Widowed, with two little children. I'd live for the kids and I'd never look at another man, although they would all look at me . . .

Fantasy _____

_____

_____

_____

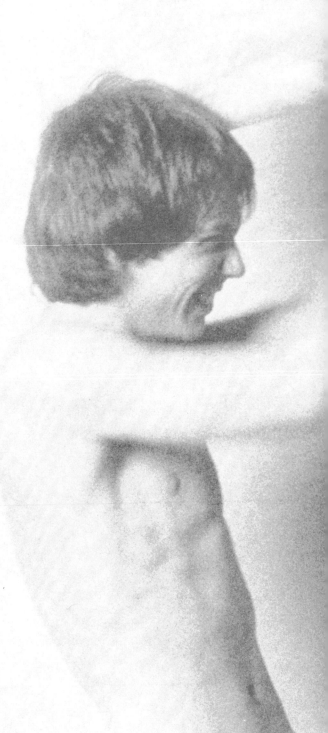

A money fantasy What if I came into a lot of money? First I'd buy a giant color television and a silver Porsche. I could send my mother to Las Vegas for a vacation. I'd want to invest in an absolutely safe venture—maybe some real estate on the Riviera. I wonder if a lot of money is going to be enough . . .

Fantasy _____

_____

_____

_____

Other common fantasies are those about revenge, failure, success, history, sex, and just the planning or replaying of the day's events. Everyone has them from time to time. They can be set off by a memory, a familiar odor, a phone call, a newspaper story, the weather, and so on. Fantasies are soothing, terrifying, wish-fulfilling, silly, and fun.

Although there are similarities between fantasies, or daydreams, and dreams, fantasies tend to be more accessible than dreams. First of all, you're awake. Second, even though both fantasy and dreams jump from scene to scene, there aren't usually the distortions of time and space in fantasy that sometimes exist in dreams. Freud called dreams the royal road to the unconscious. Fantasy reveals, at the very least, some conscious preoccupations.

Fantasies, dreams, and other thoughts all make up the inner life. They overlap and converge. The goal of this chapter is for you to start separating out from your mental meanderings the thoughts that could be called sex fantasies for clues to how you feel about sex.

WHAT IS A SEX FANTASY?

Although any fantasies may be sex fantasies, generally sex fantasies fall into three categories. There are (1) those that arouse you and lead to sex; (2) those that you have during sex; and (3) those that are not con-

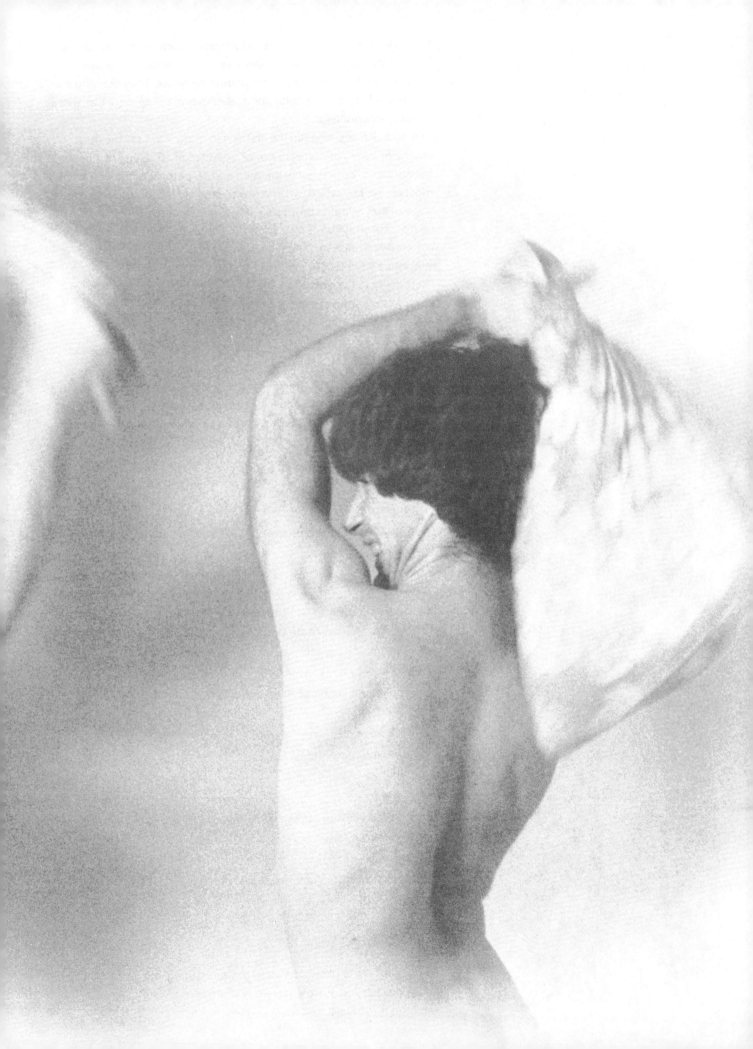

nected to any sexual activity, but which have a sexual content for you. Sex fantasies don't have to be about sex, and they can range from fleeting impulses to elaborate, long-running chronicles. They contribute to the erotic life by adding color and zest to everyday experience as well as to sexual encounters.

Alfred E. Kinsey, who did the first and in many ways still the most complete survey of sexual behavior, reported in 1952 that of those who masturbated, 72 percent of the men and 50 percent of the women almost always fantasized. A more recent study of the fantasies of women showed that women commonly have erotic fantasies during intercourse. These statistics only show that fantasy is normal, not that it is required or necessary. And they do not reflect the fact that many people aren't sure whether they fantasize or not.

In order to better acquaint yourself with sex fantasies, try having one a day. These fantasy-completion exercises are just to get you started. You may substitute and add your own at will.

Fantasy for day 1 You are in a crowded place—a store, a queue, an office. You spot someone who interests you in some special way. He or she looks at you. You hold eyes. Neither of you looks away. You move together.

Where are you? Describe the scene.

_____

_____

Describe yourself and then the other person, including appearance, posture, and so forth.

_____

_____

What might you say to each other and in what tones (jaunty greetings, shy put-downs, lewd come-ons)? _____

_____

_____

What might you do next (go for coffee, get each other's number, fade into the crowd)? _____

_____

How does this story end? _____

_____

_____

What do you like and not like about it?

_____

_____

How about improving or changing it?

_____

_____

_____

Fantasy for day 2 Now do exactly the same thing, but let the other person approach you. Follow yesterday's format, except that you play the opposite role today.

I enjoyed role 1 _____ role 2 _____ more.

I think that's because _____
_____
_____

The similarities between these fantasies and my own are _____
_____
_____

The differences are _____
_____
_____

Fantasy for day 3 Today everything goes wrong. You have your worst possible fantasy. You are forced into sex or you force someone else into it. You are impotent, unfaithful, or nonorgasmic. You are rejected. You make a fool of yourself or of someone else. Set this scene carefully, describe the characters, and give a detailed description of all the horrible things that happen.

_____
_____
_____
_____
_____
_____
_____

This fantasy was bad because _____
_____
_____

This fantasy scared me because _____
_____
_____

Fantasy for day 4 Today you get to have the best possible fantasy for you. Everything is right this time. You are beautiful, princely, poised, sexy, able. Everything happens just as you wish it would or nothing actually "happens" at all. Make yourself comfortable and let yourself go.

_____
_____
_____
_____

This fantasy was good because _____
_____
_____

I needed this fantasy because _____
_____
_____

Fantasy for day 5 Today you can do it all by yourself. Construct a common or recent fantasy if you like. If you don't fantasize very often, you may wish to use something you've read here or elsewhere for a beginning. Your setting can be exotic or ordinary. Your plot can be com-

14

plex or nonexistent. Try to describe the sensual or erotic qualities of the setting, the partner, the experience. Try to find what sex fantasy is to you.

_____

_____

_____

_____

_____

WHAT CAN YOU LEARN FROM SEX FANTASY?

Your sexual fantasies may reflect some of your sexual fears, desires, and habits. When and where you have them, as well as the role you play in them, may be clues to who you are sexually. For instance, let's say you always fantasize during arousal but not during sex. You have the idea that it is disloyal to your partner to fantasize during actual intercourse. Yet you are unresponsive during intercourse, never getting as aroused as you were during foreplay. That would seem to indicate that a fantasy might come in handy. If the loyalty issues still plague you, you might talk to your partner about it. Perhaps he or she fantasizes too.

Your own role in your fantasies may echo or reverse your usual role in life. For instance, you may be submissive and shy in your fantasies because you need to be, or usually are, in real life. Fantasies in which you are dominant may make up for or legitimize your lack of dominance in a relationship. Sometimes these fantasies can prepare you to take a new role or live with an old one.

Fantasizing that you are having sex with a stranger when you're not may be wish-fulfillment or idle eros. But you might be trying to get away from your present partner. You don't actually want to be with someone else as much as you want to pull away from involvement with this person.

Fantasizing that you are a stranger, that is, that you are more voluptuous or virile (or less so), may be a fantasy route to make up for a sense of inferiority or inadequacy sexually. Making yourself "sexier" in fantasy makes it easier to be a sexual, responsive person. Now there is no reason to change this, or any other fantasy, unless it doesn't particularly "work" for you or is boring or upsetting to you.

The content of the fantasy, as well as when it occurs and what your role is, may also reveal something to you about your sexual attitudes and concerns. Take the following examples:

Seduction fantasies These are among the most common of all sex fantasies. For women they sometimes take the form of rape fantasies and for men they might involve an especially compliant partner. In each of these extremes is an element of what society expects from men and women in sexual behavior. Many women are brought up to think they shouldn't enjoy sex. A rape fantasy means not having to be responsible for enjoying sex. Similarly men, raised to believe they should be masterful, ready, and eager, find the burden of masculine behavior relieved by a compliant partner. Fantasizing one frees you to respond more fully to sex. Elements of these extremes can be found in many run-of-the-mill seduction fantasies. They don't indicate that anything is wrong with you, only that society—not unsurprisingly—has gotten to you. Such fantasies can be a way around that society.

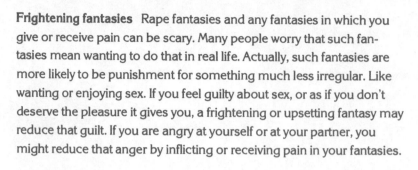

Frightening fantasies Rape fantasies and any fantasies in which you give or receive pain can be scary. Many people worry that such fantasies mean wanting to do that in real life. Actually, such fantasies are more likely to be punishment for something much less irregular. Like wanting or enjoying sex. If you feel guilty about sex, or as if you don't deserve the pleasure it gives you, a frightening or upsetting fantasy may reduce that guilt. If you are angry at yourself or at your partner, you might reduce that anger by inflicting or receiving pain in your fantasies.

Taboo fantasies Another common and sometimes scary fantasy is the one in which you are engaged in sexual activities you find "inappropriate." These include sex with animals, relatives, your best friend or your best friend's spouse, and such sex acts as anal, group, oral, and so on. You wonder if these fantasies mean you want to do what they suggest. You might very well—but in fantasy, not in the living room. Certainly fantasy is a way to experiment with and enjoy bizarre ideas.

Abstract fantasies It's a little hard to say what an abstract fantasy is about, but it isn't uncommon for people to have fantasies in which there is no plot or no particularly sexual imagery. These fantasies may feature scenes or people which evoke a certain familiar or secure mood that makes sexual responsiveness easier. Examples are glimpses of other countries, centuries, places, people. Such fantasies sometimes remove the fantasizer from what is actually happening. Abstract fantasies can heighten or diminish involvement and pleasure, depending on your needs and experience.

Pleasant fantasies Most fantasies, of course, are for fun. They add a little something extra to sex or to everyday life. Any of the above categories can be used to increase your excitement, as can anything else you find arousing. Sex fantasies in which you triumph, prevail, or succeed are almost always a pleasure.

TO FANTASIZE OR NOT TO FANTASIZE?

Some people are afraid that fantasizing is harmful. They may fear that fantasizing about sex means they'll never do it. Or that fantasizing is wasteful and unproductive. Actually, fantasizing obsessively about sex may mean not doing anything about anything. The obsession might be with avoiding work, school, family, problems. Fantasy can be an excuse, an escape, and a distraction, but it can also be entertaining and useful. If you feel that you have no control over your fantasies and that they aren't doing you any good, examine other areas of your life to see if fantasy is a harmless diversion for you or a sign that something elsewhere needs attention.

To fantasize or not during sexual arousal, with or without a partner, is something you can test out. If you generally do not fantasize during sex, you may prefer to use abstract fantasies for arousal. You may also be unaware of fantasizing. Since the people in favor of sex fantasy maintain that it enriches the sex act, you might try building a fantasy. Next time you have sex, try thinking about something other than what is happening. You don't have to have anything very detailed. Use the following lines to record your reactions. Your first try might not add a thing, but try again just to see what it's like.

_____
_____
_____
_____
_____

If you generally do fantasize during sex, try concentrating on the things around you the next time you have sex. Since the people who prefer not to fantasize then vow that it is more arousing to live in the present, you might see if they're right. Later, write down your feelings about it.

_____
_____
_____
_____
_____

People have many different responses to this experiment. Some find that a change itself is arousing and others feel that the change detracts from the experience. A few are pleased to find that they are responsive without relying on their usual routine, while others feel they are less responsive the new way.

You can add flexibility to your sexuality by playing around with fantasies. You can have them or not, you can vary them in content and style, and you can change roles in them. There is nothing wrong with continuing your usual patterns as long as they are rewarding to you. But if they are so ingrained as to be a habit or a crutch, you might want to try something new. To get more out of your sex life you might start by getting more out of your fantasy life.

CONCLUSION

Looking at your own fantasies and learning some of the concerns they reflect is just one way to start getting to know yourself sexually. In the next few chapters we'll be looking at some other ways. As we go along you can keep thinking about your fantasies. Not necessarily with a mind to changing them, but with a better understanding of what they do for you and what kind (including no kind) you find most interesting or useful. Even if you've learned something about yourself that you don't like, such as fantasies that indicate you aren't as free sexually as you thought, learning to accept yourself as you really are is better than trying to fit into some unreal mold.

Everyone has his or her own private thoughts about sex. If you feel you'd like to share yours with a trusted friend, by all means do so. Your friend may not be ready to share sex fantasies with you and you shouldn't push it. It might be easier to start with everyday fantasies or childhood fantasies and see where that takes you. Sometimes talking to another person about fantasy will release reservations and inhibitions that are related to sexual communication in general. This is a good way to start talking if you feel you want to.

In the next chapter we'll look at your sex history and some of the experiences that shaped what you fantasize about. You may wish to come back to this chapter as you read on. Some of it will probably come back to you.

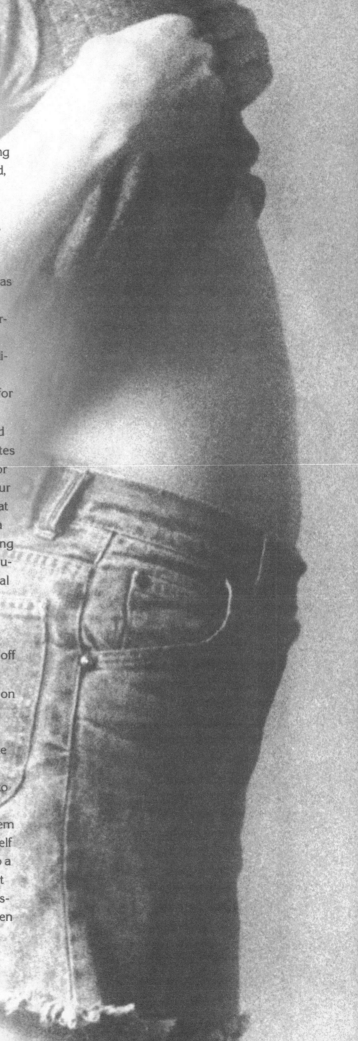

A Sex History

INTRODUCTION

A sex history is not just a list of conquests. It is a record of your entire experience with sex from babyhood on.

If you see your sex life as limited or colorless, you may be overlooking the richness of your own sexual development. After all, you've learned, or not learned, the "facts of life." You've had feelings for friends, parents, wives, husbands, lovers, and children that fit into no other category. And you've reacted to myths, facts, dirty jokes, romantic stories, movies, and other people's activities. All of these and more make up your own sexual history.

Here you will review your sexual explorations, doubts, and triumphs as a means of separating out what you think about sex right now. This chapter is to help you articulate what you've always known about yourself. The material is divided into age periods in which certain events, such as your first wet dream or your third marriage, took place. The divisions are chronological but the events are arbitrary, so read beyond your present age. Not only might some recollections be out of order for you, but you will gain some sense of the concerns of others.

Each section of this history starts with a series of questions designed to take you back. Following the questions is space for you to write notes of what flickered through your mind as you thought of yourself then or imagine yourself in the future. You may wish to write your notes in your journal or on a separate sheet rather than in this book. Remember that writing out your thoughts, whether you do long thoughtful essays or a few simple notes, is itself part of the therapeutic technique of becoming your own therapist. You can go over your notes later to look for particularly strong impressions or patterns that may affect your current sexual behavior.

After the questions in each chronological section are some comments that may or may not apply to you. They relate to some general issues that arise for many people at that particular age. They may set off new memories or just get in your way. Use them or not, as you wish.

The best possible place to take this journey into your past would be on a train trip. The next best place would be wherever you can let your mind wander uninterrupted for a couple of hours. It would be ideal to take your history all in one sitting, but because this chapter may evoke memories or fantasies you'd like to dwell on, don't feel there is any rush. You can do a section at a time and you can always come back to this chapter to go over parts of it in more detail.

This is a personal journey. No one else is along unless you invite them to be. Honest answers are the only right ones, and you can ask yourself any other questions you feel are significant. It can be helpful to talk to a friend or partner about certain subjects raised here that are important to you. If you have a friend you can talk to, consider exploring your histories together. Always start with your past. It's easier to get going when you remove yourself a little.

YOUR EARLIEST MEMORIES

Do you have any specifically sexual memories?
Do you remember any "sexual" explorations, such as:

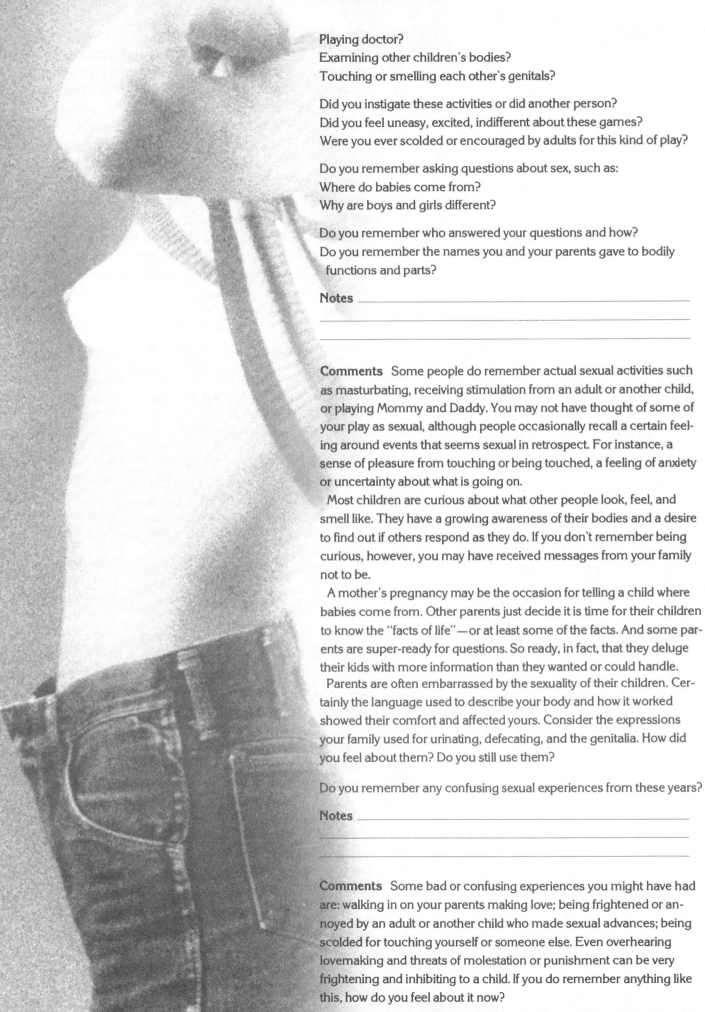

Playing doctor?
Examining other children's bodies?
Touching or smelling each other's genitals?

Did you instigate these activities or did another person?
Did you feel uneasy, excited, indifferent about these games?
Were you ever scolded or encouraged by adults for this kind of play?

Do you remember asking questions about sex, such as:
Where do babies come from?
Why are boys and girls different?

Do you remember who answered your questions and how?
Do you remember the names you and your parents gave to bodily
  functions and parts?

Notes _____

_____

_____

Comments Some people do remember actual sexual activities such
as masturbating, receiving stimulation from an adult or another child,
or playing Mommy and Daddy. You may not have thought of some of
your play as sexual, although people occasionally recall a certain feeling around events that seems sexual in retrospect. For instance, a
sense of pleasure from touching or being touched, a feeling of anxiety
or uncertainty about what is going on.

  Most children are curious about what other people look, feel, and
smell like. They have a growing awareness of their bodies and a desire
to find out if others respond as they do. If you don't remember being
curious, however, you may have received messages from your family
not to be.

  A mother's pregnancy may be the occasion for telling a child where
babies come from. Other parents just decide it is time for their children
to know the "facts of life"—or at least some of the facts. And some parents are super-ready for questions. So ready, in fact, that they deluge
their kids with more information than they wanted or could handle.

  Parents are often embarrassed by the sexuality of their children. Certainly the language used to describe your body and how it worked
showed their comfort and affected yours. Consider the expressions
your family used for urinating, defecating, and the genitalia. How did
you feel about them? Do you still use them?

Do you remember any confusing sexual experiences from these years?

Notes _____

_____

_____

Comments Some bad or confusing experiences you might have had
are: walking in on your parents making love; being frightened or annoyed by an adult or another child who made sexual advances; being
scolded for touching yourself or someone else. Even overhearing
lovemaking and threats of molestation or punishment can be very
frightening and inhibiting to a child. If you do remember anything like
this, how do you feel about it now?

The absence, illness, or death of a parent during these years can have sexual reverberations. Probably the most obvious is the absence of a role model if the missing parent is the same sex as you. Furthermore, children always think that they are responsible for whatever happens in the world. If a parent leaves or dies, you may feel that it happened because you were mad at your parent or your parent was mad at you. This can understandably produce a terrific guilt complex or a greatly exaggerated sense of your own power. Either may be related to how you see yourself later as a man or a woman.

The rigors of dealing with the oedipus complex can be pretty upsetting and confusing at this age. Supposedly, making an identification with the parent of the same sex is inspired by the desire to replace that parent in the eyes of the other parent. Feelings of jealously and rage because you cannot have Mommy or Daddy all to yourself may fade away as you get older. But these feelings are so intense in some people that it takes years to get over them.

MIDCHILDHOOD, WHEN YOU WERE FIVE TO TEN

Do you remember having pleasant sensations from touching yourself?
Were you ever punished or laughed at for doing it?
Did you know what you were doing?
Did you ever do it with anyone else?

Do you remember any changes in the way your parents or other adults
 treated you, such as:
Not letting you sleep with your brother?
Not letting you sleep with your mother?
Not letting you bathe with your sister, father, best friend any more?

Notes _____
_____
_____

Comments You may not remember any "self-pleasuring" from your early years, but by the age of seven or eight you may have enjoyed touching your genitals or rubbing against something. And you may have done this with other children, although most women and many men experience masturbation as a private matter. So private, in fact, that you may not have been aware of it at all. Even by this age you have become less open about your sexuality.

Midchildhood has been called the latency period of sexual development, but it might be better labeled the furtive period. Even if you weren't aware of sex, other people were. Parents and other or older children may have made you realize—by their attitudes toward nudity, masturbation, and sex—that there was something you didn't or shouldn't know. So your explorations went on in secret.

Do you remember trying to figure out what the word "sex" meant?
What was your idea and what did you hear from others?

Do you remember the first "sex" word you heard or used?
Where did you learn it?
What others' reactions were to it?
Did you know what it meant?

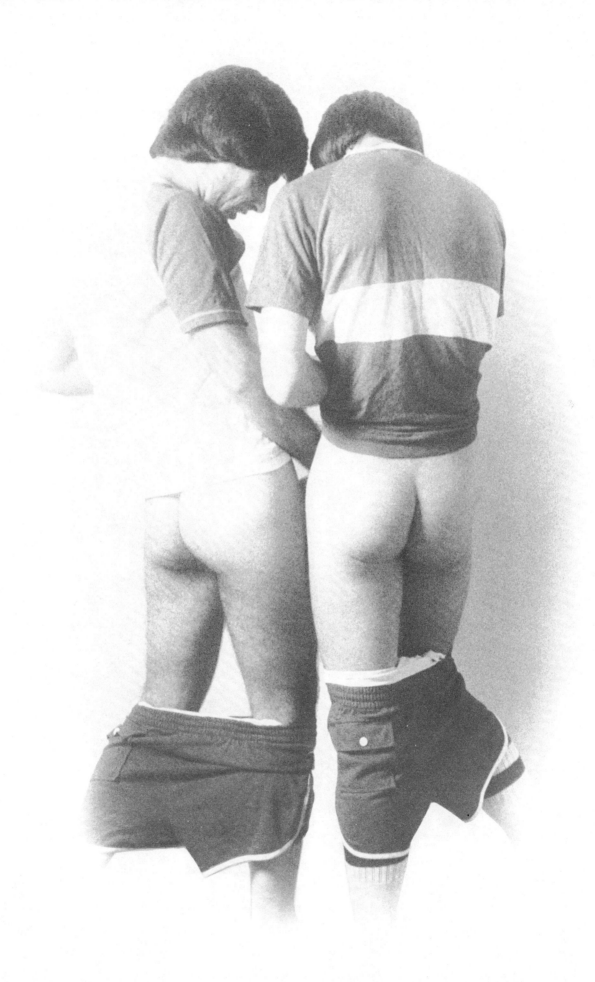

Do you remember the first dirty joke you didn't get?
Did you ever tell your parents or friends any dirty jokes?
What was their reaction?

Notes _____
_____
_____

Comments Now that you know how to talk, you start learning how not to talk. You learn from parents and teachers and giggling schoolmates that certain words are not to be uttered. You find that words like "bust," "suck," "ass," "rubber," "prick," "bone," and "hole" mean more than you thought they did.

"Dirty" words and jokes describe both excretory and sexual functions. This traditional association between sex and elimination undoubtedly originates in the efficient but confusing closeness of the genitalia to the anus and urethra—and to the erotic potential of all.

Do you remember what you learned from your friends about sex?
Was anything that you learned wildly misleading? In what ways?

How often did you talk about sexual things?

Notes _____
_____

Comments Most people learn more about sex from their friends than they learn from adults. Many children are never taught either the reproductive facts or the special feelings involved in wanting to have sex. And often parents just don't give enough information for children to be able to figure out what it is all about. Animal metaphors, scientific explanations, and love stories all leave something out.

Ignorance is the inspiration for invention. Parents often inadvertently encourage mythmaking by putting you off "for your own good" or until you are "old enough to understand." So you assume that kissing makes you pregnant, that a girl can't walk after she's had intercourse, that a boy puts his cock into a girl's asshole, that having sex means having a boy pee into you, that you shouldn't masturbate because you'll use up all your sperm, that foreplay means getting your clothes off. Even later, when you know better, some of these myths persist.

PUBERTY AND EARLY ADOLESCENCE

Do you remember the first person you were infatuated with?
Was it an older person? a relative? a friend?
Your sex or the opposite sex?

Do you remember the special feelings you had for this person?
Did you expect to feel that way?
Were you frightened or surprised by the strength of your feelings?

Do you remember something you could call a first date?
Was it with someone you cared about?
Was there anything sexual about it?

Notes _____
_____

Comments Your first love could have been for a teacher, a movie star, a chum, an aunt, even a parent or sibling. If there was something inappropriate about this attraction—and there almost always is—you had to put up with people insisting that you didn't know what you were doing, that you were too young to know what love was, that it was not love that you felt for another woman, and so on. It's impossible to appreciate what those admonitions are about when you're experiencing feelings which are unlike any you've had before. They can leave a fond memory that even now makes puppy love or the affinity you felt for the rest of the team seem stronger and fresher than anything since.

Women—Do you remember your first period?
Men—Do you remember your first ejaculation?
What did you think about it?
Had you expected it?
Were you disappointed or frightened, excited, embarrassed, or
  pleased?

Do you remember masturbating at this age?

Notes _____

_____

Comments Reactions to menstruation and ejaculation can range from guilt to pride, depending somewhat on what you expected. If you are a boy who had been masturbating secretly for years, you might fear that your first ejaculation is some sort of punishment for having "abused" your organ. Wet dreams can be a mystery or embarrassment whether you've masturbated or not. Girls are usually prepared for menstruation, but it is hard to imagine exactly what bleeding from "there" means. When you do start, the bleeding can be frightening and seem like punishment for masturbating, fantasizing, petting, and so on. Stained sheets and clothes can make both girls and boys feel bad or dirty.

   It is hard to be very late or very early developing in comparison to your schoolmates. There is a great yearning at this age to be normal, even though the only thing that seems to be normal is feeling that you are not.

   If you did masturbate at this age, you may not have known what you were doing or that anyone else did it. Incidentally, many people masturbate without reaching orgasm, or even knowing that they can.

Do you remember what your concerns about your body were at this
  stage?
Did it seem to be coming along all right?
Did you feel that parts of you were growing out of all proportion to other
  parts?
Did you think you'd never need a bra or that if you slept in your bra your
  breasts would stop growing?
Did you think that your penis was too long, too thick, too stubby, too
  circumcised?
Did you long to have more or less hair on your chest, crotch, chin, legs?

Notes _____

_____

_____

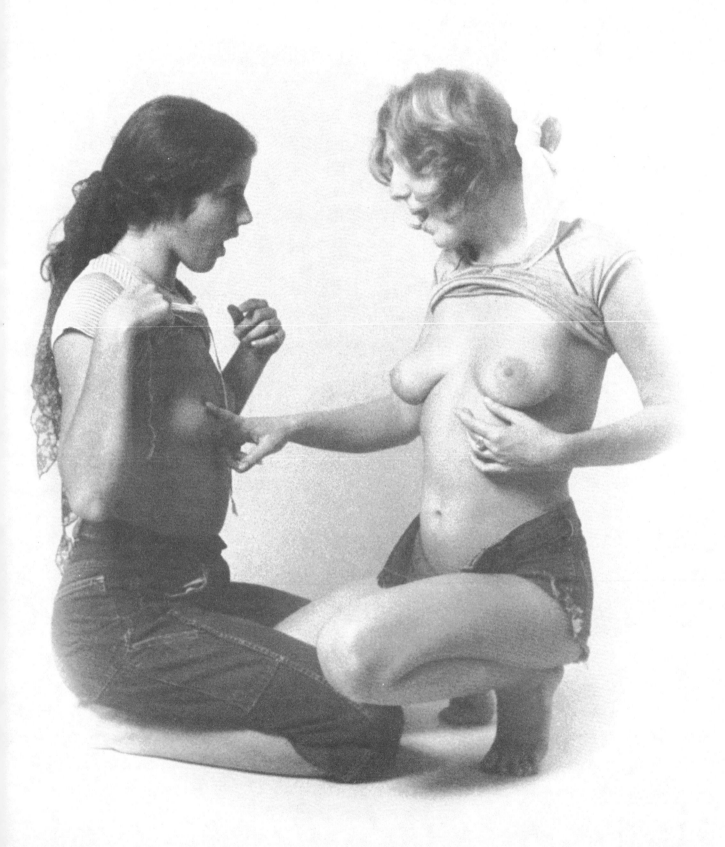

Comments Unless you were inordinately proud of your body—and few people are at thirteen, let alone thirty—you probably found those physical education classes somewhat tense. You were given to believe that you should be relaxed running around in the nude because everyone looked the same. But you knew that everybody, especially you, looked different.

Even though the size, slant, or foreskin of your penis has nothing to do with how it works, you may have felt self-conscious about however it was. If you had heard that you can tell "by the angle of the dangle if the meat's been beat," you had even more to worry about.

Women worry more about breasts and hips than about their vaginas, which, after all, can't be seen. Although breasts are sensitive and serviceable in all shapes and sizes, if yours were large you thought them bovine, if small nonexistent; if they were hard, you found them knobby, if soft, flabby; if pert, they were pointy, and if full, they were pendulant. It is hard to be right at this age.

Do you remember what you knew about the opposite sex?
Did you know what men and women looked like nude? Did you want to?
Did you know about erections and periods and jock straps and bras?

Did you know the mechanics of sex at this point?
Do you remember what words like "fuck," "intercourse," "ball" meant to you then?
How about words like "rape" and "sodomy"?

Do you remember learning other things about the other sex, such as who was smarter, more sensitive, more ambitious, more athletic, more loving, etc.?

Notes _____

_____

Comments You may have known everything about your own sexual and reproductive capacity without ever being able to put it together with that of the opposite sex. You may have had exciting sexual experiences or feelings without knowing how they connected to the words and facts. You may remember looking up words, trying to find out what things like "to have carnal knowledge" meant.

You didn't have to have an erection in the school cafeteria to worry about what would happen if you did. You didn't have to start your period in class to live in fear that you might. If you had such an experience, review what you did about it. Perhaps you have a clearer memory of this happening to someone else, although most teenagers are too self-conscious to worry about others.

In addition to all the information about how bodies work, both boys and girls are being indoctrinated into their roles as men or women. Having to play a role may be ridiculous, but most teenagers are not secure enough to question that. Many experience much uncertainty and doubt about being masculine or feminine enough.

Do you remember conversations you had with your friends about sex?
If so, write the subjects here:

Notes _____

_____

31

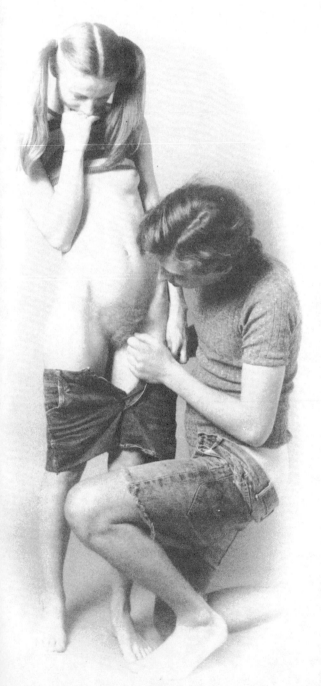

Comments Try to remember how you did talk to friends, if at all. By being vague and mysterious you kept your activities secret but suggestive. By being boastful you could have played what you felt was a required role. Your conversations could have demonstrated a need to do or feel what you thought was expected. If this was the case, it could have set a pattern in which you even now find it difficult to be straightforward about sex. You either pretend to be disinterested or all-knowing, despite never really learning anything that way.

Write down a sexual or romantic fantasy that you had in early adolescence. If you can't remember one specifically, write down what you think you spent a lot of time thinking about then.

Notes _____

_____

_____

Comments This is the age where fantasy really comes into its own. Sex is not really available to you, even though you have all this equipment suddenly ready to go. So you test out in fantasy some of your longings and desires. Some people have what could be called explicit fantasies, full of nude people and sexual acts. Others have love, seduction, or submission fantasies in which everything is suggested but not seen. And some people have abstract fantasies. The fantasies you cherish at this age sometimes recur throughout your life.

YOUR FIRST "SEXUAL" ENCOUNTER

Who was it with—a man? a woman? a long-time friend? no friend at all? a relative? a prostitute? What sort of encounter was it and what made it different from previous encounters—heavy breathing? intercourse? almost intercourse?
Where did it happen?
Did you plan or expect it?
Did you use birth control? Did you wish you had?
Did you have an orgasm? Did your partner?
How did you feel afterward—glorious? guilty? tired? tranquil? hungry?
How do you feel about it now?

Notes _____

_____

_____

Comments Most early encounters are awkward and exciting. It is often difficult to say when the first experience was, since you could have been creeping toward it for some time. It may have been pleasant, traumatic, or unresolved. Even when you know what you want, sex takes practice.
   Men, whose sexuality can only be described as urgent during these years, are almost always out of phase with women partners, who, for cultural and physiological reasons, need much more stimulation. A man may be able to come and come again within a short period of time at this age, while the woman has no orgasm at all. A woman might well wonder why he wanted to do it and what he liked about it. For her, there just wasn't enough time or touch to get aroused. And if intercourse did occur, it may have cut off the pleasure and excitement she was feeling from fooling around.

It can take years to achieve real sexual satisfaction—but you don't know that in the beginning. If you have an unpleasant first experience with sex, you might not want to try again. Bad experiences might be those that leave you pregnant, guilty, infected, confused, or rejected, any of which can make you see sex as something to fail at.

Naturally, a glorious first encounter can set a good tone for the future. Even an awkward, tenuous experience with an understanding partner can make you want to try again. And trying again is often the best way to build confidence.

YOUR FIRST LONG AFFAIR OR MARRIAGE

Do you remember why you were first attracted to this person?
What do you have in common?
What do you not have in common?
What keeps you together?
What keeps you apart?

Are there things about your sex life that you want to change but do not know how to?
Do you want to change or have your partner change?

Are you at all disappointed in the sexual part of your relationship?
Do you feel you or your partner doesn't respond as you expected?

Do you ever talk about sex with your partner?

Notes _____
_____
_____

Comments First affairs are usually a combination of love or affection for the other person and a desire to find out what a long-range commitment means. Sometimes, it is true, people marry or get involved to escape unhappy home situations, to avoid being alone, or because they are forced into it by pregnancy or economic dependence.

Inexperience and shyness can make it hard to right things at this point. You don't know how things are supposed to be. You think maybe this is all there is to it or that something is wrong with you or your partner. You may read the marriage manuals or ask your friends—subtly of course, because you don't want them to know that anything is wrong. But you have trouble applying all that advice to your particular situation.

Many sexual problems are the result of the myths and misinformation you received about sex when you were younger. Not only facts, but also expectations, can be distorted. If you find things not working out as you assumed they would, you don't know what to do.

Furthermore, if you can't talk to your partner about it, it is hard to make things better. He or she may think everything is all right. But if you don't know what your partner thinks, it's hard to test your own feelings and thoughts about it.

Some so-called sexual problems are really related to other problems you don't talk about, such as money troubles, dominance and privacy issues, and just the physical space problems of living with someone else. These will be considered in later chapters.

NOW A REVIEW OF YOUR TWENTIES

Think of some of the people who have been meaningful to you over
these years, especially lovers, children, spouses, and parents.

If more than one lover is in your review, what was similar and different
about them? If it's parents you're talking about, how did they affect
your sexual life style, if at all?

What changes in your sex life have children brought?

If your lovers have been the same sex, how have your parents and
friends reacted?

Have you had any health problems during these years?

Notes _____

_____

_____

Comments People tend to repeat themselves. You may notice in your
cavalcade of lovers that many of the people you are attracted to are
similar. Your spouse may have characteristics of a parent or sibling.
You may treat your children as you were treated. No doubt people are
attracted to familiar figures because they are comfortable figures. Of
course it's fine to marry dear old Dad—as long as your partner marries
dear old Mom.

You may have sought a completely unfamiliar partner because you
didn't want to fall into the pattern your parents did. If your father was
domineering, you may have wanted a milder man in order to offset
what you knew to be a destructive relationship. Unfortunately, you
sometimes get more than you bargained for. Even though you knew
you didn't want to be dominated, you're so familiar with the submissive
role that you find yourself not giving it up.

Or, you might be a woman or man who is continually attracted to the
"wrong" kind of partner; that is, the partner who is inaccessible or rejecting. That might mean you don't really want someone who is "good
for you." You could be unwilling to be committed. You could seek painful or dead-end relationships because you feel unworthy of "good"
partners. You might also have had a rejecting or remote parent whom
you grew used to. It may seem punishing or irrational to seek that in a
partner, but for you it is comfortably familiar.

You might also be attracted to those who complement you, who fill in
your gaps. Someone who can be smart when you're stupid, serious
when you're silly, weak when you are strong. This works beautifully in
mystical unions, but is a problem when two people become so inter-
twined that neither can function independently.

If you are gay, exactly the same principles of attraction and familiarity
apply. You have the additional problem of accepting yourself as gay
and then assuring others they should do the same, particularly your
family. How you resolve their identity crisis depends a lot
on how much self-respect you have. If your parents or friends helped
you gain that self-respect, they probably will accept you. If not, yours
will be a continual battle over standards and rights not unlike that of
"loose" women, confirmèd bachelors, and childless couples. Their
families and friends all hate to see them wasting themselves.

Physical problems during this time of your life can affect your sexual
life. Bladder or vaginal infections, venereal disease, and childbirth are

all possible sources of discomfort. These will be discussed more fully later in the book. For now, consider whether any physical symptom has stood in the way, figuratively or literally, of comfortable or satisfying sex for you.

NOW YOU ARE IN YOUR EARLY THIRTIES

What is your sex life like now?
How often do you have sex?
Is this more or less than ten years ago?
With whom do you have sex?

Have you had any sexual problems?
With new people or with familiar people?
Have you talked to anyone about your problems?

Notes _____
_____
_____

If you are married or with someone now—
What role does sex play in your relationship?
Do you and your partner experiment more or less than you used to?
What does your partner think of sex?
Has either of you had an affair?
Have your friends?
Have you talked about it?

Notes _____
_____
_____

If you are not married or with someone now—
Do you want to be in some sort of relationship?
Why or why not?
What has happened in previous relationships?
What are the advantages and disadvantages of being alone now?

Notes _____
_____
_____

If you have children—
Do your children ask you about sex?
What do you tell them?
What have your children done to or for your relationship with your part-
   ner, your parents, your ex-partner, or anyone else?
What are your incestuous feelings toward your children?

Notes _____
_____
_____

If you do not have children—
Do you want children?
Do you think that children would change your life, especially your sex

life, in some way? How do you feel about getting involved with someone who has or wants children?

Notes _____

_____

_____

Comments This is a great time for comparisons. Your kids are doing
what you used to do and you want to find out from your parents just
what that was. Your friends are settling down or starting up, either of
which makes them less accessible to you. You in turn become involved
in your family, your work, your aloneness, your togetherness, and compare that to other life styles you know about, including your own at
another time.

It is also a time for making decisions about children, marriage, work,
and sex. You might ask yourself if you are the sexual person you want to
be. If you are experienced enough or "good" enough. If you should try a
commune, an older woman, a young boy. You wonder if you are doing
what you want to do.

PUT YOURSELF IN YOUR LATE THIRTIES

What role does sex play now in relation to your roles as father, mother,
  worker, friend, etc.?
How many affairs have you had or considered having at this point?
Did you tell anyone about them?

Did you find you had less or more time for sex during these years?
Have you done anything in the sexual sphere that you are ashamed of?
Have you done anything special you'd like to do again?
Have your children had experiences with sex that recall your own anx-
  ieties at their age?
What were they?
Are you still anxious about these things?

Notes _____

_____

_____

Comments The late thirties are a time for reflecting on what has been
and what can be in the time that is left. Women, who reach their sexual
summit during these years, may become restless with males whose
sexiest time was in their teens. There are no sound physiological explanations for this mismatched peaking yet, but there are some other explanations. Most women this age are no longer having and caring for
babies. But they may be caring more about themselves—looking for
new careers or different lives. Then there is the "new wrinkle syndrome," which is the feeling that with menopause coming on and new
wrinkles appearing daily, you'd better get it all in while you can. So,
many women feel a new kind of freedom, an all-or-nothingness, and a
willingness to experiment which extends to sex.

Men, on the other hand, may begin to feel a little less interested in having sex, even if they are still very interested in thinking about it. A demanding partner, a demanding boss, and demanding children can
make you feel more put upon at this time than at any other in your life.

You, too, are wondering if this is the life for you. There you are questioning yourself and your partner starts questioning you, too. She's freer now and wants more from you. Or, she's busier now and wants you to give her more emotional support than you are used to giving.

Children, who rarely think their parents are sexual, can make you feel even worse. There is a certain competitive-defensive feeling about seeing your children begin to handle sex. You're either protecting them because they weren't as sure as you were or you're resenting them for being surer.

You may be regretting your missed opportunities now as much as the ones you followed up on. Some people are haunted by homosexual adventures, unwanted pregnancies, premature marriages, abortions, acrimonious separations, unusual sex acts, extramarital affairs, and

other events in which they were involved. There is also the self-berating because you didn't have the guts to go to the Mazola party, to follow that man on the street, to proclaim your love, to change your sex life.

These years can be particularly satisfying for those who can stay in tune with their kids, their relationships, careers, sex, and themselves. The attempts to stay in tune, however, can be exhausting. The pressures of trying to control everything can make this a time of mid-life crisis. It's hard to keep things together, and sex is often the first to go.

NOW YOU ARE IN YOUR FORTIES

How is your marriage or relationship at this point?
How is not being married?
What are your children up to?
Are you jealous of your daughter's freedom, husband, future?
Does your son's life drive you crazy?

What do you think of your sex life now?
Have you had any bad sexual experiences?

Do you have any physical problems?

Notes _____
_____
_____

Comments These years seem to be particularly vulnerable ones for marriages. You who were staying together until the kids left home, suddenly have no more excuses. Changes in jobs, living situations, goals, and avocations can mean adjustments that upset one or both partners. Sometimes one is more interested in preserving the marriage than the other. This makes you both feel guilt, sorrow, anger, pity, and/or remorse. You may feel very depressed that you spent so much time with someone you have nothing in common with any more.

Because of the special relationship children and parents share, rebellious acts on the part of your kids can throw you into disproportionate despair. Bringing hippies to dinner, marrying into their own sex, living with "the wrong sorts," all represent a loss for you of your influence and power over your children. And it comes at a time when you feel you are losing power over yourself, especially sexual power. You are doubly dispossessed.

Some men experience impotence for the first time in their forties. There is no magic cure for it and it's hard to know why it happens.

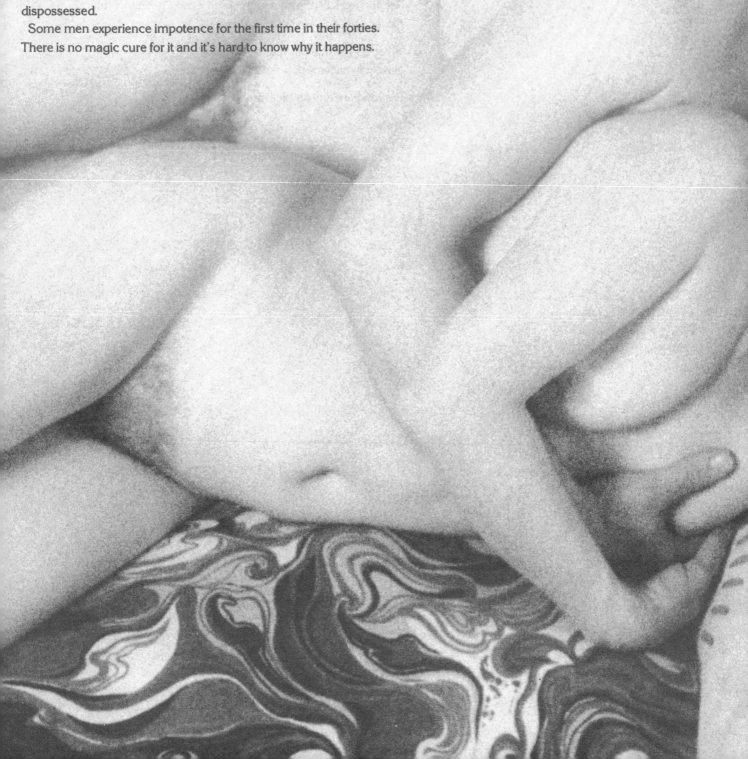

Probably, at this age anyway, it is the result of trying to do something you don't really want to do but feel you should. How many men have the nerve to tell their wives or mistresses to just go watch TV? Men are supposed to be "up" to it all the time. No matter that you were up all night, that you just had sex with your wife, that you have something on your mind. (Impotence is discussed further in Chapter 9.)

Many women are still experiencing the increased interest in sex that began in their thirties. But they may feel "all that" isn't appropriate any more. If their husbands and lovers seem uninterested in sex, some women give up before they should. Naturally menopause can be a real barrier to satisfactory sex for a while. If you feel achey and depressed, you aren't likely to be too interested in sex. But that passes. If you haven't given up sex entirely, you'll find your pleasure in it increasing as your emotional and physical health return to normal.

Someone who never liked sex much anyway may embrace the idea of waning sexuality. A woman can use the menopause as a way out. A man can use the male menopause, although not too much is known about that right now (which may be an advantage). Researchers think men may also go through a period of hormone imbalance without, however, loss of reproductive capability. Both men and women can use age or health as excuses at any time.

Some people have a period of great sexual activity in their forties, when they run around in almost wild abandon. This may be a reaction to fear of impotence or declining attractiveness. It seems to be an attempt to get others to confirm that you are still alluring. If someone will sleep with you, particularly someone new, you still have it.

Actually, the more active you've been, the more active you'll continue to be. People who have had regular sex, or even irregular sex regularly, tend to continue that pattern into old age. It's the people who never were very fond of sex who sometimes use this as a time to slow down.

FROM ABOUT FIFTY TO AROUND SIXTY-FIVE

Have you gained interest in sex lately?
Have you lost interest?
How about your partner(s)?
Do you feel sexually freer than you used to?
Do you feel anxious or depressed about sex?
Do you have any physical problems?

Notes _____

_____

_____

Comments Some people experience new sexual vitality during these years. After all, the kids are out of the way, you know what interests you sexually now, and you're not so reluctant to tell your partner what you like as you may have been when you were younger. Sex seems more relaxing than ever before. There's a sense of freedom and the willingness to spend time on yourself and your partner for what may be the first time in your life.

If you aren't prepared for physical changes, you could have some sexual difficulties now. Women sometimes experience pain during intercourse as the vaginal walls become thinner and there is less lubrication.

43

Uterine contractions during orgasm are sometimes quite sharp. Hormone replacement therapy can help keep the genital tissues soft and moist as well as reduce the contractions. This somewhat controversial therapy consists of finding the right dosage of estrogens to be taken orally on a regular schedule. There are also local medications for this problem. Ask your doctor.

Although women can continue to have multiple orgasms all their lives, the orgasmic contractions aren't as intense or numerous as they once were. Generally, however, women continue to have an interest in sex even though the frequency of sexual activity may gradually decrease.

Sexual activity in men seems to diminish more rapidly than in women, but interest in sex by no means disappears. Unlike women, men do continue to be able to have children. Men notice fewer contractions and lessening intensity of orgasm just as women do. Some other normal changes for men are a longer time between erections (even when ejaculation has not taken place), less forceful ejaculations, less tightening of the testes, and quicker loss of erections. Sometimes hormone replacement therapy is useful, although so far it has not been as helpful to men as to women. Accepting changing sexual patterns in yourself is more helpful since none of the above symptoms indicates less pleasure from sex but simply a gradual decline in frequency.

Surgery to the reproductive organs as well as other illnesses can be traumatic. Men sometimes need prostate surgery because the prostate gland has increased in size and is pressing on the bladder. Such problems as heart disease, cancer, and any physically debilitating diseases naturally affect your sex life because they affect you, period. If you have a serious illness, you should ask your doctor for some specific guidance regarding sexual activity. It may be more harmful, psychologically and physically, to cut yourself off completely than to engage in some moderate sex activity.

Women have many of the same problems. Removal of the uterus or breasts can make you feel as bereft as the loss of a loved one. Other illnesses can make you too depressed or anxious to be very interested in sex. But do consult with your doctor. You may be counting yourself out before you need to.

If you are in reasonably good health and give yourself time to enjoy and explore your changing sexual responsiveness, these can be years of rediscovery. Some couples start communicating with a candor and vivacity that they could never have had when they were younger. They are able to spend more time arousing each other and enjoying more polymorphous, less genital sex.

NOW YOU ARE PAST SIXTY-FIVE

Do you find that you are still very much interested in sex, but no one
  treats you as if you were?
What would you like to change about your sex life?
Are you sexually happy with your present partner?
How often do you partake of some sexual activity?
Is this enough for you?

Do you fantasize more or less than you used to?

Notes _____

_____

Comments If you aren't rich and famous (and even if you are sometimes), to be interested in regular sex when you're over sixty is to be a dirty old man or a hungry old lady. There just is not a whole lot of appreciation for the sexual concerns of those over sixty-five. Even doctors—let alone husbands, wives, and children—don't acknowledge that the drive for sex, just like those for food and sleep, goes on. Yet masturbation rates for this age group increase, probably due to the presence of drive and the absence of available partners.

Most people are interested in sex all their lives and are perfectly able to enjoy it always. As long as you are healthy and interested in sex, there is no point in going without at this age.

EIGHTY AND BEYOND

Would you still enjoy sex if you had a willing partner?
Are you relieved "all that" is over?
Do you live in a family or institution where you have no privacy?
Do you wish your family would suggest dating for you instead of baby-
  sitting?
Do you have a good sex life?

Notes _____
_____
_____

Comments Older people who are interested in maintaining an active sex life sometimes find that there aren't the opportunities they might wish. Lack of partners is one problem. Lack of privacy is another. Residential and nursing homes often have open-door policies that make any kind of sex play awkward. Living with your family can be just as bad.

Even if you have the chance and you are in good health, you may not know how aging affects arousal. For instance, both men and women need more stimulation than they did when young. People who have never touched themselves or their partners on the genitals may find this hard to start at this age. However, communicating about your needs and finding the privacy to satisfy them are as important at this age as at any other.

CONCLUSION

This is not the sort of form you can go back over and add up your score. But do go back and read through your notes. Then use this last space to write down some things about yourself you left out. You know more about yourself than any form can elicit.

Last notes _____
_____
_____

No matter where you stopped this history, you have traveled some distance. You have gone through growing up, having good and not so good experiences, and you have developed some tastes and opinions out of those experiences. In the next chapter we'll examine how your history comes out in your attitudes. You cannot change your history but you may be able to change your attitudes.

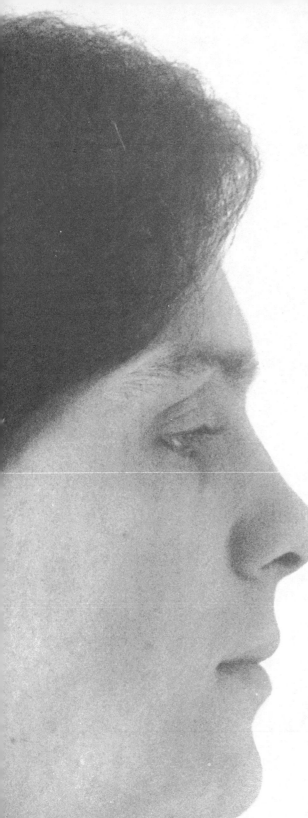

An Attitude Survey

INTRODUCTION

Your attitudes toward sex can influence your sexual behavior in many ways. This survey is designed to help you find out what your attitudes are and how they affect you. No one is asking you to change your attitudes, but rather to acknowledge that you have them. Beneath your attitudes, which are sometimes adopted because they are socially acceptable, are your real feelings. You should try to find out how well your attitudes do reflect your real feelings.

On the pages which follow you will find several passages and photographs covering subjects that may amuse, arouse, disgust, or confuse you. After each entry is a space for you to write down your initial reaction to the idea presented. It is important to capture your first impression before you can censor it. For instance, you may like something you feel you shouldn't, or you may feel uncomfortable about a subject you intellectually approve of. Often the best way to find your honest feelings is to record your reaction as fast as you can. If you find yourself dawdling around looking for the right words, skip to the next entry.

After you've written your initial reaction, read the statements that follow. Next to each statement is a line from YES across to NO. Your assignment is to draw a line bisecting the scale wherever you feel you fit. The closer to YES you draw the line, the more you agree with the statement. The closer to NO you draw the line, the less you agree with it. Here is an example of a neutral response:

I am totally at ease taking a survey of my attitudes.

YES ——————/—————— NO

You should, incidentally, be a little suspicious if you find you are having nothing but neutral responses.

There are blank spaces under each entry for you to write in your own statements when you'd like to. If you'd prefer to use a separate sheet or your journal for remarks and additional thoughts, don't hesitate to do so. Although many of the subjects raised here are to be dealt with later in the book, some are not. You may find it useful to explore many of your attitudes now, especially in conjunction with facts from your history from the previous chapter. The goal is self-knowledge and eventually self-acceptance. The therapeutic technique of looking for yourself in these pages is the beginning of this process.

Dwayne Hoover, incidentally, had an unusually large penis, and didn't even know it. The few women he had anything to do with weren't sufficiently experienced to know whether he was average or not. The world average was five and seven-eighths inches long, and one and one-half inches in diameter when engorged with blood. Dwayne's was seven inches long and two and one-eighth inches in diameter when engorged with blood.

Dwayne's son Bunny had a penis that was exactly average.

Kilgore Trout had a penis seven inches long, but only one and one-quarter inches in diameter....

...Patty Keene had thirty-four-inch hips, a twenty-six-inch waist, and a thirty-four-inch bosom.

Dwayne's late wife had thirty-six-inch hips, a twenty-eight-inch waist, and a thirty-eight-inch bosom when he married her....

His mistress and secretary, Francine Pefko, had thirty-seven-inch hips, a thirty-inch waist, and a thirty-nine-inch bosom.

His stepmother at the time of her death had thirty-four-inch hips, a twenty-four-inch waist, and thirty-three-inch bosom.

Kurt Vonnegut, Jr., Breakfast of Champions

MEASURING UP

Notes _____

_____

_____

My penis is about average.	YES _____	NO
My breasts are about average.	YES _____	NO
I am comfortable looking at another man's penis.	YES _____	NO
I am comfortable looking at another woman's breasts.	YES _____	NO
I am always a little uncomfortable taking my clothes off with someone of my own sex watching.	YES _____	NO
I am always a little uncomfortable taking my clothes off with someone of the opposite sex watching.	YES _____	NO
I feel ill at ease wearing boxer shorts.	YES _____	NO
I feel ill at ease not wearing a bra.	YES _____	NO
I have measured my penis.	YES _____	NO
I have measured my bosom.	YES _____	NO
I would let someone else measure my penis.	YES _____	NO
I would let someone else measure my bosom.	YES _____	NO
Jokes about the size of breasts really make me self-conscious.	YES _____	NO
If I were better endowed physically, I would be more relaxed and forthright about sex.	YES _____	NO
Most women can't feel the difference between a large penis and a small one.	YES _____	NO
_____		
_____	YES _____	NO
_____		
_____	YES _____	NO

The fact is that the size of the penis or the bosom has nothing to do with how much pleasure either can give and receive. But that does not lessen the anxiety both men and women feel about the size of their sexual paraphernalia. No matter how stacked your front or long your organ, there is always someone who's better than you.

If you have not thought before about how your perception of your physical adequacy influences your sexual behavior, spend some time now reflecting on it. We will examine this phenomenon more closely in the next chapter.

Susan Gilbert

TOUJOURS GAI

Notes _____
_____
_____

I don't like to think about these people having sex.	YES _____	NO
The prospect of growing old and losing my sex drive really depresses me.	YES _____	NO
I don't feel people my age should have sex any more.	YES _____	NO
I sometimes wonder if my parents still "do it."	YES _____	NO
The idea of an older person having sex with a much younger one is really disgusting.	YES _____	NO
I'm embarrassed to let people I meet now know that I am still interested in sex.	YES _____	NO
One of the good things about old age is that you find there is a lot more to life and love than sex.	YES _____	NO
I feel uncomfortable talking about sex with an older person.	YES _____	NO
_____	YES _____	NO
_____ _____	YES _____	NO

Sex, including intercourse, is something you can enjoy all your life as long as you are healthy and have a willing partner. But society isn't very tolerant of the sexuality of older people. Sex among the aged seems to be the subject of much derision for those who aren't there. You'll notice it in the jokes and comments that people make, even people who are old enough to know better. When you hear such remarks, look for your own reaction and try to analyze any signs of queasiness, pleasure, or lack of response that you experience.

AUTOEROTICISM

Notes_____
_____
_____

I have masturbated recently.	YES _____	NO
I think probably that most of the people I know masturbate.	YES _____	NO
I would feel uneasy if someone watched me masturbate.	YES _____	NO
I would like to watch someone else masturbate.	YES _____	NO
Masturbation is wrong and should not be indulged in by anyone.	YES _____	NO
I have thought of masturbating but I really don't know how to do it.	YES _____	NO
I'm sure my children masturbate.	YES _____	NO
I think my parents probably never did masturbate, although my father might have when he was a boy.	YES _____	NO
I'd feel furious and rejected if I found out that my partner masturbates.	YES _____	NO
I'd be relieved to find out my partner masturbated.	YES _____	NO
I feel it's fine to masturbate when you don't have any other outlet.	YES _____	NO
Somehow the word "masturbation" strikes me as dirtier than the act.	YES _____	NO
I feel it is all right for children to masturbate each other.	YES _____	NO
I feel guilty when I masturbate.	YES _____	NO
I've considered teaching my children how to pleasure themselves.	YES _____	NO
_____	YES _____	NO
_____	YES _____	NO
_____	YES _____	NO

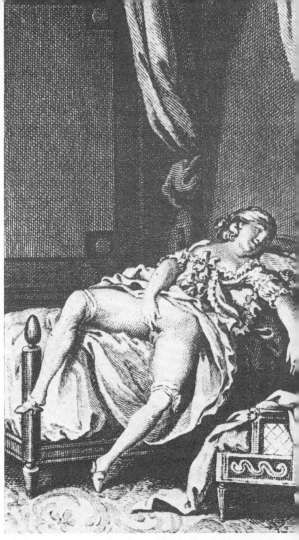

from Caylus, Thérèse Philosophe

There are many myths surrounding autoeroticism, mostly concerning the bad things that will happen to you if you do it. Your hands will turn hairy, you will go crazy, you will use up all your sperm, you won't be able to have a "vaginal" orgasm, you won't love your partner. None of these is true but their popularity can leave an imprint on you.

If you have never masturbated, imagine how and why you might go about it. Examine the prejudices or expectations you come up against when you look at yourself as a potential autoerotic. How does this comment by Jacqueline Susann strike you? She was allegedly speaking of Philip Roth, the author of Portnoy's Complaint—a book about masturbation among other things. "Well, he's a good writer, but I wouldn't want to shake hands with him."

If you have masturbated, examine how you feel about it, as separate from how you think you should feel about it. Where do the shoulds come from and how much, if at all, do they influence your behavior? Perhaps they do not influence your behavior but do touch on your attitudes toward the behavior of others.

"Hi"—softly, and with a little surprise, as though I might have met her somewhere before...

"What do you want?"

"To buy you a drink," I said.

"A real swinger," she said, sneering.

Sneering! Two seconds—and two insults! To the Assistant Commissioner of Human Opportunity for this whole city! "To eat your pussy, baby, how's that?" My God! She's going to call a cop! Who'll turn me in to the Mayor!

"That's better," she replied.

And so a cab pulled up, and we went to her apartment....

Philip Roth, Portnoy's Complaint

THE FIRST STEP

Notes _____

_____

_____   _____

I know it's fashionable to talk dirty and be direct but I prefer a romantic approach.	YES _____ NO
To make a clear sexual proposal and be rejected is really degrading.	YES _____ NO
I am reluctant to proposition women because I don't want them to think I'm just another guy on the make, although I am.	YES _____ NO
If my partner wants sex and I don't, I feel guilty.	YES _____ NO
I wish my partner would do the initiating sometimes. I'm always cast as the heavy who has to have it.	YES _____ NO
I never know how to show my partner that I am interested in sex.	YES _____ NO
My partner just doesn't understand that I'm not always up for sex the minute I get home.	YES _____ NO
If my partner, or anyone else, wants sex when I don't, I end up putting them down when I don't really mean to.	YES _____ NO
_____	YES _____ NO
_____	YES _____ NO

Who should take the first step is one of the most consistent and common complaints that both singles and couples have about sexual interchange. Feelings of rejection, guilt, fear, and inhibition seem rampant around this subject. People who never take first steps may feel exploited. People who always do may yearn for a change.

Look at your own patterns of initiating or not, whether it's intercourse or just a social contact. Your own fears and hesitations can sometimes be spotted in others.

THE TIE THAT BINDS

Notes _____
_____
_____

Living together is all right, but I don't think I'll really feel we are committed to each other unless we get married.	YES _____	NO
I don't know why anyone would get married these days.	YES _____	NO
I should know better by now, but each time I get married I think it's forever.	YES _____	NO
Marriage just means having a friend you can really count on.	YES _____	NO
I don't really believe that people should live together if they aren't married.	YES _____	NO
I want very much to get married, but so far I just haven't met anyone I want very much to marry.	YES _____	NO
To me marriage means having a home, children, some stability, and a partner I enjoy.	YES _____	NO
I often wonder what I'd do if I weren't married or if something happened to my partner.	YES _____	NO
My partner and I made a mistake and now we're trapped because of the kids.	YES _____	NO
Sometimes I just don't think that I am the marrying kind.	YES _____	NO
_____	YES _____	NO
_____	YES _____	NO

Despite all the criticism of marriage and the talk of alternative life styles, people seem to go on getting married. Consider some reasons you think people want to get married. Think about whether or not these reasons apply to you, and to what degree. Then think about whether these reasons are the same as your parents', your friends', and your partner's.

And she was close. Oh, she was close so much of the time. Like a child on a merry-go-round the touch of the colored ring just evaded the tips of her touch....I turned her over suddenly on her belly, my avenger wild with the mania of the madman, and giving her no chance, holding her prone against the mattress with the strength of my weight, I drove into the seat of all stubbornness, tight as a vise, and I wounded her, I knew it, she thrashed beneath me like a trapped little animal, making not a sound, but fierce not to allow me this last of the liberties, and yet caught, forced to give up millimeter by millimeter the bridal ground of her symbolic and therefore real vagina. So I made it, I made it all the way—it took ten minutes and maybe more, but as the avenger rode down to his hilt and tunneled the threshold of sexual home all those inches closer into the bypass of the womb, she gave at last a little cry of farewell, and I could feel a new shudder which began as a ripple and rolled into a wave, and then it rolled over her, carrying her along....

Norman Mailer, <u>Advertisements for Myself</u>

UP YOURS

Notes _____

_____

_____

I think of anal sex as being a homosexual practice.	YES	_____	NO
That seems so dirty to me.	YES	_____	NO
I have touched my anus but I don't think I'd like to have anyone else do that.	YES	_____	NO
Anal sex doesn't hurt you if you are clean and you move slowly.	YES	_____	NO
Anal sex in excess will make your colon fall out.	YES	_____	NO
Sometimes I really enjoy defecating but I certainly don't think of it as a sexual thrill.	YES	_____	NO
I'm very excited by anal stimulation.	YES	_____	NO
Anal stimulation interests me but I can't feature asking someone to do it.	YES	_____	NO

Anal sex is practiced by both homosexuals and heterosexuals, but it is by no means prevalent among either. It is preferred by some couples to vaginal intercourse, or at least as a variation to vaginal intercourse. The only dangers are from rushing in, rather than moving millimeter by millimeter, and from infection if the penis is moved to the vagina afterward without being cleaned.

Feelings about anal sex are closely related to attitudes about defecation and bodily functions in general. The anus is an erogenous zone in both men and women, but people sometimes feel it is an inappropriate one. If you have never touched your anus erotically, you might imagine doing it to see what feelings of repulsion or excitement that arouses.

I awakened at noon to find the blood welling up between my legs. If I parted my thighs even a little, the blood would gush down and stain through the mattress. Foggy and half-dazed as I was, I knew to keep my legs together. I wanted to get up to search for a Tampax, but it was hard to get out of that sagging bed without parting my legs at least a little. I stood suddenly and blackish-red rivulets began to inch their way down the inside of my thighs. A dark spot of blood glistened on the floor. I ran to my suitcase leaving a trail of glistening spots. I felt that heavy and familiar pull in my lower belly.

Erica Jong, Fear of Flying

THE MONTHLIES

Notes _____

_____

_____

I'd be mortified if that happened to me.	YES _____	NO
I feel very uncomfortable when women insist on talking about that.	YES _____	NO
I really think menstruation is a beautiful thing and should never be regarded as a nuisance.	YES _____	NO
I'm very interested in sex when I'm menstruating.	YES _____	NO
I have some hesitation about making love to a woman who is having her period, especially if she likes oral sex.	YES _____	NO
At least you can't get pregnant when you're on the rag.	YES _____	NO
I feel a little uneasy when women talk about having the curse, being on, etc.	YES _____	NO
I would feel comfortable inserting a Tampax in a woman I knew.	YES _____	NO
_____	YES _____	NO
_____	YES _____	NO

Women experience menstruation in different ways, depending on their religion, associations, history, mothers, and individual physiology. Men seem to pick up their attitudes from the women they are close to. Although blood from the uterus is sterile, flowing as it does from between the legs seems to make it unmentionable no matter what the real feelings associated with it are.

Consider advertisements for sanitary napkins. There is much mention of the absorbent qualities of the product, but the word "blood" is never used. Think about how often anyone refers to menstruation as bleeding. Think about looking at a used Kotex or Tampax. Listen for how your friends and acquaintances refer to the monthly cycle.

Gustave Courbet, "Le Sommeil"

SOME OF MY BEST FRIENDS . . .

Notes _____

_____

_____

I feel quite comfortable about homosexuality although I am not homosexual myself.	YES _____ NO
I have had some experiences I would describe as homosexual in tone.	YES _____ NO
I know I should be open-minded but I really don't know how people can do that.	YES _____ NO

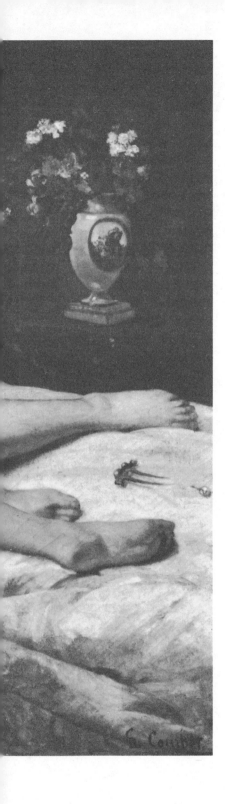

I would feel fine bringing a homosexual friend home to meet my family. YES _____ NO

I think it's really unfair to assume that female gym teachers or male interior decorators are gay, but I do it myself. YES _____ NO

Photographs like this one really excite me. YES _____ NO

I can't help it, I am uneasy leaving my children with a homosexual babysitter. YES _____ NO

It would be all right with me to have a homosexual friend see me in the nude. YES _____ NO

Most homosexuals just haven't met the right person of the opposite sex. YES _____ NO

I think anyone who makes derogatory remarks about homosexuality is probably a latent homosexual. YES _____ NO

I enjoy having homosexual friends. YES _____ NO

I feel almost all homosexuals benefit from professional help. YES _____ NO

One of the best ways to look at homosexuality is to become aware of the homosexuality in yourself. Very few people, according to Kinsey and others, are strictly homosexual or strictly heterosexual. Most go through a period of attraction to their own sex while growing up, and continue to have friendships which have a sexual component.

Choose a friend of your own sex whom you can imagine being close to sexually. Think about what it would be like to kiss this person, to touch him or her. Examine your feelings of fear or distance or pleasure. Remember that a fantasy won't hurt you.

I am homosexual and I'm really proud of it, although I have had some bad times. YES _____ NO

I'm homosexual and I desperately wish I weren't. YES _____ NO

I really object to gay liberation. I've made a place for myself and I don't need them screwing up all I've strived for. YES _____ NO

I don't know anyone else who is gay. YES _____ NO

I'd like to have children. YES _____ NO

I'd prefer to have gay friends. Straights are always so righteous about us. YES _____ NO

I think most straight people are afraid of me. YES _____ NO

_____

_____ YES _____ NO

_____

_____ YES _____ NO

Sometimes gay people are harder on themselves and on other homosexuals than the heterosexual world could ever be. If you are gay, consider how you feel about your homosexuality in relation to other life styles, such as those of your family or friends. Then think about what comfort or pain you receive from the straight world versus the gay world.

3 Men and 3 Women Convicted of Rape

Three men and three women were convicted in Superior Court Wednesday of sex crimes against a young Puerto Rican mother of two in March, 1974, in East Los Angeles.

Jurors found one of the women guilty on three counts of rape for "aiding and abetting" the males in their sexual assaults on the woman, according to Dep. Dist. Atty. Robert K. Gosney, prosecutor in the month-long mass trial of the six.

The three women and one of the men were convicted on one count each of another sex offense, oral copulation, and all six defendants were found guilty on two other counts of the same offense.

Gosney said the women were convicted along with the men because California law holds all persons acting in concert during the commission of a crime responsible for the crime.

He said the 21-year-old Bell Gardens mother had accompanied the three women acquaintances to the Ramona Gardens housing project where she was assaulted and brutalized during a period of four to five hours.

Sentencing was set for Sept. 3 in the court of Superior Judge E. Talbot Callister.

Gosney said each of the counts carries a maximum penalty of five years to life in prison.

RAPE

Notes _____

_____

_____

How could those <u>women</u> do that?   YES _____ NO

I have to confess that I always read those
  articles.   YES _____ NO

Sometimes I think every man is a potential rapist.   YES _____ NO

A man who is the victim of a homosexual rape
  does not suffer in the way a woman does if she
  is raped.   YES _____ NO

If prostitution were legalized, rape would be
  far less common.   YES _____ NO

A reasonably healthy woman who doesn't want
  to be raped, can't be.   YES _____ NO

Some days they just drive me crazy with their
  short skirts and their tits hanging out. If I
  could just touch <u>one</u> of them, just <u>one.</u>   YES _____ NO

I don't like to admit it, but I have pretended
  that my lover was raping me while we're making
  love.   YES _____ NO

I have fantasized about how I would foil a rapist.   YES _____ NO

I would be sexually stimulated hearing a woman
  tell about having been raped.   YES _____ NO

Every woman, in her heart of hearts, wants to
  be taken by force.   YES _____ NO

_____

_____ YES _____ NO

Rape has been called a crime against property and a crime against Mother, but that doesn't make it any easier to explain why it seems worse than most other crimes. Attitudes toward rapists and their victims range from sympathy to outrage; almost everyone has something to say about it. Most people read the newspaper articles with a mixture of titillation, horror, and perplexity.

Try to analyze the next rape story you read or hear. At the same time that you are looking for the author's attitudes, check your own.

...I lay on my back like a dead man, the only thing alive being my prick. I felt her mouth closing over it and the sock on my left foot slowly slipping off. I ran my fingers through her long hair, slid them round under her breast, moulded her bread basket which was soft and rubbery like. She was making some sort of wheeling motion in the dark. Her legs came down over my shoulders and her crotch was up against my lips. I slid her ass over my head, like you'd raise a pail of milk to slake a lazy thirst, and I drank and chewed and guzzled like a buzzard. She was so deep in heat that her teeth were clamped dangerously around the head of my cock. In that frantic, teary passion she had worked herself up to I had a fear that she might sink her teeth in deep, bite the end of it clean off. I had to tickle her to make her relax her jaws. It was fast, clean work after that....

Henry Miller, <u>Sexus</u>

NAKED LUNCH

Notes _____

_____

_____

This stuff just isn't relevant to me—I think
  I'll skip on ahead. YES _____ NO

I was brought up to think that enjoying oral sex
  indicated you were homosexual. YES _____ NO

If a woman sucks a man's cock, it means she
  really likes him. YES _____ NO

If a woman sucks a man's cock, it means (1) she
  knows how to get rid of him in a hurry, or (2) she
  doesn't want to get pregnant. YES _____ NO

My wife wants me to do it but frankly it makes
  me gag. YES _____ NO

Sometimes I go down on my partner even though
  I don't want to. YES _____ NO

I never know what to do with the ejaculate. YES _____ NO

Homosexuals probably get more pleasure from
  oral sex than heterosexuals do. YES _____ NO

Oral sex is okay as long as it is just a preliminary
  leading to intercourse. YES _____ NO

It is very hard to tell or show someone that
  you'd like oral sex. YES _____ NO

I like it better than anything else. YES _____ NO

I enjoy performing oral sex for my partner but
  I don't want it done to me. YES _____ NO

I like kissing very much, especially long, deep,
  passionate kissing. YES _____ NO

I'd like to try oral sex, but I really don't know
  what to do. YES _____ NO

_____ YES _____ NO

_____ YES _____ NO

_____ YES _____ NO

Oral sex means kissing, sucking, or licking the genitals of another person, occasionally at the time that the other person is doing the same to you. Some people do not like the taste or texture of semen or of vaginal secretions, but there is nothing inherently wrong with them. Semen, which is estimated to average less than 36 calories per ejaculate, can make you neither fat nor pregnant.

Your attitudes toward oral sex depend on your experience and your expectations. If you have always thought of oral sex as being irregular or queer or if you've had some bad experiences, your attitude will be negative. Good experiences obviously make you more positive.

CHILD'S PLAY

Notes _____
_____
_____

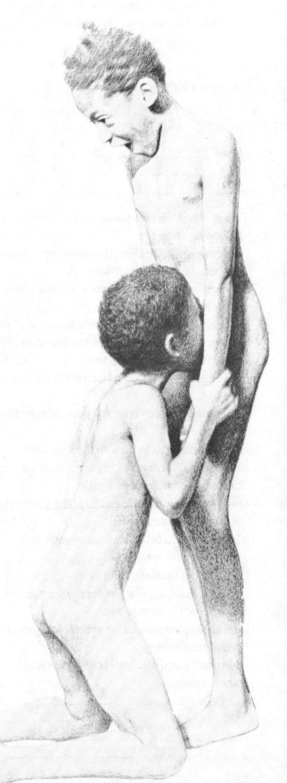

I would have to break that up.	YES _____	NO
I wish I'd started that young.	YES _____	NO
Children don't really have any sexual desires until they reach puberty.	YES _____	NO
Children should watch their parents making love so they'll know what to do.	YES _____	NO
My parents felt uncomfortable talking to me about sex.	YES _____	NO
I feel it's all right for children of opposite sexes to sleep together when they are little.	YES _____	NO
Children of the same sex probably shouldn't ever sleep together.	YES _____	NO
I have a friend whose interest in my little girl really sort of worries me.	YES _____	NO
I am very afraid that my child might be harmed sexually by an adult.	YES _____	NO
I wish my father had taken me to a whorehouse when I was fourteen.	YES _____	NO
If my kid walked in on me having sex, I'd tell him to get the hell out.	YES _____	NO
If I walked in on my children messing around, I hope I'd have the presence of mind to explain to them what they were doing.	YES _____	NO
I think children are probably frightened seeing adults having intercourse.	YES _____	NO
_____		
_____	YES _____	NO
_____		
_____	YES _____	NO

There are many taboos concerning children and sex. Everyone is always trying to decide what is all right for children to know, to witness, and to do. Some of the emotional turmoil around this subject is related to adults' confused feelings about their own sexuality. It is also wrapped up in sexual feelings that adults find occasionally they have toward their own and other children.

Think about how and when you gave your child, or other children, guidance on sexual issues. Is it when they ask, when they do something

Gerald Gooch, "Black Children"

you consider dangerous in some way? Describe a dangerous or loaded situation that has or might have happened. Consider how much your reaction depended on your being a "good" parent, teacher, or relative and how much was beyond your control. Even if you don't know children, think about the conflicts that might arise for you in dealing with their sexuality.

_____

In order to obviate confusion, let us first define what we regard as normal sexual intercourse. It is not altogether easy. All rigid definitions and sharp distinctions are particularly difficult in sexual matters. I think the most comprehensive and exact definition is as follows: That intercourse which takes place between two sexually mature individuals of opposite sexes; which excludes cruelty and the use of artificial means for producing voluptuous sensations; which aims directly or indirectly at the consummation of sexual satisfaction, and which, having achieved a certain degree of stimulation, concludes with the ejaculation—or emission—of the semen into the vagina, at the nearly simultaneous culmination of sensation—or orgasm—of both partners.

Theodor Hendrik van de Velde, M.D., Ideal Marriage

_____

CARNAL KNOWLEDGE

Notes _____

_____

_____

Now that sounds good to me. YES _____ NO

I'm not very concerned about simultaneous orgasms. YES _____ NO

I don't feel satisfied if my partner doesn't have an orgasm during intercourse. YES _____ NO

I would like to know what is considered normal sexual behavior. YES _____ NO

I feel you shouldn't have intercourse until a certain emotional commitment has been made on both sides. YES _____ NO

I feel let down or even guilty if I'm bored during sex. YES _____ NO

I really only enjoy intercourse when I'm on top. YES _____ NO

Sometimes I wonder if it is really good for me to have carnal knowledge of so many people. YES _____ NO

I'm disappointed if sex play doesn't lead to intercourse. YES _____ NO

I like to have sex once a day but my partner thinks once a week is plenty. YES _____ NO

I'm very annoyed and embarrassed when we stain the sheets. I always try to have a tissue handy. YES _____ NO

I don't think that coitus is necessary in a relationship. You can have good sex and good times without intercourse. YES _____ NO

_____

_____ YES _____ NO

There are many variations in attitudes toward intercourse, including some new ones since Dr. van de Velde wrote his book. Your attitude depends somewhat on your generation, your religion—even one you no longer practice—and your friends and associates.

Issues of frequency, positions, and coming together will be discussed in later chapters. For now, start thinking about how you communicate your feelings about intercourse to someone with whom you are or would like to be having sex.

MOTHER'S MILK

Notes _____
_____
_____

Rupfer, "Simon und Vera"

I would like to suck milk from a breast just to
  see what it tastes like.   YES _____ NO

I've reached orgasm just having my breasts
  stimulated.   YES _____ NO

I feel awkward if a woman wants me to suck her
  breasts.   YES _____ NO

Although I guess I wouldn't do it even if I had
  the chance, I sometimes fantasize that I am
  sucking and holding another woman's breasts.   YES _____ NO

There aren't enough breasts in the world for me
  to satisfy my desire to nuzzle them.   YES _____ NO

I feel uncomfortable if a man wants to fondle
  my breasts.   YES _____ NO

Men generally don't like to have their nipples
  touched or nibbled.   YES _____ NO

I don't care how natural it is, when I'm around
  a woman who is nursing her baby, I gawk.   YES _____ NO

I don't like to nurse my baby in public.   YES _____ NO

My wife thinks it's fine for her to nurse in public,
  but I don't.   YES _____ NO

I am very aroused watching another woman nurse
  her baby.   YES _____ NO

Sometimes I think they are just showing off.   YES _____ NO

I got very turned on nursing my baby, at least
  at first.   YES _____ NO

I don't think nursing is necessary.   YES _____ NO

_____

_____   YES _____ NO

Nursing among adults as a stimulating part of lovemaking is quite common. The return to breastfeeding in the past few years has brought some feelings toward nursing and breasts more out in the open. Reactions to nursing mothers as well as decisions to breastfeed may involve more than the merit of mother's milk. Some women, however, who are not particularly excited by breast manipulation, may find it hard to understand a lover's insistence on that activity. Some men, who thought it was a great idea, find that the actual experience doesn't do much for them. Couples who like it may see it as a relaxing pastime not necessarily leading to intercourse.

CASE 238. Z., age fifty-one, superintendent, enamored with his own daughter since her puberty. She had to leave home and reside with relatives abroad. He was a peculiar, nervous man, somewhat given to drink, without manifest taint. He denied being in love with his daughter, but the latter stated that he acted and behaved towards her like a lover. Z. was very jealous of every man who ever approached his daughter. He threatened to commit suicide if she ever married, and on one occasion proposed to her that they should die together. He knew how to arrange things so that he could be always alone with her, and overwhelmed her with presents and caresses. No signs of hypersexuality. Did not keep a mistress and was looked upon as a very decent man.

Richard von Krafft-Ebing, <u>Psychopathia Sexualis</u>

A CLOSE-KNIT FAMILY

Notes _____

_____

_____

I sometimes find myself wanting to touch or hug
   my child in a not altogether innocent way.   YES _____ NO

I still get a little testy when one of my parents
   fondles me.   YES _____ NO

When I was young I was always hoping to see my
   parents nude, but they were very modest.   YES _____ NO

I feel bad about it, but I just don't feel right
   having my children stare at my penis.   YES _____ NO

I think I married a woman much like my sister.   YES _____ NO

I'm very close to my family. We all touch and
   kiss each other a lot.   YES _____ NO

I find it a little shocking to think about my
   mother's pubic hair or my father's penis, but
   I don't see what that has to do with incest.   YES _____ NO

If I knew someone who was involved in incest,
   I'm not sure how I'd react.   YES _____ NO

I don't like to talk about sexual matters around
   my brother.   YES _____ NO

_____   YES _____ NO

_____   YES _____ NO

The prohibitions against incest arose more out of fear of disrupting the family than out of fear of genetic abnormalities. In fact, many royal families practiced incest to keep the blood lines pure. But it is not acceptable behavior for most folks in any culture. Evidently the taboos reflect the possibility that people who live in close proximity will think of such things.

Incest is not very common but there are tensions and rivalries in all families which may be attributable to underlying sexual feelings that can never be expressed. Sometimes these feelings are impossible to see as sexual, given all the prohibitions against seeing family members as sexual. But when you think how familiar and available family members are to each other, it seems odd that sexual feelings wouldn't involve them.

By the way, many people enjoy reading case histories like this one for their prurient value. People who are never aroused by pornography or romances find that "science" sometimes is especially interesting to them.

PORNO

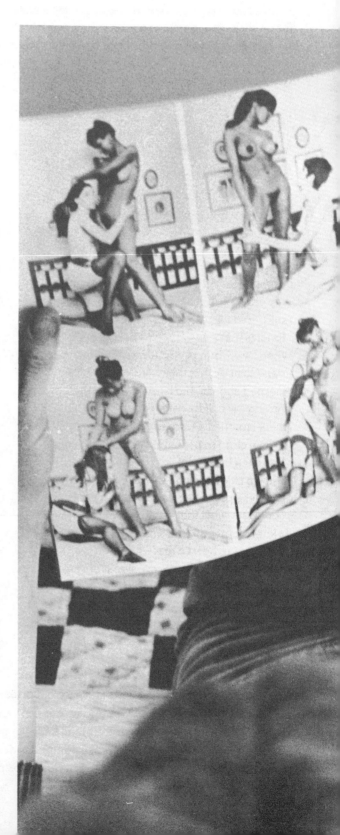

Notes _____

_____

_____

Hey! Where can I get some of this?!!	YES _____	NO
I don't care if other people read this stuff, but it just isn't for me	YES _____	NO
I really need something like this to get interested in sex.	YES _____	NO
It's all right for adults but I don't think children should have access to material like this.	YES _____	NO
Pornography really degrades women.	YES _____	NO
Pornography is so artless it just doesn't arouse me at all.	YES _____	NO
I'm too embarrassed to go into a porno shop or a porno movie.	YES _____	NO
When people talk about pornography I always come off sounding very liberal, but I'm really not as free as I think I should be.	YES _____	NO
I don't think pornography should be legal.	YES _____	NO
I don't really like pornography but if it's around I'll read it.	YES _____	NO
The trouble with pornography is that it encourages people to laugh at sex and disguise their feelings of arousal or disgust.	YES _____	NO
_____	YES _____	NO
_____	YES _____	NO

It is hard for many people to describe why they object to or enjoy pornography. Pornography has been around from the walls of Pompeii to underground Victoriana. Even now, very emotional battles rage over what is obscene and what the freedom to read includes—and for whom. Although studies show that pornography is not related to sex crimes, many people still feel that it is. They also feel that the availability of pornography shows moral turpitude in a society. Yet for many people forbidden or hidden sex is more fun. Because porno isn't on every newsstand, you have to seek it out—and that in itself can be exciting.

As with other sexual subjects, attitudes toward pornography may echo attitudes toward your own sexuality. See if remarks you hear or make in any way reflect comfort or lack of comfort with sex. If possible, expose yourself to pornography by going to a "dirty" movie.

"It's my Donald. We have an open marriage."

OPEN AND CLOSED

Notes _____

_____

I would like to be sophisticated and casual, but
the thought of my partner sleeping with someone else makes me sick.   YES _____ NO

I would feel rejected if my partner told me she
or he was having an affair.   YES _____ NO

I don't care what my partner does as long as it's
done discreetly.   YES _____ NO

I occasionally feel that certain friendships I
have with the opposite sex could blossom if I
weren't married.   YES _____ NO

Affairs just aren't worth the trouble.   YES _____ NO

Why have hamburger out when you can have
steak at home?   YES _____ NO

I would never tell my partner if I had an affair. YES _____ NO

My partner and I have talked about what would
happen if one of us were attracted to someone
else.   YES _____ NO

Running around by either partner is usually a
sign that the relationship is in trouble.   YES _____ NO

My partner and I feel our relationship has been
strengthened by our extra-curricular activities. YES _____ NO

Sometimes I wonder if I could still attract someone other than my partner.   YES _____ NO

I don't know why people get so excited about
infidelity.   YES _____ NO

_____
_____   YES _____ NO

Some of you may feel very threatened by the idea of an open marriage
yet wonder if it is the thing to do. Others may feel it isn't difficult at all.
The idea that it is natural for men to have affairs and not for women has
changed recently. That is threatening to many men, let alone women.

   You are probably already aware of the subject from movies, television,
and general conversation. If you have never talked to your partner
about open marriage, maybe you should test your feelings by bringing
it up. If you find you can't bring it up, that should tell you something.

64

Franz von Bayros

THE BIRDS AND THE BEES

Notes _____

_____

_____

Wow! Now, that is exciting.	YES _____	NO
I never think of my pet having a sex life.	YES _____	NO
Watching animals copulate really excites me.	YES _____	NO
I get a little embarrassed when someone's dog starts nuzzling my crotch.	YES _____	NO
I'm embarrassed if my pet has an erection, especially if there are other people around.	YES _____	NO
I have attempted to get my dog to rub up against my genitals but he seems to prefer his own kind.	YES _____	NO

I don't believe people should have sex with
  animals because the animals have no choice in
  the matter.   YES _____ NO

I'm not sure why but I would like to see someone
  have sex with an animal.   YES _____ NO

_____   YES _____ NO

_____   YES _____ NO

You may find this rather bizarre, especially if you haven't thought of
animals as having erotic potential. It is bizarre, yet sex with animals is an
idea that persists in the literature and art of most countries as well as in
the myths and fantasies of most peoples. Although it occurs rarely, it
continues to have a fascination mixed with repugnance for many
people. Your dealings with animals may reflect some of your feelings
about your own sexuality.

   Other unusual sexual practices, such as fetishism, exhibitionism, necrophilia, sadomasochism, and so on, are also more common in fantasy
than in life. Your attitudes toward them, as separate from whether you
want to do them or not, will often tell you something about yourself. Of
course, any sexual activity which becomes debilitating or obsessional
can be a serious problem. This aspect will be dealt with in Chapter 13.

   The word love, as used today, means romantic love—a concept that did not
exist before the troubadours in the Middle Ages and did not really assume its
horrendous sickness until the nineteenth century. My attitudes about sex are
closer to Petronius, to Rome and Greece, than they are to the sickness of the
Middle Ages, the obsession with self that led to the vulgar romanticism of the
nineteenth century.

   …What we would regard today as normal—the frenzy a man ideally should
feel for a woman—the Greeks and Romans treated as a fever, an illness that
would pass. That's how they viewed what we regard as romantic love, and it's
my idea of it.

Gore Vidal
"The Truth About Gore Vidal—Right From Gore Vidal"
by Curtis Bill Pepper

LOVE

Notes _____

_____

_____

Sex without love is really empty.   YES _____ NO

I am sometimes sexually attracted to people that
  I don't even like, let alone love.   YES _____ NO

To me love means having someone to really care
  about.   YES _____ NO

Love is painful sometimes.   YES _____ NO

I don't think you've ever really been alive if you've
  never been in love.   YES _____ NO

Vidal wouldn't like this but I don't feel complete unless I have someone I love.   YES _____ NO

I have a physical reaction to being in love.   YES _____ NO

I want very much to love someone but first I
have to find someone who loves me.   YES _____ NO

Romantic love is still in style if you want it
to be.   YES _____ NO

I know I shouldn't feel this way, but the word
"love" implies obligation and guilt to me.   YES _____ NO

_____   YES _____ NO

_____
_____
_____   YES _____ NO

Writers, philosophers, and many others have tried to describe what love
is. Isolate your own ideas and compare them to what you read or hear.
It's a large and confused subject but you should have a sense of what it
means for you. Use your journal to evaluate Vidal. If possible, talk to a
friend or partner about your ideas on love.

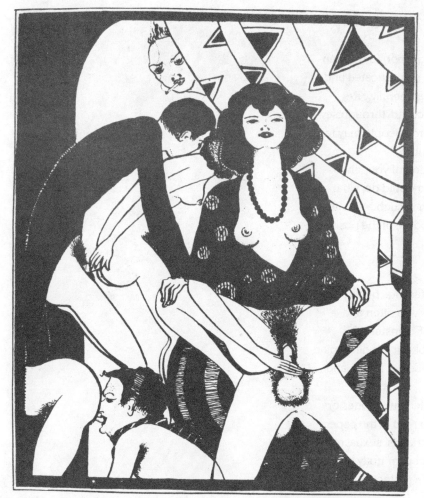

Count Alexis, His Memoirs

TOGETHERNESS

Notes _____
_____
_____

I like to kiss everyone goodbye after a party.	YES _____	NO
I would like to go to an orgy but no one has ever invited me.	YES _____	NO
Sometimes I fantasize about picking up a young hitchhiker and bringing him/her home to play with.	YES _____	NO
If I were in a group situation I would probably be impotent. Either that or I'd be overlooked.	YES _____	NO
I like to lie on a crowded beach with all those other bodies around.	YES _____	NO
When my partner and I are sitting around with friends, I fantasize something sexual just happening.	YES _____	NO
I like group sex but my partner is very jealous in such situations.	YES _____	NO
Those things are always better in your imagination than in real life.	YES _____	NO
The idea of taking my clothes off in a large group of people scares the pants off me.	YES _____	NO
_____		
_____	YES _____	NO
_____		
_____	YES _____	NO

Sex for more than two at a time has long held a fascination for human-kind. Usually such practices are associated with the sophisticated and well-to-do, who have the means to flout conventional morality. Recently, however, it seems to be discussed, if not practiced, through several levels of society. With its increased publicity, some people may feel they ought to try it or that they are missing something.

Try to place yourself mentally in a group sex situation of your choosing. Imagine what you would do and what the others would do, what you would like and not like about it. If you have been in such a situation, even if it involved just kissing or fondling, examine some of the positive and negative aspects you encountered.

CONCLUSION

This has just been an introduction to exploring the feelings behind your sexual attitudes. In the next few days, try to stop every so often and evaluate a reaction you are having to a sexual idea. For instance, if someone at a party or in the office tells you a dirty joke, try to determine what you do and do not like about it, why you do or do not laugh, and how comfortable you feel listening to it.

If there is no party or office in your near future, look at magazines or billboards. Think about your response to things you read in the paper, to your children's embarrassing questions, to your friends' sexual references or complaints. If you find that you blandly accept or hotly reject most everything, try to find out if it is necessary, even protective, for you to do so.

Think about having someone else look over the marks you made on this attitude survey. If you knew that that were going to happen when you started, would you have made different marks? You might have made yourself appear more liberal, more conservative, more or less interested in some of the categories. Think about who, if anyone, you would be willing to show your journal or this book to.

For one last check of attitudes, look at how you drew the lines throughout this chapter. You may have been firm and sure or wispy and wavering. You may have erased a lot; you may have gone through it hurriedly with no second thoughts, on paper, at least. You could have used a pen, a pencil, or a crayon. And, of course, you may have just made mental marks, protecting yourself right from the start. By now you have erased all evidence of any lines just in case some nosy visitor starts poking around your library.

It is absolutely all right to protect your privacy, just as it is all right to find in yourself feelings of disgust and pleasure toward taboo subjects. The important thing always is to be aware of what you are doing and why you might be doing it.

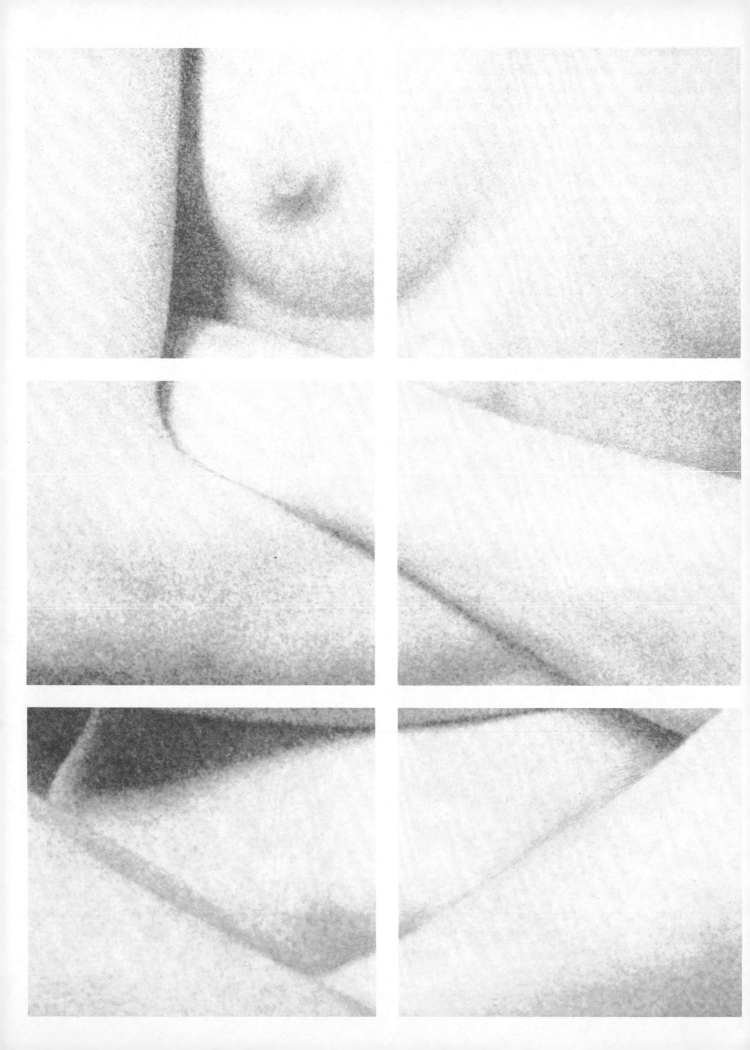

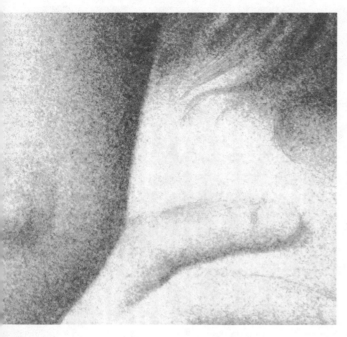

Your Body

INTRODUCTION

There are days in your life when your body seems perfect. You take an extraordinary pleasure in how it looks or feels. This might be after hard physical activity, while sunning or swimming, during lovemaking, after a fast or feast, when you are wearing something new, when you are just getting over a cold or the flu.

But these moments of pride and confidence don't seem to last. No matter how your body is, you wish sometimes it were otherwise. Feeling bad about your body can affect your behavior and inhibit you both socially and sexually. Conversely, feeling inadequate socially or sexually may be the result of feeling awkward or uncomfortable with your own body.

THE EVERYPERSON GALLERY

Let's see what you are dealing with. On the following pages you will see some familiar disembodied body parts. You are to consider each part of your own body separately. Circle the one on the page that is closest to your own. If none is close, sketch a facsimile in your journal.

As you are considering each possibility and choosing the best one, think about what that particular piece of yourself means to you. Consider the feelings, if any, you associate with it and where they come from.

After you've thought about these parts of yourself, try putting them together for a group portrait. Draw a rough unprofessional outline of your own body and include especially the parts from this gallery that made you hesitate, blush, or laugh.

Feet

Look for signs of care, shoes, health, age in these feet and then in your own. Circle the ones here that most resemble your own.

Legs

Look for hair, veins, flab, and muscles along your legs. Then check out the shape and detail of your knees.

Hips and Crotch, front view

Women—Look at the varieties of pubic hair growth. Is your own curly, sparse, thick, dark, light?
Men—Check out pubic hair, scrotal sac. Is your penis slanted, circumcised, erect?

Hips, back view

Note hair showing, pimples, dimples. Who here is most like you?

Back

Look at musculature, shoulder blades, spinal column, and love handles. Note signs of physical condition, sex, and age.

Abdomen

Are you plump, thin, solid bellied? Do you have any scars? Is there a navel here like yours?

Chest

Note differences in shape within as well as between the sexes. Check nipples, including color and hair growth.

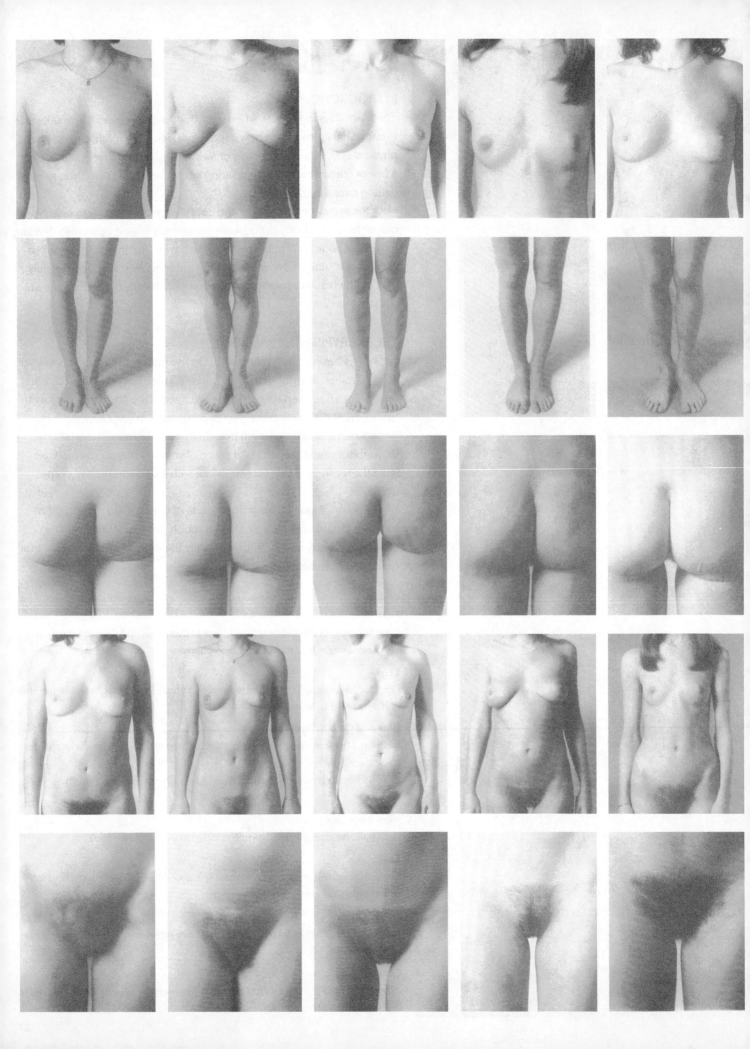

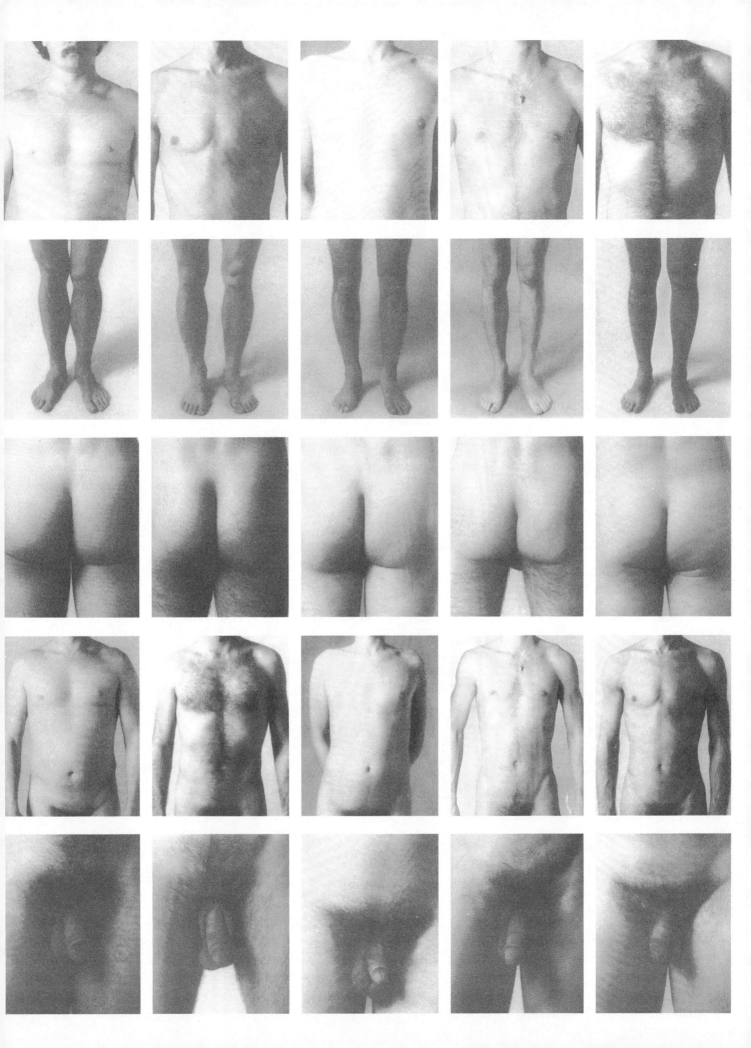

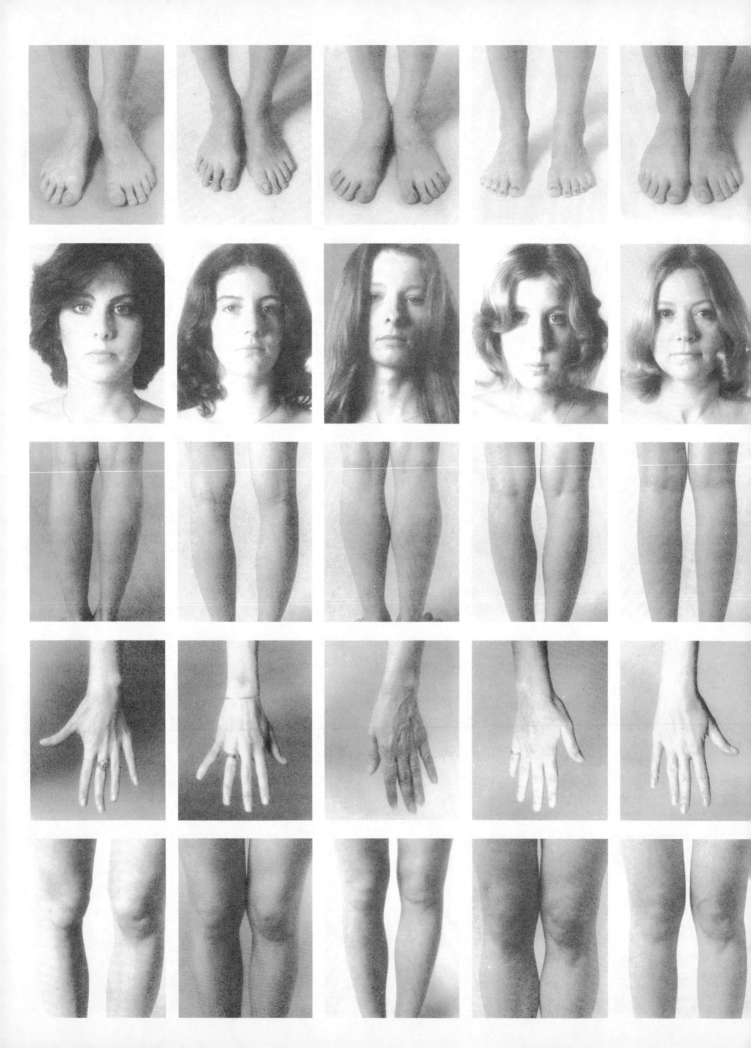

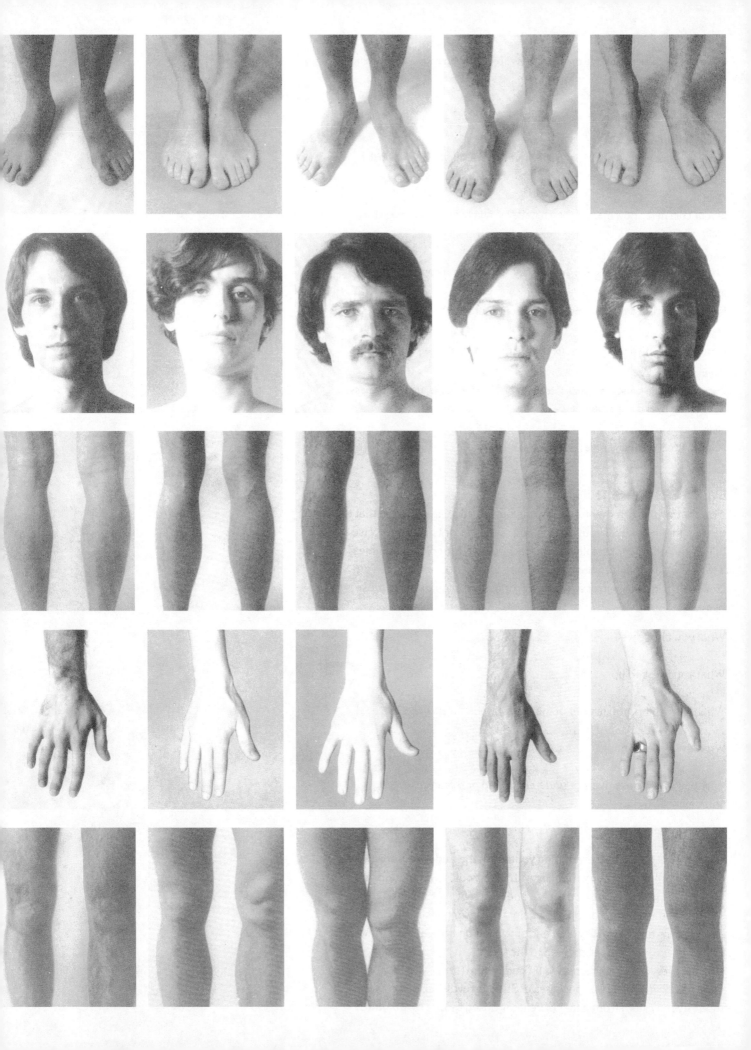

Arms

Does one of these arms have muscles, veins, freckles, or hair growth anything like yours?

Hands

Look for your shape of hand, nails, palms.

Neck and shoulders

Look for grace, strength, lines in the neck and slopes, curves, breadth in the shoulders.

Chin

Is your chin here? How many do you have? Any intimation of wattles, recession, clefts, sliding?

Ears

Think about your own ears. Are they pierced, lobed, hairy, flapping?

Mouth

Is your mouth like any mouth here? How about your teeth?

Nose

Noses come turned up, bulbous, freckled, large and small, fixed.

Eyes

Eyes may be the most individual of features so look for shape, make-up, glasses, lashes, brows, and not expression.

Hair

Note how hair color and style reveal age, sex, life.

EVERYPERSON VS. THE REAL YOU

Now that you have a mental picture of yourself you can compare that to the real thing. Take off your clothes and stand in front of a mirror. Use a full-length mirror if possible and look at yourself from different angles. Try to judge how close your choices were to what you see before you. Now, still using the mirror and your composite as a guide, fill in these blanks:

What you chose well _____

_____

What you messed up _____

_____

What, if anything, you left out of the assembled composite _____

_____

What the Gallery left out _____

_____

Why you might have over- or underestimated or misrepresented yourself _____

_____

You may not be used to examining yourself in the nude. Your mistakes come from not really being familiar with your body. Even though you have more right to look at it than anyone, you may feel inhibited doing so. This comes from prohibitions against nudity in our society and the associations among nudity, sex, and sin which go back at least to Adam and Eve—rarely pictured dressed to the teeth.

Nearly everyone is embarrassed by nudity sometime, whether their upbringing was puritan or permissive. Shame, revulsion, or excessive modesty may stem from a fear of being aroused by one's own nude

body. Even pride in one's body can affect behavior if that pride is seen as inappropriate or unnatural.

If you feel you aren't up to snuff in the buff, you may not want to look at your body. If your body is not the way you think it should be, looking at it just depresses you. Familiarity, for you, breeds contempt. You might consider where and when you feel this inadequacy, and whether or not you have a specific reason. Did anyone ever tell you that you were inadequate physically? Probably not. But if so, they may have been projecting their own body image problems onto you.

You might have tried to make up for the sense of inadequacy by misrepresenting yourself. Everyone does this to some degree and it is probably healthy in moderation. What isn't healthy is wallowing in your imperfections. Some people become almost aggressive about their worse features and thrust them on others.

When people put themselves down, others have to decide whether to be sympathetic or liars. If you put yourself down, you may be imploring: "Accept me anyway," or "Tell me it isn't true." People do use inadequacies to get other things they want.

If you left anything out of your body picture, you may feel ashamed of it, sad about it, or a little hesitant to have it. Before you excuse your omission by saying that you just forgot, think about what that part means to you. Maybe you left it out because it used to look better than it does now—and you prefer to remember it as it was. Maybe you never really liked it. Maybe you had a conflict of interest because no one but you, or everyone but you, likes it.

If you went through this section without feeling both good and bad about your body, you'd better back up and try again.

MORE EVERYPERSON

It isn't enough to know your body just from looking at yourself in the mirror. How does it look up close? Do you know how it smells and tastes?

Go back and do a very minute visual examination of your body. You should be nude and you can use a mirror for the parts you can't see well. Start with your feet and look at them carefully. What is the texture and shade of the skin on your soles? Look at the way the hair grows, the bones protrude. Examine the shape of the arch and the toes. Continue on to your calves, thighs, hips, navel, neck, and head. Get to know your body.

How would you feel if someone else examined you this closely? _____

_____

What would you want them not to notice? _____

_____

What would you point out for special attention? _____

_____

Has anyone ever examined you like this? _____

_____

Have you examined anyone else like this? _____

_____

This kind of close examination incorporates another sense, touch. When you go over your body this time, try to concentrate on how it feels to touch your toes, knees, abdomen, penis, breasts, ears, etc. Can you distinguish between touching and being touched? How does it feel to rub your skin the wrong way, to find areas of your body that are highly sensitive and others that are almost numb, to feel soft places, rough places, hairy places? The skin is our largest and most varied organ. Check it out:

What of yours do you like to touch? _____

_____

What do you like to have other people touch? _____

_____

What, if anything, do you find unpleasant to touch? _____

_____

What, if anything, do you feel self-conscious, uncomfortable, or nervous having someone else touch? _____

_____

Smell is an important and often unsung sense. Think about your body scents. W. H. Auden once said that everyone loves the smell of his own farts. You may have noticed that your urine smells strongest when you first get up and that perspiration changes with your activity and your diet. Smells of tobacco, garlic, sweat, perfume, semen, and soap can be picked up on other people as well as yourself. Examine yourself carefully with your nose and then fill in these blanks:

Genital juices tend to smell sweet, faint, foul, or _____

_____

There is a difference between clean sweat and stale sweat. It is _____

_____

I feel uncomfortable if someone wants to smell my _____

_____

I think vaginal sprays, toothpaste, antiperspirants, after shaves and perfumes are _____

_____

People who smell of _____ really make me feel _____

_____

Taste isn't as strong a sense as smell but it does have the advantage of being in the mouth, generally considered to be more erotic than the nose. You may not be used to licking or kissing your body, but you'll see that your sense of touch is extended by using your lips and tongue as receptors. Ear wax has its own special, bitter flavor. Your hands and hair often carry other flavors as well. Taste anything you can reach.

I didn't know my menstrual blood tasted _____

_____

I didn't know my semen tasted like _____

_____

I didn't know my underarms tasted like _____

_____

I didn't know my knees tasted _____

_____

I knew my_____ tasted like _____

_____

Your body makes all kinds of fascinating sounds. You can hear your heart beating, but it is impossible to distinguish the movement of different heart valves. (Next time you are around someone with a stethoscope, ask to listen to yourself.) You can also hear digestive noises. If you have a willing friend or lover around, try listening to his or her heart and tummy. You can hear muscles singing if you flex your biceps close to your ear. And you probably have joints that creak or crack sometimes.

Your body is also affected by sounds which make it relaxed, tense, or excited. Some of these might be music, traffic, sighing, wheezing, voices, rain. Listen to the sounds of yourself and the sounds around you.

Are there any specific sounds which you associate with making love?

_____

_____

How do you feel if someone wants to lay his or her head in your lap?

_____

_____

What kinds of sounds affect your mood to the extent of affecting your body? _____

_____

Your sense of your body isn't limited to one sense impression at a time. There are several situations listed below in which you may be acutely aware of your body. Put yourself into the setting and describe in detail your reactions. Include as many sensual responses as you think would be involved.

You're at the beach. (What do you think of your bathing suit? Are you proud of your body? How do the sun, water, and sand feel against your skin? How do they smell? How does the wind taste? What effect do the sounds of waves or other people have on you?)

Notes _____

_____

_____

You are trying on clothes in a very crowded, noisy shop where you have to share a dressing room.

Notes _____

_____

_____

You are sick and have taken to your bed.

Notes _____

_____

_____

You are sitting on a toilet and there is someone else in the room, watching you or just chatting with you.

Notes _____

_____

_____

You are being examined by a doctor.

Notes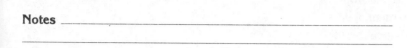

These are just a few examples of when and where you might be particularly aware of your body, how it feels, smells, and so on. Try to think about what makes you comfortable or uncomfortable in these situations. Would you have been happier on a nude beach? an empty beach? Do you like to try on clothes wherever you are? It might make a difference to you if the person watching you on the toilet were an adult or a child, if the doctor were a man or a woman, and so on.

The point of these exercises is not to make you comfortable in all situations under all conditions, but rather to make you aware of how you feel in very varied settings.

WHERE DO FEELINGS ABOUT BODY IMAGE COME FROM?

Comparison is a basic mental process which goes on all the time. If you didn't know when you were comfortable in the preceding section, how could you know when you were uncomfortable? Comparisons between your body and other bodies begin in infancy when you first separate your body from the world around you. Later, you start comparing yourself to your parents. When you are a child you are always faced with the fact that you are smaller and less powerful than the rest of the world. Your desire to be able to control your body and your environment as easily and nonchalantly as adults do can lead to feeling that you can't compare to them.

That sense of inferiority persists when you get a little older and find that there are people whose physical development somehow outstrips yours. You can feel inferior even if you are ahead of your classmates in body development. The young person who matures early physically may be treated as more mature emotionally or socially than she or he is able to be.

Comparisons seem to be inevitable. The girl or boy who towers over her or his classmates, who is fat or thin, will almost always feel uncomfortable with her or his body, at least for a time. Feelings like these can linger even after your body changes. If you don't compare yourself to your friends, you might have an older sibling or parent to measure up to. And these comparisons go both ways. You may not be as pretty as A or as athletic as Z, but you are surely more attractive than D and a better dancer than C.

The idealization of women's bodies, and more recently men's, in magazines and pin-ups gives you something to compare yourself to if you should get bored pitting your body against those of your friends and relatives. There is a big conflict surrounding these and other cultural ideals. They are, many of them, truly lovely to look at, but we usually see them at their very best. The ideal is maintained with soft focus, make-up, silicone, airbrushing, hairdressers, good dentistry, and careful lighting.

The effect of this glamorization is to make you wonder if everyone else looks beautiful all of the time. Even when you reject the movie star image as unrealistic, you wonder if other people reject it too. Or do they expect you to look like the pin-ups? Women have worried about this for years; and men, who have seen no reason for women to object to their talking about boob sizes, are now being threatened by the idea that women might think all men are hung like the male pin-ups. Actually, whereas you may regard the idealization of the opposite sex as simply good fantasy material, the idealization of your own sex can be quite threatening.

Another aspect of beauty in the media is the commercial one. Pleasant as it may be to be sold a product by an attractive person, most advertising seems designed to make you feel bad about yourself. The implication is always that you could be attractive too, if only you smelled, tasted, looked, or felt better. Irrational as you know such a pitch to be, there is always a longing for the magic formula.

Comparison, as you grow older, can also be with a younger you. You may long for the days when you could count on your body to hold up. You could stay up all night, play thirty-six holes of golf, and stuff a wild bikini. Your hair wasn't gray, your legs didn't bag at the knees, and your hands weren't coated with liver spots. Now you've lost your teeth and your hair and, perhaps, your body image.

Loss is something everyone experiences in body image terms— whether you've lost anything real or not. You experience loss when you first compare yourself to your parents and find youself lacking. You experience it when you compare yourself to cultural ideals and find you're missing something you never had. You experience it when you lose your youth. The fact of the loss can almost be taken for granted. How it affects your behavior and self-image can't.

BODY IMAGE AND SELF-IMAGE

It is natural to have a conflict between the image you have and the image you want. In this section we'll examine how you confront and resolve that conflict.

First of all, you may feel that people do not see you as you really are. You seem to be always fighting the stereotyping of your body image. You may be plain, but you are not beautiful inside. You may be tall, but you don't play basketball. You may be fat, but you are not jolly. You may be handicapped, but you aren't brave. You may be beautiful, but you aren't happy.

Think about the assumptions you make of others according to their body images. You may expect men with big noses to have big penises, women with big breasts to be good in bed. People who stand up straight could be uptight and physique freaks could be latent homosexuals. These are very prevalent myths that are useful to consider in terms of how your response to these people is influenced by such assumptions.

It would be grand if you could love your body without qualification. If you didn't compare yourself to anyone else or fall victim to your own stereotyping. If you thought you were the greatest looking, smelling, and tasting morsel around. You may not be able to do that totally, but just to savor the role of the happy native, try this exercise.

Below are some body types with spaces to add more. For each body, list here or in your journal all the lovable, attractive, erotic qualities you can think of—a fat body is a sea of billowing bulges, a garden of fleshy folds, an infinite source of warmth and security.

A thin body is _____

_____

A strong body is _____

_____

A deformed body is _____

_____

A small body is _____

_____

A _____ body is _____

_____

A _____ body is _____

_____

If you didn't praise your own body type much, you need more practice. Now try this exercise again, writing down repulsive characteristics of these bodies. This can be a cathartic way of getting to your real feelings about your own body. If you can say why you don't like it and why you do, you can move closer to accepting it.

When you think about having a different body, you may also think about how personality is shaped by the body. You might think you would be a different person if you had a different body. Actually maybe you do have a different body. You could be, right now, wearing a wig, dentures, make-up, a padded bra. Your body could have been changed by plastic surgery, dieting, exercise, contact lenses. That could make you feel attractive, confident, and proud; but it might also make you skulk around fearful of being uncovered or of having the fat, wrinkly person inside you break out. There is certainly nothing wrong with making yourself attractive as long as you don't feel you are living a lie. The important thing is to still be you when you lift your toupee or take off your girdle.

Everyone has rituals which make them feel better about their body— even when they don't feel bad in the first place. Some rituals are long and expensive, many are simple and everyday. They range from getting a tan or growing a beard to taking a bath or eating a peach. Make a list here of some things you know will give you a lift:

_____   _____
_____   _____
_____   _____
_____   _____
_____   _____

Why don't you do something from this list right away? The book can wait.

Most people also find that clothes affect how they feel about themselves and their bodies. Clothes change your mood, make you feel festive, sporty, or businesslike. They give you status and position and define your age, class, profession, even politics and interests sometimes. Describe here an outfit of yours that makes you feel particularly smart, comfortable, and composed:

_____

To analyze this description, you could think about when and where you would wear this outfit. If it is something you wear to work, think about how it compares to other things you wear to work and how it fits in or out with your fellow workers. Maybe it reflects an ideal of yours. It could be something you wear only when alone, which might indicate that you are most comfortable then. If it doesn't flatter you in the least, you may be saying that you feel best when you play yourself down. If you couldn't think of any outfit in which you feel comfortable, you're just being stubborn.

Deciding what to wear and dressing may say something about body image. If you agonize over what to wear and take hours pulling yourself together, are you trying to look your best or are you afraid you, not your clothes, won't be acceptable? If it takes you no time at all to throw something on, you could be confident that you usually look fine or else convinced that no amount of preparation would help.

The way you carry your clothes once you get them on is another body image test. If you slink around hoping no one will notice what you're wearing, you may be hoping no one will notice you yourself. If you are inclined to drape your draped body over the nearest group, you may want to get close, to be absorbed, to be absolved. An erect carriage may mean aloofness, pride, or tight clothes. Before trying to figure out what messages you send, think about some you receive from people you know. Their movements, gestures, ways of wearing clothes could tell you something about their body image. So could your own.

Sometimes resolving conflicts about your body image calls for more than taking care of your body, dressing up, or walking tall. Sometimes you have to change your behavior. You should consider whether or not your body image affects your behavior. If you don't think any clothes look good on you, you might never go out. If you think your body is ugly, you might never make love in the nude. If you think your toes are too smelly, you might never let anyone suck them.

CONCLUSION

When it gets right down to it, you are faced with the fundamental injustice of life. You aren't perfect and even if you are you won't last forever. It doesn't seem fair but that's the way it is. Once you've acknowledged that you are hugely—or even slightly—disappointed, you have two recourses. The first is to like yourself a little more anyway. To this end you can get to know and appreciate your body, and you can do the things for your body that you know will make you feel good.

Secondly, you can get angry at anyone who doesn't accept you as you are. One of the reasons cultural ideals and other objects of envy get you down is because you don't stand up for yourself. Maybe it is time you did.

Sexual Anatomy and Physiology

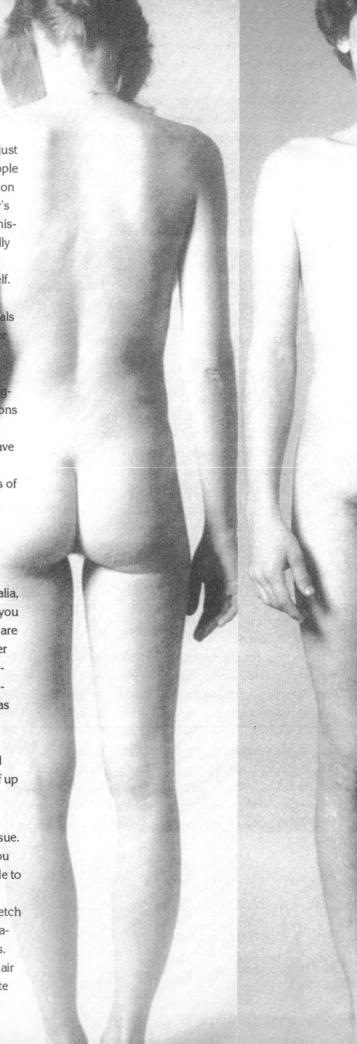

INTRODUCTION

All the body image problems discussed in the previous chapter are just heightened when you narrow your sights to your genitalia. Even people who don't feel particularly sensitive about how they look to the man on the street feel shy or nervous when confronting their own or another's sexual anatomy. The endless taboos on sex in this society and the misguided romanticism of the airbrush mentality keep people from really looking at their sex organs.

Often this leads to regarding your genitals as separate from yourself. You see desire and drive as necessary functions, with sexual intercourse as an activity carried on by a third party made up of the genitals of both partners. The naming of the genitalia, or using "he," "she," or "it," can be examples of this.

The isolation of the self from the sex reinforces feelings of shame, doubt, and self-consciousness about sex. This leads to widespread ignorance about the sexual anatomy, its physiology, and the implications of sex and reproduction.

To integrate your sex into your self in a positive way, you have to have a clear picture of your external genitals. You also have to know what goes on inside your body sexually. And you have to weigh the effects of conception and contraception on your sexuality. Here we'll address each of these issues.

THE EXTERNALS

We will begin with a thorough self-examination of the external genitalia, that is, what you can see or feel yourself. Find a private place where you can be alone and uninterrupted for a few minutes. Men and women are described at the same time, so if you wish to do this with your partner you may. If you don't have a partner or don't want to do it with someone, at least the first time, take note of the anatomical similarities between the sexes for future reference. If your partner is the same sex as you, look for the differences within your similarities.

To see the whole genital area clearly, you will need a mirror and a flashlight or lamp. You should direct the light between your legs and either squat over the mirror or use pillows or a chair to prop yourself up so you can see your reflection easily.

Start with your anus. It is all puckery and usually pinkish in color. Examine the hair growth if any, and look for protrusions of rectal tissue. You may wish to hold your buttocks apart in order to see better. If you gently nudge the center of the anus with your finger, you may be able to see it draw in.

The anus may also contract when you touch the perineum, the stretch of skin between the anus and the scrotum in men or the anus and vagina in women. The perineum is often quite sensitive to soft touches. It is usually a darker color than the surrounding skin and often has hair growing wispily around it. If you have ever had surgery to the prostate gland, the vagina, the uterus, or the anus, you may be able to detect

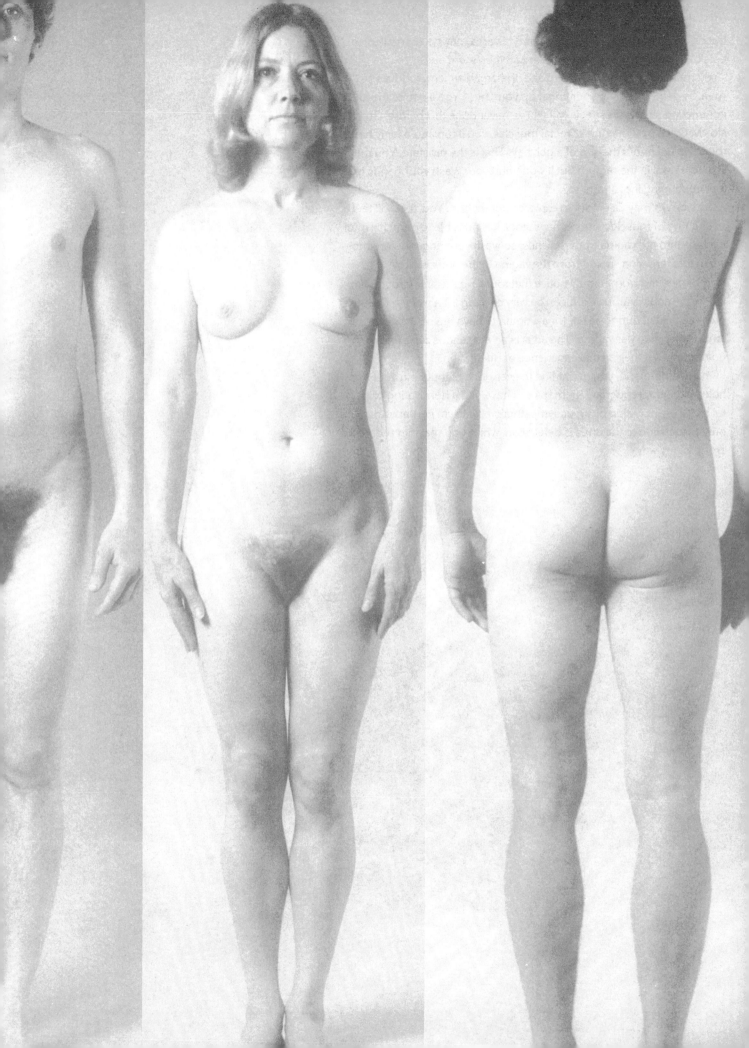

traces of stitches along the perineum. This area may be cut (called an episiotomy) or torn during childbirth and then sewn up.

You men can feel the prostate gland, the organ which produces semen, by gently pushing your finger up your anus. You'll notice the anus contracting strongly, especially if you've never done this before. Go slowly. Once past the ring of rectal muscles, you'll run into a fairly hard, round object about the size of a golf ball. That is the prostate. You may also feel stool in the rectum but it won't hurt you. Wash your hands before continuing if you want to.

You women may also want to explore your rectum. You, too, will feel a strong ring of muscles and perhaps stool. It is possible to carry harmful bacteria into the vagina from the anus, so wash your finger before moving in that direction. Going from the vagina to the anus is okay.

Both men and women may notice that touching the area around and inside the anus is arousing. It can be very exciting for a man to have the prostate tickled during sex or for a woman to have the penis inside her anus rather than her vagina. The anus is an erogenous zone for many, no matter what their sexual experience or orientation.

On the other hand, you might find the very idea of touching your asshole absolutely repugnant. Perhaps you have had a humiliating or painful rectal examination by an unsympathetic physician. Perhaps your only association to the anus is defecation, which you may not regard as erotic in any way.

If you wish to experiment and possibly expand your knowledge and attitudes toward anal eroticism, have a bowel movement before you start experimenting. Wash the anus thoroughly. That means wash the outside area with soap and warm water and insert a soapy finger up and around the anal muscles just inside. Some people might like to take an enema, which has erotic potential in itself. Finally, rinse the soap away and pat yourself dry with a clean towel.

To make the insertion of an exploratory finger easier, you may wish to use a lubricant. You can use Vaseline, hand cream, or, best of all, you can buy a sterile lubricating jelly in the drugstore which is water-soluble and easy to clean off. Warm whatever you use between your fingers before you start.

You may decide that you still don't think this very interesting. Some people find that pressure on the prostate or the rectum is more painful than thrilling, more uncomfortable than arousing.

If you are just winging along here not doing the exam as you read, either because you feel you already know all this or don't need to know it, why don't you take a few moments right now to describe below what your anus and genitalia are like.

_____

_____

_____

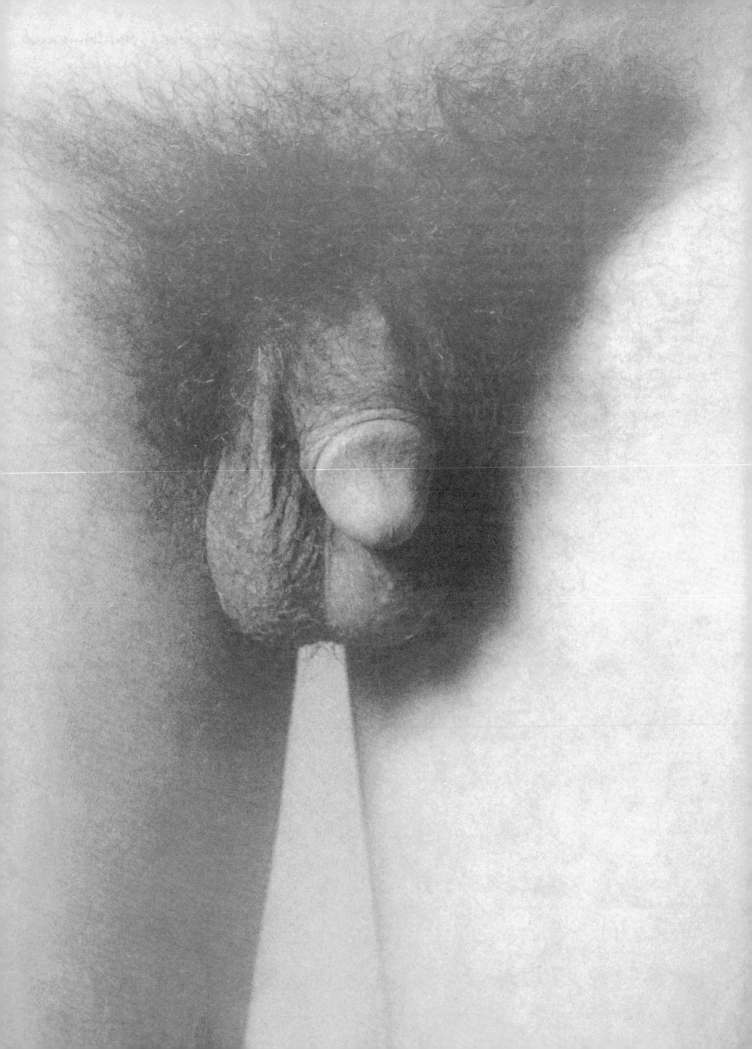

Now, let's do a close inspection of the labia majora and the scrotal sac. These parts of the female and the male respectively are said to be homologous, that is, they are similar in origin and structure. In the first weeks of intra-uterine life, all embryos are female. In about the tenth week, those whose genetic code so prescribes become male. But the sex organs of both develop out of the same tissues.

The labia majora or outer lips of the vagina are hairy on the outside and hairless and moist on the inside. They are also a darker color than the surrounding tissues. If closed together they would look like the scrotal sac, which has a line up the center, giving the appearance of being fused from two parts. The scrotal sac is also hairy and a darker color than the skin around it.

The scrotal sac is a multi-layered pouchy structure, heavily pocked with what are actually sweat glands. These glands control the temperature inside the sac where the testes are making sperm. The ideal temperature for sperm production is slightly below body temperature. That is why the scrotum draws closer to the body in cold weather or cold water, and hangs farther from the body in warm weather or water.

Inside the scrotum you can feel the two testes, which are almond-shaped and about 1 inch in diameter. The left one is usually lower than the right one but they work just as well the other way around. You can also feel some of the tubes which carry sperm into the prostate gland. These will be discussed in more detail later.

Often people think that the skin of the scrotal sac resembles the skin of a plucked chicken, whatever its clever thermostatic function. Somehow all those marble statues lead you to expect a tight package of majestic smoothness. The scrotum is tight just prior to ejaculation but most of the time it just hangs there. That wouldn't do in marble, but it'll do fine in you. There is much variation in the shape and texture of the scrotal sac—some men have fat balls, some have loose balls, some have light hair growth, and so on. Use the space below to describe yours or the one you are examining.

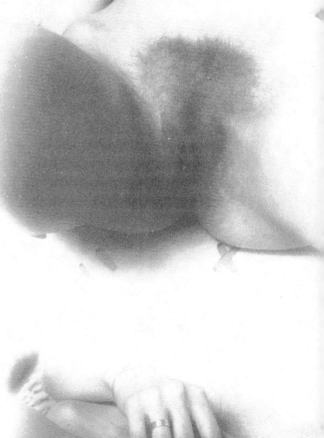

_____

_____

_____

Inside the labia majora are the labia minora, or inner lips to the vagina. These are hairless on both sides, pinker and moister than the outer lips. They are connected to the clitoris in front and they fade into the labia majora and the perineum behind the vagina.

Both sets of lips kind of flap around and overlap each other. They certainly are not perfectly in place all the time. When you are aroused, the lips fill with blood, seem to fill up the space between the legs more completely, and form a cushion to protect the vagina and clitoris. There are many variations in the size and shape of the vaginal lips. Some inner lips are longer than the outer ones. Women who've had children tend to have lips that are fuller and wider than women who haven't given birth. Use the space below to describe yours or the ones you are examining.

_____

_____

_____

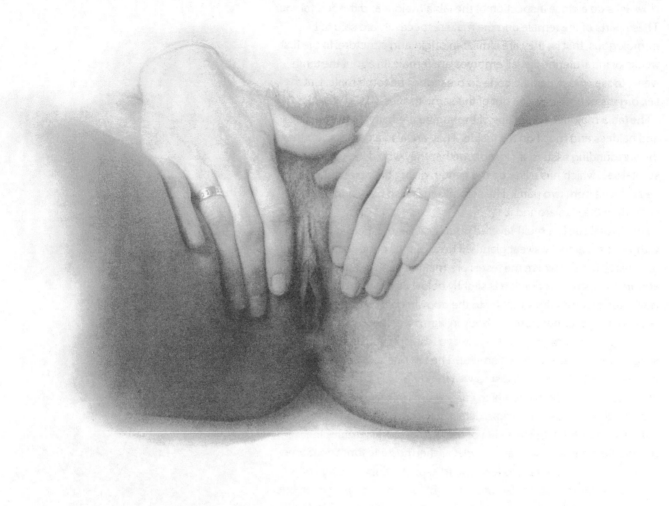

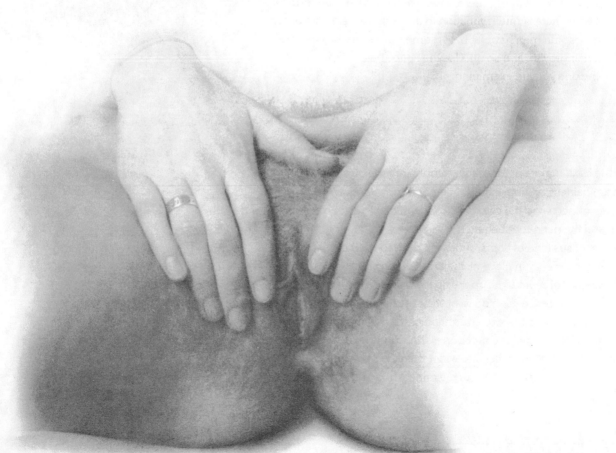

Inside the minor lips, starting at the top, are the clitoris, the urethra, and the vagina. The clitoris looks like a small bump, the urethra is a little hole, and the vagina is a somewhat larger hole. Sometimes you can see traces of the hymen around the edges of the vaginal entrance.

The hymen is a piece of membrane which stretches across the vaginal opening and is found only in human females. There is usually one or more small openings in the hymen through which menstrual blood passes out and Tampax, a penis, or a finger can pass in. If there is no opening at all, which is rare, a doctor could cut one. A penis passing in may tear or break the membrane, but if the membrane is elastic, and many are, it may just stretch to accommodate the penis. Some women are born with little or no hymenal tissue.

The hymen is the subject of many myths and superstitions regarding virginity. If a woman doesn't have a cherry, as it's called, she's no virgin. The only visible evidence that a woman is no longer a virgin is a little blood from the hymen tearing during first intercourse. Supposedly, if she doesn't bleed on her wedding night, she wasn't pure.

Actually, hymens are often broken during sports, the classic being horseback-riding. Some women never had one anyway. Others are highly elastic. Slow, gentle penetration of the penis could stretch the hymen without breaking it. If you are a virgin, you can stretch your own hymen (if you have one) by gradually inserting one finger into your vagina, then two fingers, and possibly three.

Breaking or tearing of the hymen, with or without bleeding, usually doesn't hurt if the woman is sexually aroused and lubricating from the vagina, or if she is involved in sports. Even a rushed or inexperienced entry which tears the hymen isn't particularly painful for very long. Why women have them, though, other than to make up myths about, remains a mystery.

Right past the hymen is the muscular entrance to the vagina. If you gently pull the vagina open, you'll see that it is quite pink and that there is a sort of waffly pattern to the inside skin. This ring of muscles opens easily during arousal and childbirth but it may be quite tight at other times—whether you want it to be or not.

It may be difficult for you to figure out how to control this ring of muscles. It is relatively easy to squeeze or push with your anal muscles, but you may not know where to start with the vaginal muscles. Actually, these are the same muscles that you would use to stop the flow of urine. You can pretend you are doing that and feel a little pressure on your finger inside the vagina. If you can't seem to do that now, next time you urinate—and possibly for several next times—practice stopping and starting the urine flow. Once you can do it while urinating, you'll be able to do it dry.

To tone these muscles and improve your control over them, you should squeeze 100 times a day, 10 times at once. You can do it anywhere—on the bus, at your desk, during a movie. No one will know. Once you can actually feel the squeeze when you put a finger in your vagina, you can cut down to ten or twelve squeezes a day just to keep in shape. This may take several months to learn, so be patient. The advantages are being able to insert Tampax or birth control devices easily, being able to tolerate a gynecological examination, and being able to increase the friction between the vagina and the penis for more pleasure for you and your partner.

Doctors often recommend that women who have given birth do this exercise to restore the natural flexibility and tone of the vaginal muscles. They used to take an extra little stitch in the episiotomy to tighten the vagina. This was called the "husband's knot"—not necessarily a delight for the wife.

The vagina is usually between 3 and 4 inches in length but it expands enormously during childbirth and, if the muscles around the entrance are healthy, can contract to close around a finger. The idea that the vagina is too large or too small for a particular penis is rather remote. During arousal the vagina lubricates, expands, and then closes down to facilitate and accommodate just about any penis.

If you feel that your particular vagina doesn't do this, there are some things you can try. First, and most important, do the exercises above. Next, choose the positions that increase friction between the penis and the vagina. If, for example, you feel that the penis is too small and your vagina too large, you should use positions in which the legs are close together and the heavier person is on top. This will increase both friction and pressure. If you feel that your vagina is too small and the penis too large, you should use positions where there is little pressure and friction, such as on your side or standing. You should also be sure that you are aroused. If you are not lubricating, this might not be the best time to try anything. If you don't have much natural lubrication, sterile jelly or saliva will help.

To continue with your self-exam. Beyond the entrance to the vagina you can feel the soft moist walls in the inner vagina. These walls balloon out when something is inside the vagina and lie flat the rest of the time. The vagina rather resembles a pocket in this respect.

Near the top or back of the vagina you should be able to feel the cervix, which is the entrance into the uterus. You may, if you have long fingers, be able to feel the bottom of the uterus itself. It is important to know where the cervix is. Many birth control devices depend on having this passageway protected.

The cervix feels like a lump with a dimple. The dimple is the passage into the uterus. The lump is usually quite hard compared to the surrounding soft tissues. It is between 1 and 2 inches in diameter. One of the early signs of pregnancy is the softening of the cervix—but of course you couldn't detect that unless you knew what the cervix usually felt like.

The cervix is one of the most common sites for cancer in the female, which is why it is important to have regular Pap tests. The doctor takes a smear from the cervix and has it tested for cancer cells. If, during your regular self-exam, you feel anything unusual, you should check with your doctor immediately.

The clitoris is connected to the vagina by the minor lips. This is an extremely important connection since it is the movement of the penis or whatever is in the vagina that indirectly—through the minor lips— moves and stimulates the clitoris. The clitoris is the most sexually sensitive organ in the female body. (The vagina has relatively few nerve endings compared to the richly endowed clitoris.) In fact, the clitoris is an exclusively sexual organ, the only one in either male or female. It is the connection between the clitoris and the vagina via the minor lips that means there is no difference between an orgasm from direct clitoral stimulation and an orgasm from having something in the vagina. An orgasm is an orgasm is an orgasm, as we will discuss further in Chapter 7.

Examine the clitoris closely. It has a little hood, a head, and a shaft just like the penis. If you touch it carefully in the center, it seems to slide around. It isn't fixed in the same way that the penis is, and during sexual excitement it retreats under the hood so that you can hardly feel it at all. This actually signals a high point of arousal. It is usually a soft pinkish color, which becomes darker during sexual stimulation.

The mons pubis or mons veneris, the "mount of Venus," is the fleshy, hairy area covering the pubic bone. It is the most visible part of the female genitalia. The hair and fat here protect both the male and female during intercourse. In examining this part of the sexual anatomy, note particularly your reaction to the pubic hair. Is there too much or too little for your taste? Should it be, or not be, shaved, dyed, curled, waxed? What do you like about the way the hair grows, its texture, and color? Note your observations here.

_____

_____

_____

Now let's take a look at the penis. It, too, has a hood, a head, and a shaft; but often the hood, prepuce, or foreskin, is removed shortly after birth. This is called circumcision. If you have been circumcised, you'll

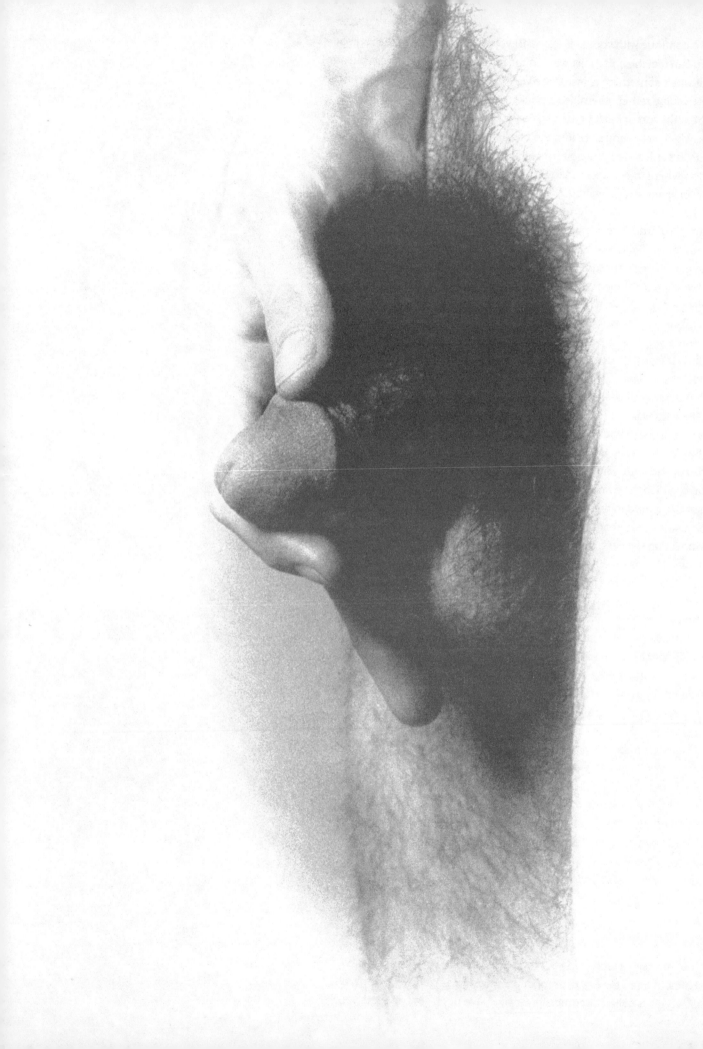

be able to see how the penis changes color about one-third down from the tip. The foreskin is removed for religious and, more commonly, for health reasons, since germs tend to breed under it. If you are not circumcised, it is important to keep that area clean.

People have some funny ideas about circumcision. They think that their penis would be larger or more sensitive if they had or didn't have a foreskin. But the foreskin doesn't affect sensitivity one way or the other and the diameter of the penis is measured at the base, so the foreskin couldn't influence that figure. Some men hope that impotence or premature ejaculation could be cured by circumcision. Unfortunately, these troubles tend to be psychological and are not changed by surgery.

The penis is made up of three cylinders which are full of blood vessels. These vessels engorge with blood to bring about erection. There are no bones in the human penis. Erection is a response to neurological impulses which trigger the vasocongestion. It is hard to distinguish the cylinders when the penis is flaccid, but you can feel them when it is erect. The underside cylinder, the one closest to the scrotum, houses the urethra and makes up the head or glans of the penis.

The glans is the most sensitive part of the penis, especially where that narrow vertical strip of skin, the frenulum, joins the horizontal ridge, the corona. This is the part of the male anatomy most similar in erotic potential to the female clitoris. The penis is attached at the base to strong pelvic muscles which control ejaculation and urination. This makes the penis seem more fixed than the clitoris. Men to not have voluntary control over these muscles and it is impossible to move the penis much except for small, jerky movements. You cannot will an erection or ejaculation.

The average size of the penis calm is 3 or 4 inches long. The average size excited is 6 to 6½ inches. The diameter changes from about 1¼ to 1½ inches. This is only the average, however. There are variations both ways. Erect penises tend to be closer in size than flaccid ones. That is, a small penis may double in size when erect, whereas a large one would change much less. Penile size is more related to heredity than to the size of your nose or your thumb.

The penis varies in angle when erect and even when flaccid. The penis in the photograph, incidentally, is semi-erect. Some penises lean to one side or the other, some are bowed, some are hooked. Erections vary, too, with the person, his age and his health. These interesting variations have nothing to do with fertility, potency, or satisfaction.

If you feel that your penis is too large or too small for your partner, take note of the suggestions on page 92 for the woman who thinks her vagina is too small or too large. It is not possible to enlarge your penis by pulling on it or exercising or taking vitamin E. It is the way it is always going to be.

Sometimes both men and women allow unhealthy attitudes toward their genitals to dictate behavior. If you are reluctant to ask a doctor about a problem concerning your penis or vagina or let your partner know how to stimulate you, you may be letting inhibitions about your body stand in the way of your health and pleasure. Also, if you are obsessed with the unsightliness or inadequacy of your genitalia, you may be centering feelings of self-hatred on a specific part of yourself rather than on such issues as commitment, responsibility, fidelity, and so on,

which may be more to the point. People have many ways of denigrating themselves to get out of changing or facing difficult situations.

Although the breasts are not primary sex organs, many women and some men find that their nipples are second only to the clitoris or glans of the penis in sexual sensitivity. Examine your nipples. Women's breasts are made up of more than a dozen lobes of tissue which produce milk and which open into the nipple. Men's breasts are an underdeveloped version of the same. For both men and women the nipples, which are centers of nerve responsiveness, become erect during sexual arousal. Some people want to be touched on or around the nipples and others don't. The sensitivity of the nipples in either women or men is unrelated to the size or shape of the breasts.

Before discussing the internal genitalia and what goes on that you can't see or feel, think about how you felt doing this self-examination. If you felt silly, self-conscious, or uneasy sitting there with your penis in your hand or your finger up your vagina, you probably need to look at yourself "scientifically" more often. It's natural to feel awkward or embarrassed, but it is your body and you should know as much about it as you can for your mental and physical health.

If you weren't able to do this self-exam at all, don't give up. You can do it in stages. Start in the dark. Just feel your genitals. Get comfortable having your own hands exploring yourself. Then add a little light, perhaps from the next room. Gradually come out in the open and start looking at yourself.

Or, you can start by just looking at yourself and not touching at all. Take off your drawers and look. Don't explore. Then put your clothes back on and do the same thing a little later. When you are comfortable doing that, start your explorations.

If genital odors annoy or upset you, make sure you are quite clean when you start your exam. Later, you can become more familiar with your body scents.

You don't have to examine everything at once. If you feel overwhelmed, stop. Just study the scrotal sac or the anus or the clitoris at one sitting. If you are doing this with a partner, examine him or her the first time. Then you may be readier to bare your own breast the next time.

If it is devastating to even think of letting someone else in on this exam, maybe you haven't accepted your body yourself yet. Your reactions can vary from extreme self-consciousness to total objectivity, depending on who you think has the right to examine you. If you don't think you have the right above all others, keep practicing.

THE INTERNALS

The internal genitalia are just as important to your health and enlightened self-knowledge as the external genitalia. They are also significant in the control of birth, which we'll be discussing soon.

Let's look at the travels of the egg and the sperm through the reproductive systems of the female and the male. Each is produced by a gonad (that which generates), the testes in men and the ovaries in women. The word "testes" is Latin for witness, and derives from the Roman practice of putting the hand on the testicles when making an oath or testament. The word "ovary" derives from the Latin ovum or egg, as does the word "oval" or egg-shaped.

97

The female

There are about 400,000 eggs in the ovaries at birth, but only 200 to 400 are used during a woman's lifetime. Of these, the first is released during puberty when the woman is between ten and sixteen, with the average being about thirteen. The first menstruation or period is called the menarche, and may not follow ovulation or release of an egg regularly in the beginning. By the late teens, however, most women release an egg about two weeks before each menses. This is not the same as two weeks after each menses, as will be seen below.

When the egg is released, it passes from the ovary to the Fallopian tube and is fertile for twelve to thirty-six hours. The ovary is similar in shape to the teste but smaller and the tubes, which are each about 4 inches long, are not actually attached to the ovaries. A chemical or electrical attraction draws the egg from the ovary up into the tube.

It takes the egg about a week to travel down the tube to the uterus. If it is fertilized along the way it will stay in the uterus, otherwise it will disintegrate.

The uterus itself is a strong elastic muscle of several layers. It is hollow and shaped like an upside-down pear. It is usually tilted forward. Perfectly normal uteruses, however, are tilted backward or rest in a middle position. The nonpregnant uterus is a little smaller than its owner's fist.

A fertilized egg attaches itself to the wall of the uterus, where it feeds on the nutrient inner layer which has been building up there since ovulation. The embryo grows in the uterus until it is ready for the outside world, at which time strong contractions of the muscle layer of the uterus push it out.

The cervix or neck of the uterus is also muscular and highly elastic. It is through the cervix that sperm, menses, and babies pass, as well as infections and their medications. The cervix becomes quite soft during pregnancy and dilates naturally before childbirth.

The vagina or birth canal is well supplied with blood vessels which swell during sexual arousal, but it has few nerve endings. Although the reproductive function of the vagina matches that of the penis, the similarity in sensitivity and structure is between the clitoris and the penis.

Just inside the vaginal entrance are the Bartholin's glands. It used to be thought that these glands supplied vaginal lubrication during intercourse and that this fluid was essential for conception. Then Masters and Johnson found that the vaginal lubrication during arousal comes from the "sweating" of the vaginal walls, due to the vasocongestion of the blood vessels behind them. The Bartholin's gland secretion seems rather to lower the natural acidity of the vagina, thus making it a better environment for sperm. These glands occasionally get infected and are treated with suppositories and other medications.

The male

Sperm are produced in the testes (testicles is the Latin diminutive of testes and teste and testicle are the singular forms). The sperm are produced in the thousands of tiny, twisty tubes, called the seminiferous tubules, of the testes. The sperm regularly move from there into the epididymis, on top of each teste, evident during the self-exam.

There seems to be some kind of selection process in the epididymis where unfit or old sperm are discarded. (Old would be up to about six weeks.) Since sperm production is a continual process from puberty

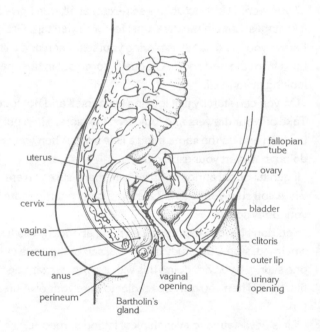

FEMALE SEXUAL ORGANS

uterus — fallopian tube — ovary — bladder — cervix — vagina — clitoris — rectum — outer lip — anus — urinary opening — vaginal opening — perineum — Bartholin's gland

on, it is not possible to run out of sperm. The number per ejaculate does decrease a little over the years.

The vas deferens, which is not unlike the Fallopian tubes in form and function, is the route from the testes to the prostate gland. During arousal of the male, sperm move from the epididymis up to the prostate gland, where they mix with the seminal fluid to form semen. It is this passageway, the vas, which is cut and tied for male sterilization, vasectomy.

The sperm make up only about 2 percent of the semen. The rest is supplied by the prostate gland. Even so, there may be up to 600,000 sperm per teaspoonful—average size of each ejaculate—of semen. Given the tortuous route to the egg, a regular sperm count of under 200,000 per ejaculate is usually classified as infertility.

After the sperm leaves the vas, it enters the seminal vesicles, on either side of the prostate gland. These chambers appear to supply a fluid which helps the sperm move quickly once inside the vagina. Next, the sperm is carried into the ejaculatory ducts inside the prostate gland. These ducts receive the seminal fluid from the prostate and mix it with the sperm. The seminal fluid is quite alkaline, which is good for the sperm.

The prostate gland, that golf ball you felt during the self-exam, lies just under the bladder. The urethra passes right through the prostate. Thanks to a couple of important little valves, urination and ejaculation are separate and discrete functions. Some people claim to be able to control these valves in such a way that the ejaculate flows up into the bladder and is later eliminated through the urine. Not only do they preserve their vital fluids this way but they don't get anyone pregnant.

Most men experience retrograde ejaculation, as this is called, involuntarily. If it happens to you, see your urologist. It may be caused by an undetected illness or a medication you are taking for something else.

Prostatic surgery may result in dry ejaculation, but you will still be potent and orgasmic. Prostatic surgery is sometimes called for if the prostate gland enlarges and presses down on the bladder, causing pain on urination and ejaculation. This is usually a problem only after fifty years of age. Because of the danger of cancer of the prostate, one of the most common cancers in men, you should have an annual check-up by a urologist once you pass fifty.

The Cowper's glands, right under the prostate, are similar to the Bartholin's glands in women. They seem to secrete a fluid which reduces the natural acidity of the urethra just prior to ejaculation. This fluid often appears on the tip of the penis during arousal. It is clear as compared to the cloudy color of semen, though it can contain sperm.

The penile urethra is the 8 or so inches of tube from the bladder to the tip of the penis. It is through here that the semen passes out of the penis, aided by the action of the ejaculatory muscles at the base of the penis.

THE SEX HORMONES

Puberty is that stage in early adolescence when everything starts to change. Girls start to develop breasts, wider hips, and pubic and underarm hair. Boys develop full-sized prostate glands and penises, pubic and facial and underarm hair, and broader and taller builds. Both start producing sex hormones.

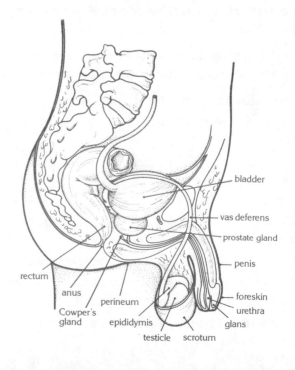

MALE SEXUAL ORGANS

bladder
vas deferens
prostate gland
penis
foreskin
urethra
glans
rectum
anus
perineum
Cowper's gland
epididymis
testicle   scrotum

The pituitary gland in the brain releases hormones into the bloodstream of both male and female which stimulate the production of testosterone in the male and estrogen and progesterone in the female. These sex hormones in turn stimulate the production of sperm and eggs, and are responsible for the other changes as well.

In the female estrogen, progesterone, and the pituitary hormones regulate ovulation, pregnancy, menstruation, and more. When the pituitary no longer sends or receives messages from the ovaries, which produce estrogen and progesterone, ovulation ceases. This is called the menopause.

In the male the pituitary hormones regulate the production of testosterone in the testes throughout life. But testosterone is also produced in the adrenal glands of both men and women. If a grown man is castrated (testes removed), he will no longer produce sperm but he will still have drive and potency from the testosterone in the adrenals. A woman who is castrated (ovaries removed) will not ovulate but her interest in sex will not be affected. Evidently adrenal testosterone is associated with sexual drive in both men and women.

It is difficult to determine whether certain moods trigger hormonal changes or if the hormones influence the mood. In any case, it does seem that higher hormonal levels are associated with increased drive —not just for sex but for life. People seem to have higher confidence and assertiveness when sex hormone levels are up and to feel depressed and listless or irritable when they are down. This is seen most clearly in the female menstrual cycle. Most women have at some time experienced premenstrual blues or general crankiness when hormone levels are low—just before and during menstruation. And many women feel best when hormone levels are high—at or about the time of ovulation.

Since hormone levels in both men and women are cyclical and vary with health and stress, you should take these into account as your own therapist. That is, there are times when you really cannot expect to be interested in sex. These are times when you are under extreme pressure from work or family, or when you are physically ill. If these are constant rather than occasional or cyclical problems for you, do check with a physician.

Here is a little quiz on some of the material covered so far. Please fill in the blanks. It covers both the externals and the internals.

The uterus is about the size of _____.

Menstruation occurs when _____ levels are _____.

The _____ is an erogenous zone for many people.

The _____ is the only exclusively sexual organ.

The scrotum in the male is homologous to the _____ in the female.

The _____ and _____ glands in women and men affect acidity in the reproductive tract.

Sperm live best in an _____ environment.

The vas deferens connects the _____ to the _____.

Sweat glands in the scrotum help control _____.

Seminal fluid from the prostate makes up about _____ percent of the ejaculate.

Retrograde ejaculation is when the _____ goes into the _____ instead of the _____.

The labia tend to be a _____ color during sexual arousal.

The penis has _____ bones in it.

The cervix feels like a _____.

_____ affects sex drive in both women and men.

CONTROL OF BIRTH—CONCEPTION AND CONTRACEPTION

So far we have looked at the functions of sex and not the implications of sex. No matter how carefully you separate drive and reproduction, you haven't really been thorough until you've examined how they fit together. Sex can lead to pregnancy—and that means something to those who are trying to prevent the connection, as well as to those who are trying to make the connection.

What follows about conception and contraception is for both men and women. Much of the responsibility for the control of birth has been taken away from men lately. Although this has its positive aspects for women, who finally do indeed own their own bodies, there are negative implications for men who wish to evaluate their feelings about fathering children, whether they ever intend to have them or not.

Many people, given the availability of better birth control (including abortion), have separated sex from pregnancy. In Victorian times, sex was supposed to be only for procreation. Passion was considered impolite. Nowadays it is sometimes as difficult to bring passion and pregnancy together as it used to be to keep them apart.

If you have ever made someone pregnant, or been pregnant accidentally, think about the reasons why. Of course accidents happen, but rather than thinking about what went wrong, think about what may have unconsciously gone right.

People have pregnancies for reasons that are not always accidental. Turn your thoughts around to think about what was going on in your life to make an accident happen then. A man might want to know if he

could make someone pregnant. A woman could have lost a relative or lover she needs to make up for. Unwanted pregnancies happen when school or a job is ending and people are wondering what will come next. A couple that is growing apart may feel that their differences can be addressed only over an issue as important and immediate as pregnancy.

Sometimes people get pregnant because they are using mind control instead of birth control. You think it won't happen to you, that you will be lucky or will get away with something. Sometimes these chances are really tests against the self, the partner, or the fates. Other issues may make one need to test oneself, but sex is where the acting out takes place.

You could of course really want to be a parent even though you aren't trying consciously to be one. You could feel that children will complete or fulfill some expectation you have of yourself. You might be thinking that a child would make you feel young again or that it would make you feel more grown up. You could be thinking that a child would bring you and your partner closer together.

All these kinds of subjects come up for the people who cannot get pregnant, too. Although some people really are infertile, sometimes other issues are in the way. Perhaps you don't feel committed to your partner or secure in her or his commitment to you. You may have hidden fears about inherited or even acquired traits of yours which you worry would be passed on to your child. You could be concerned about being too old or too young to be a parent.

Both trying to get pregnant and trying to prevent pregnancy can make your sex life frustrating. The pressure of having intercourse at the exact right moment for conception can do away with any pleasure from the sex act itself. Fear of pregnancy can make both partners uncomfortable, rushed, or furtive. Yet there is help available. It is far better to consult with both a urologist and a gynecologist if you want to have children and haven't been able to than to blame each other and end up ruining your relationship. Despite the embarrassment of asking a doctor or druggist for birth control devices, it is better than never achieving any pleasure or comfort from sexual union.

On the next few pages are some facts about how people conceive and how that can be interrupted. This is only a brief summary of the information available. If you wish to know more, consult your doctor. If you don't have a doctor, call your local Planned Parenthood or public health office.

CONCEPTION

If you want to have a child, you should have intercourse as close to the time of ovulation as possible. It was mentioned earlier that ovulation occurs approximately two weeks before menstruation. The menstrual cycle is based on Day 1 being the day menstruation begins. The last day in the cycle is the day before the next menstruation begins. Thus, a woman who has a 26-day cycle would probably ovulate on the 12th day after she started menstruating. A woman with a 30-day cycle would ovulate on or near the 16th day. This calculation is based on having regular cycles, that is, of the same length each time.

The easiest way to be certain when ovulation takes place is to chart your temperature with a basal body thermometer for several months.

By taking a reading every morning before getting up, you will be able to spot the low point of the cycle each month. This happens just prior to ovulation. After that, your temperature stays up for the rest of the cycle. Since the egg is fertile for about one and a half days and sperm live for three to five days, intercourse is most likely to result in pregnancy between five days before ovulation and one day after. There are some very sophisticated new tests for ovulation which your doctor or clinic can tell you about.

A woman who has irregular periods even occasionally would have to take her temperature daily and have intercourse when her temperature dips. It wouldn't be very helpful to bother with a chart unless the irregularity is regular, such as every other month or every third month.

Other ways to increase the chances of conception are to have a high sperm count, increase the alkalinity of the vagina, and use a rear entry position for intercourse. You get a high sperm count by abstaining from sexual activity several days prior to ovulation. You can increase the alkaline environment of the vagina by douching it with two tablespoons of baking soda dissolved in one quart of water just prior to intercourse. Entering the vagina from behind means that the sperm will be deposited closer to the more alkaline cervix.

Female orgasm tends to weaken the acidity of the vagina, making it

favorable to sperm. So the woman should by all means enjoy herself.

A couple concerned about having children because the woman is older may wish to consider amniocentesis. This is a procedure to determine whether or not a fetus has one of the genetic defects more common in the offspring of older women. The doctor extracts some amniotic fluid in the fourth month of pregnancy. If tests show anything wrong, the couple can consider abortion.

CONTRACEPTION

To prevent pregnancies, it is also important to pinpoint ovulation. However, even the most regular of menstrual cycles can become irregular sometimes. There is no absolutely safe time. Ovulation is affected by health and stress; a woman who is upset, ill, or under unusual pressure could ovulate early, late, or more than once during her cycle. This uncertainty can of course affect sexual functioning and will be discussed later.

It is this fact, plus the rare but known instances in which the sperm live up to seven days, which makes the rhythm method of contraception so unreliable. The rhythm system requires that a couple do not have intercourse for several days before and after ovulation. You must calculate ovulation carefully and, even more important, you must both be willing to abstain.

The oral contraceptives, of which there are many, suppress ovulation—and where there is no egg there can be no fertilization. However, if the pill is not taken regularly, there is a chance that the woman may ovulate and possibly become pregnant. Many women seem to feel that missing a day or two doesn't really matter. It can. Also, some people think that they can stop taking the pill for a few days, a month, or even longer and they will still be protected. They are wrong.

The pill is a very effective, low-risk contraceptive. Statistically, it is medically safer than abortion and sterilization, but some women can't take it, some women don't like to take it, and all women have to take it under a doctor's supervision.

The IUD is also highly effective. It is a little object which is placed by a doctor in the woman's uterus. No one knows for sure how the IUD works, but it appears to keep the egg from implanting in the uterine wall. Most have tiny strings which hang out of the cervix so that the woman can check to be sure that it hasn't been expelled during a menstrual period. Losing it without detecting it is the biggest risk IUD users take.

Both these methods are unnatural in that they require a woman to have a foreign object in her body or her bloodstream. Some women feel uneasy about that and prefer to use a diaphragm, have their partner use a condom, or both.

The diaphragm is a round rubber device that fits around the cervix and keeps sperm from getting into the uterus. It must be fitted by a doctor or nurse to the individual woman. Because it is a little awkward to insert, a woman may like to have her partner help her put it in, or she might like to wear it all the time. If you decide to wear it all the time, be sure to take it out daily, wash it off, and check for flaws. Use a contraceptive foam or jelly just before intercourse to ensure that the entrance to the uterus is fully protected.

Condoms are the most available method of birth control around and they are very effective if used properly. Some men complain that they cut down the pleasant sensations of being in the vagina, but diaphragms and pills and IUDs cut down the pleasure of sex for women sometimes, too. It is often fairer to share the responsibility by relying on the condom at least some of the time.

Condoms must be put on as soon as you have an erection because of the danger of the Cowper's gland secretion and of coming unexpectedly. Because penises get soft soon after ejaculation, it is important to pull out of the vagina shortly after coming. Hold onto the rim of the condom to be sure it comes with you. There is talk about condoms breaking, but they are more likely to slip off. To guard against breakage, don't pull them on too tight. Try to leave a half inch at the tip if you are using one that doesn't have a little tip for semen.

Contraceptive foams are not the most effective means of birth control but they are better than nothing. Used in combination with a diaphragm or condom, their effectiveness goes up. Foam is always better than jellies, creams, or suppositories, which do not get as well distributed in the vagina. These methods all contain a chemical that kills sperm, so they should <u>not</u> be washed out of the vagina for six to eight hours after ejaculation. Some people are allergic to these substances. If either of you notices an itching or irritation, try a different brand or a new method.

All these methods require cooperation and planning on the part of both partners. If you know what you are going to use and you have it ready, you don't have to lose spontaneity at the time of intercourse. You can make the application of these devices part of your act, with the man inserting the foam or diaphragm and the woman putting the condom on him. If you are comfortable with your choice of birth control, you know how to use it, and your partner is involved too, you are doing your best.

Because even your best can fail, you should know that abortion is a reliable, safe, and relatively easy method of birth control. It is obviously easier—financially, physically, and psychologically—to prevent pregnancy; but if it does occur and you wish to consider abortion, ask your doctor.

Abortion in the first twelve weeks of pregnancy is usually performed as an outpatient service by vacuum aspiration. In this ten-minute procedure the uterus is literally vacuumed out. The egg and uterine lining are removed. A woman will generally feel some cramping and have some bleeding for a few days afterward. Because she can get pregnant again right away, it is essential to secure birth control before resuming intercourse.

Sterilization is the best method of birth control if you are ready for it. If you are sure that you do not want children or more children, you can have your tubes tied. In the male, the tubes are the vas deferens, which can be severed and tied under local anesthetic in your urologist's office in about fifteen minutes. If you are a woman, the Fallopian tubes will be cut and tied under general anesthesia.

As with all questions of birth control, which of you is going to be sterilized can be an issue. Costs and the general health of both parties are considerations. If one of you thinks she or he might like more children some time or children by someone else, the other person should be the one to be sterilized. If one of you is terrified by the required procedure, perhaps the other should be the one to have the operation.

Other methods of birth control, such as douching, withdrawal (coitus interruptus), keeping the legs or fingers crossed, and abstinence haven't been discussed because they are either no good or no fun.

You will use best and enjoy most the birth control method that is best for you. Despite the high effectiveness of the pill, a woman who is unhappy with it may feel resentful toward her partner and unable to enjoy sex with him. A man who feels he shouldn't have to use the condom all the time may resist or refuse the sexual advances of a partner who leaves all that up to him.

In any case, all methods of birth control should be the choice of both partners. Even though it is the woman who carries and cares for babies, the man is part of it too. The woman who makes all the decisions and the man who makes none are denying something implicit in their decision to have sex at all. A woman who has an abortion or is sterilized without consulting her partner may be overlooking the fact that men have feelings too. The man who doesn't care what the woman does may be ignoring his own rights and responsibilities.

Here are a few questions on conception and contraception:

The best time to conceive and contra-ceive is _____.

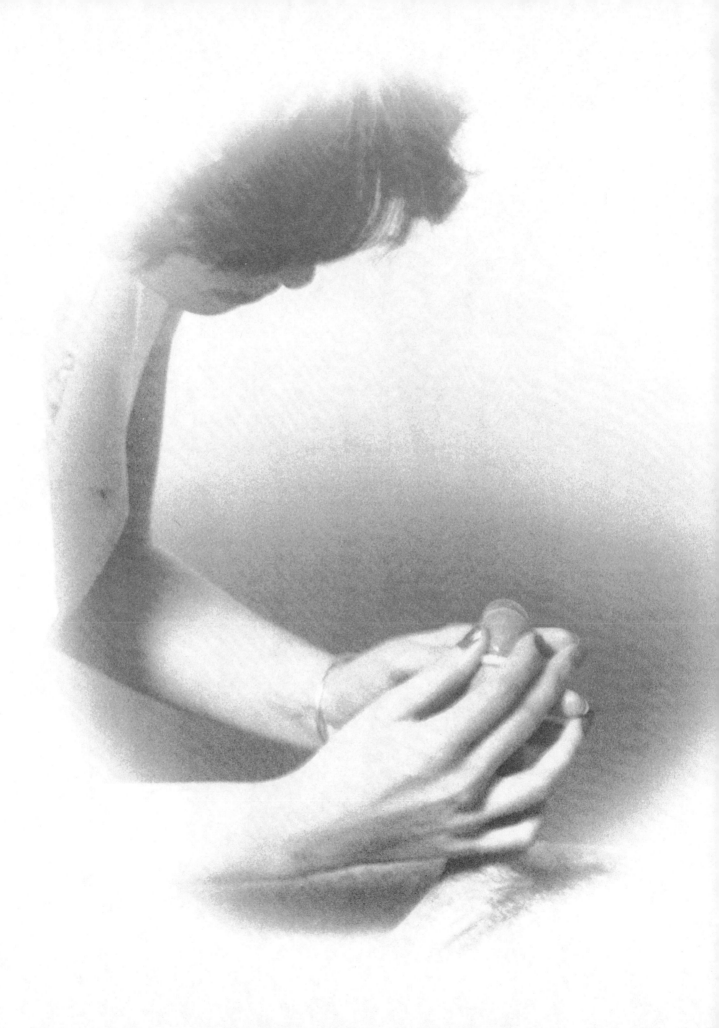

The pill _____ ovulation.

Sterilization means tying the _____, for both men and women.

Women with _____ menstrual cycles shouldn't rely on the _____ system.

Abortion is safe and fairly painless during the first _____ weeks of pregnancy.

_____ may be desirable if the woman is over thirty-five.

An _____ environment is favorable to sperm.

You should use _____ with the diaphragm.

Some people are allergic to _____.

A woman should check her _____ strings after each _____.

Body temperature _____ before ovulation.

Sperm can live up to _____ days.

If you didn't answer all of these, you'd really better read this section again.

CONCLUSION

Anatomy and physiology of the sexual organs involves more than knowing where everything is and how it all works. You also need to think about what meaning these facts have for you. You may think it is all very romantic not to know certain things about yourself or your partner. You may even think it isn't nice to wonder. But ignorance really isn't very romantic. You can know yourself and still experience love and passion.

Arousal

INTRODUCTION

Sexual arousal is a state of physical and emotional tension exciting in itself and essential for intercourse or orgasm. It is impossible to have satisfactory sex without physical arousal, but it is possible to be physically aroused without really desiring sex. The trick is to know how to be aroused when you want to be.

Arousal is not simply an erection for a male and vaginal lubrication for a female. These most obvious signs of readiness for sex are preceded and accompanied by other physiological changes, including increased pulse rate, muscular tension, dry throat, wet palms, and various tingling or warm feelings throughout the body. These physical signs are usually dependent upon or influenced by one's feelings for the setting, the partner, the circumstances, and one's self. Thus, there is a whole constellation of physical and emotional reactions which affect arousal.

BARRIERS TO AROUSAL

Most people manage to become aroused most of the time. But if you don't get aroused at all or when you think you should, you may start thinking that you are asexual, frigid, inadequate, oversexed, or incompetent sexually—fears that many people have had at one time or another. It's those fears that make you lose confidence in your sexuality and feel at the mercy of forces you don't control.

At the root of these insecurities there is often a simple lack of familiarity with your own arousal. Because there is a pervading sense in this society that it is egotistical to concentrate too much on yourself, you don't get to know what you like and what you are capable of. Sex then becomes a performance, with orgasm as the goal. All the sensations and feelings that are associated with being aroused are lost in the rush to climax.

Ignorance about arousal can make you dependent on routine or myth. You try to accept what you heard aroused someone else. You rely on techniques and activities that aroused you in the past. You assume that you should be turned on by something you read, someone you're with, something they do. You look for the right formula. And in the process sex and arousal become a chore.

There is no question that there are real barriers to arousal which dampen anyone's ardor. These are distracting outside pressures, ill health, bad experiences with sex, and insensitive partners. You do have to make allowances for yourself. If you are run-down mentally or physically, you have to wait until you feel better. If you've had bad experiences or partners, you have to relearn what arouses you. If you are having sexual problems with your present partner, you may each have to learn what arouses you individually and then as a couple.

You also have to convince yourself that it is all right to be attending to your own sexuality. Cultural barriers to sexual self-knowledge include the feeling that concentrating on yourself is self-centered, immodest, and a sign that you are unable to relate to other people. If you are a man, you are supposedly born knowing all there is to know about sex. If you are a woman, you're supposed to let some man instruct you. Yet if you can't relate to yourself sexually, it is very hard to relate to anyone else.

Obviously, the more ideas you bring to this subject, the more confused you can get. You can't bank on formulas, other people, society. So, start at the beginning with no ideas about how arousal should be and no grand expectations that this chapter offers the formula you've been waiting for. Even if you know all about your own arousal, approach this chapter as an opportunity to rehearse all that you already know.

TURNING ON

The first thing that you have to capture is the recognition of arousal itself. You need to know when you are aroused, even if you aren't going to do anything about it right then and there. Maybe there are times when you find that your heart is beating, you are flushed or stirred, even though there is no clear-cut object of your interest around. Or, there could be times when you feel warm and relaxed with someone but you have no physical signs of sexual arousal even though sex is on your mind. That's fine. These stirrings can be preludes to more intense arousal and they are pleasant in themselves. Your job now is to identify the moods, circumstances, and people that bring them about.

Described below are some broad categories of arousal. Try to find something in each that is familiar for you. In the space provided or on a separate sheet you can write out your own similar experiences of arousal.

Sensual stimulation Into this category fall all the physical settings and sensations that arouse you. These might range from an awareness of your surroundings to specifically sexual stimulation. For example, such things as the time of day, the place, certain scents, foods, and kinds of accidental and intentional touch belong here. Make a list of the places and things that arouse you, such as the subway, ice cubes briefly on your testes or nipples, the smell of sweat or chocolate chip cookies, the Botanical Gardens, marijuana, cherimoyas, a church, and so on.

_____   _____
_____   _____
_____   _____
_____   _____
_____   _____
_____   _____

Mental stimulation Here you can put down all the things you think about sexually that arouse you. Include sex fantasies, forbidden sexual pleasures, and sexual expectations. For example, anticipating sex is arousing, thinking about someone you want is arousing, memories are arousing. Make a list here of the ideas that turn you on, such as the idea of sex with your brother, sex in a public place, sex in the future. Or, list the nonsexual, but to you sexy, ideas that arouse you.

_____   _____
_____   _____
_____   _____
_____   _____
_____   _____
_____   _____

Human stimulation Last but not least are the types of people and social situations that you find arousing. Make a list of the personality and physical types you are attracted to, the social situations you like to be in, the emotional, verbal, or sexual support you get from others that makes you feel sexual. For example, witty banter, lovemaking in the next apartment, political conventions, small and strong men, could each give you a thrill.

_____   _____
_____   _____
_____   _____
_____   _____
_____   _____
_____   _____

In looking over your lists, see if you've been true to yourself. Are these really things that do arouse you or are they things you think should arouse you? If they aren't your very own, cross them out. Spend some time observing your own reactions in different settings with different people before you make a new list. Your list doesn't have to be very long—just very personal. If you didn't make a list at all, it isn't too late. Sometimes seeing things in print, even in your own crabbed hand, arouses you more than mental musings.

Another thing to consider in examining the lists is whether or not you use what you know about yourself. That is, if morning sex, square dances, or sports arouse you, do you see that you participate in such activities regularly? If candlelight, dominant partners, and flannel sheets are known to arouse you, do you do anything special to see that they are available? Having sex with someone you care about, someone who is aroused, someone who talks to you could all affect your arousal. And they are all things you can control to some degree. Setting the scene for yourself, asking a partner for something that pleases you, concentrating your thoughts on arousing images are all ways of encouraging your own enjoyment. Sharing your thoughts and preferences with a partner and listening to theirs can be arousing as well as fair.

Finding it hard to do these things or to think this way isn't odd or abnormal. It just shows that you haven't spent enough time trying to develop your arousal potential. You may know what arouses you and yet not do anything about it. Trying just one thing at a time is the best way to start. Use the space below to write down where you'll begin.

_____

_____

_____

_____

TURNING OFF

It is just as important to know what doesn't arouse you as to know what
does. This is particularly true if you find that you aren't aroused when
you want to be or think you should be. It is also important for those of
you who become aroused and then inexplicably lose interest. Many
people just don't credit the fact that arousal patterns change and everyone isn't aroused by the same things or at the same time. For instance,
you may have found that alcohol was very stimulating to you sexually a
few years ago, but now it tends to make you sleepy. Or perhaps you
just don't like to have a backrub, no matter who gives it to you or when.

Often continuing practices that are not arousing is sheer force of

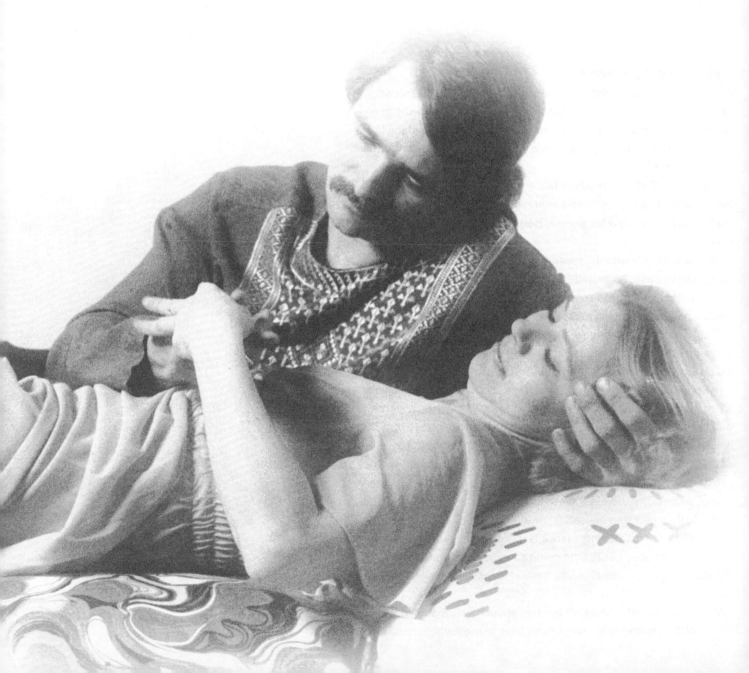

habit. It is difficult to change patterns, to try new things. Even if you aren't particularly happy with things as they are, it can be more threatening to you or to your relationship to try something different. And if you have tried things that failed, it is even harder.

Losing arousal once you have had it may also be a habit. You may have never learned how to maintain it or developed the confidence that it will return. Losing arousal with a particular partner may have something to do with the relationship or the partner, rather than with physical changes in you. It could be your way of saying you don't care any more or that you feel too many demands are being put on you.

The type of self-consciousness called for here, where you have to analyze and dissect your arousal, can really turn you off. You might think you'll lose everything. You won't, but that doesn't mean you won't feel bothered and reluctant doing it.

Look over the previous section and then, using it as your guide, list some things that do not arouse you. Include current practices and partners if they apply.

_____

_____

_____

_____

TURNING ON TO YOURSELF

Now we'll look at autoeroticism, the ways in which you can arouse yourself when you are alone. You may arouse yourself by being in an exotic place, fantasizing about a movie star, touching something in an erotic way. But most specifically, autoeroticism is masturbation, whether to orgasm or not.

You may think it's pretty silly to talk about masturbation. You're reading this book to get away from solitary sports, to get some new ideas, to learn how to relate to other people. Besides, you already know about masturbation.

Yet, many people who do masturbate don't think of it as being of much use to them. It's regretted, not paid much attention to, considered remote from other sexual concerns. Some people don't really know what they are doing and others don't appreciate that the details of self-arousal are translatable to arousal with another. Furthermore, knowing how to arouse yourself helps you understand that others become aroused in similar, if individual, ways.

There are, of course, many prohibitions to exciting yourself sexually when there is no prospect of engaging in sex with another person. One of these taboos concerns the idea of waste. This goes back to times when underpopulation was a problem and it made sense to have a lot of children just for economic survival. Now that overpopulation is the problem, masturbation is not considered a direct threat to the preservation of society. But there is a sense that one must have something better to do than play with oneself.

The taboo against self-indulgence is related to the puritan ethic. You should be busy all the time doing something productive. Hence the slang use of the word "masturbation" to indicate wasting time or energy.

Another source of ambivalent feelings about masturbation is the idea that it is second-best. People who have to masturbate must be

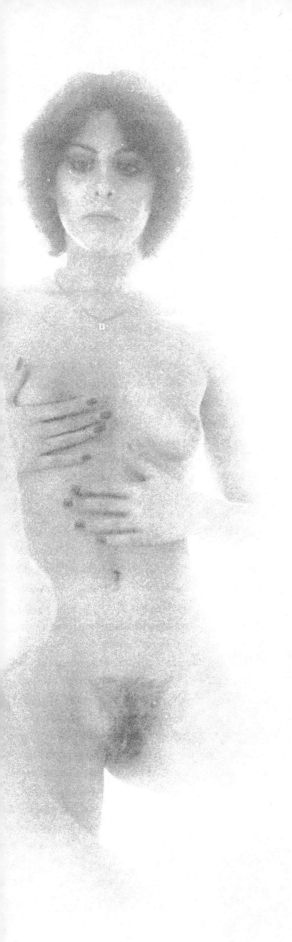

sad, desperate, and unable to deal well with other people. The only "real" sex is sex with someone else. The person who has sex with him– or herself can't or won't get a partner. That's one reason why married people are horrified to learn that their partner masturbates. They either feel inadequate and rejected or bitter about being indirectly imposed upon. Masturbation is rarely considered a pastime pleasurable in itself and a positive way of mediating the differing drives of partners.

People who do use masturbation effectively in a relationship may masturbate alone or with the partner when they feel interested in sex and the partner doesn't. They might also masturbate to arouse the partner or themselves before and during intercourse.

Much of the guilt about masturbation comes when you are growing up. Most children are not encouraged to touch their own bodies in any way and certainly not genitally. Parents who are amused when their children play doctor may not be at all amused by a child who masturbates. So, many children grow up with a well-ingrained sense that masturbation is unhealthy and bad.

The ironic thing about guilt is that it is usually instilled to protect you. Parents may not be protecting children against masturbation itself but against "what it can lead to." For instance, masturbation is considered inferior to "real" sex, and children who masturbate may therefore never be able to enjoy sex with a partner. Or masturbation might lead to "getting in trouble," by which most parents mean an unwanted pregnancy which would be a lot of trouble for them too. Or masturbation could lead to becoming obsessed with sex.

Actually excessive masturbation and unwanted pregnancies, among teenagers anyway, come from emotional needs more than physical ones. As for relating to other people, those who have masturbated as children have an advantage in that they know what they want erotically from a partner. Masturbation can be an escape, but so can not masturbating. Looking at masturbation as evil or immoral can be a way of escaping a reluctance to touch your own body or take responsibility for your own arousal. Not acknowledging the different drives between you and a partner may indicate a refusal to give up rigid expectations for compatibility.

Because the body is capable of pleasure, it would seem that its owner has the right to that pleasure in whatever way pleases her or him. Masturbation is certainly not the only kind of sexual pleasure, nor the best or the worst one. It is, however, one that is readily available and certainly a means of learning precisely just what one's own body responds to and in what ways.

If you feel squeamish or bored by the idea of reading on, and you've eliminated all those questions about what in your history or experience accounts for this, try to go ahead with the attitude that it won't hurt you. This is just another kind of self-knowledge. Masturbation may be surrounded by mystique and taboo, tedium and disappointment, but it is also a great source of pleasure and relaxation.

A guide to a guide
This guide is separate for men and women, but you should read over both parts. It might come in handy when you are with a partner. You can do this with your partner if you wish, but it is probably best to be alone the first time.

Some people like to set a scene for themselves, mentally or physically, by using the information about themselves from earlier in the chapter. You might also like to use some kind of lubricant, as described in Chapter 5, for touching the genitals. In addition to sterile jelly, lubricants are vaginal juices, saliva, soap (if you are in a bath or shower).

It is particularly important during this exercise to concentrate on arousal and not on orgasm. Don't try to do too much at one time. If you are tired or frustrated, sore or too excited, rest and return to it later. You want to learn the elements of arousal, how it ebbs and flows. Some people get upset because they can't maintain arousal or it's over so fast that they don't remember it. Here you are trying to recognize and control arousal.

Guide for women

Most women masturbate by rubbing or stroking the area just beneath the mons veneris with their hand. But there are other ways. Crossing the legs and squeezing the upper thighs together to apply pressure to the mons area is one. Another is pressing against a bed, a tree, a partner. Some women masturbate by stimulating other parts of the body, especially the breasts, vagina, or anus. You can also use a vibrator or something else that you hold in your hand and then apply to erogenous areas. Deep vaginal penetration with a vibrator, a finger, or a banana isn't usually as thrilling as stimulation to the minor lips and clitoris, although many women feel an aching or itching inside the vagina.

Certainly what you are thinking about is an important component of arousal. Physiologically, arousal is a response to stimulation of nerve centers in the lower spinal cord. This response can come from physical stimulation to the erogenous areas of the body or from images and fantasies in the brain. Very few people can become aroused to orgasm by

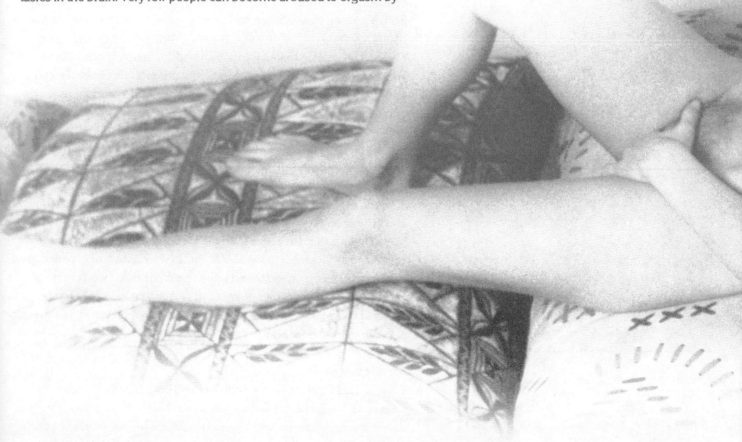

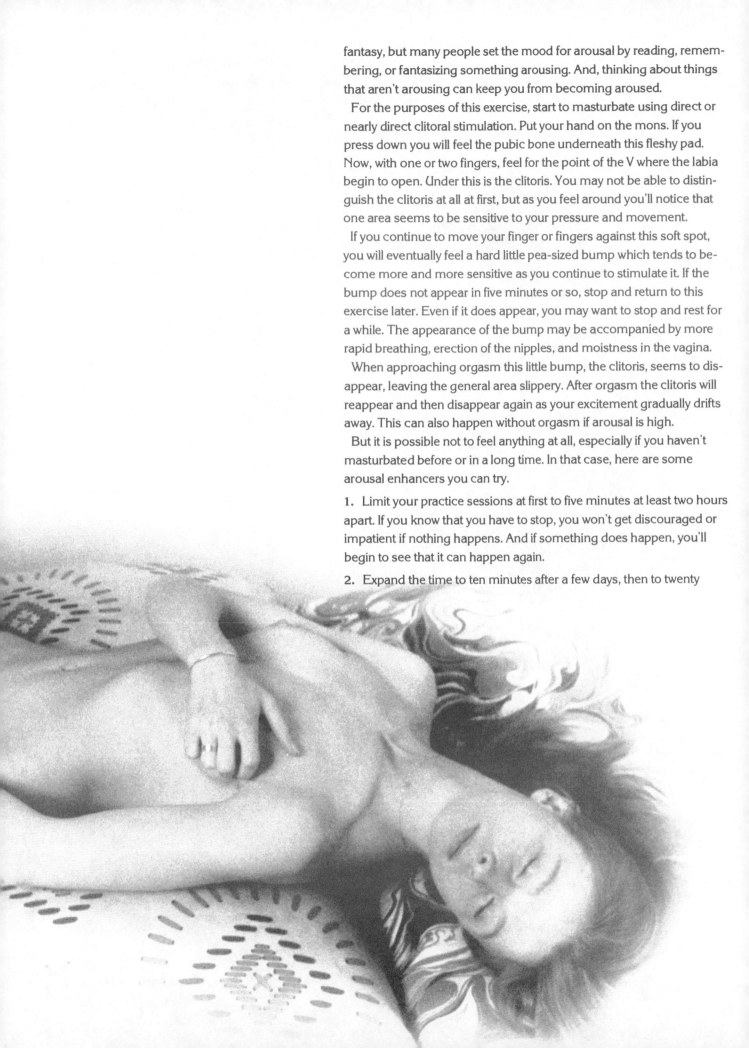

fantasy, but many people set the mood for arousal by reading, remembering, or fantasizing something arousing. And, thinking about things that aren't arousing can keep you from becoming aroused.

For the purposes of this exercise, start to masturbate using direct or nearly direct clitoral stimulation. Put your hand on the mons. If you press down you will feel the pubic bone underneath this fleshy pad. Now, with one or two fingers, feel for the point of the V where the labia begin to open. Under this is the clitoris. You may not be able to distinguish the clitoris at all at first, but as you feel around you'll notice that one area seems to be sensitive to your pressure and movement.

If you continue to move your finger or fingers against this soft spot, you will eventually feel a hard little pea-sized bump which tends to become more and more sensitive as you continue to stimulate it. If the bump does not appear in five minutes or so, stop and return to this exercise later. Even if it does appear, you may want to stop and rest for a while. The appearance of the bump may be accompanied by more rapid breathing, erection of the nipples, and moistness in the vagina.

When approaching orgasm this little bump, the clitoris, seems to disappear, leaving the general area slippery. After orgasm the clitoris will reappear and then disappear again as your excitement gradually drifts away. This can also happen without orgasm if arousal is high.

But it is possible not to feel anything at all, especially if you haven't masturbated before or in a long time. In that case, here are some arousal enhancers you can try.

1. Limit your practice sessions at first to five minutes at least two hours apart. If you know that you have to stop, you won't get discouraged or impatient if nothing happens. And if something does happen, you'll begin to see that it can happen again.

2. Expand the time to ten minutes after a few days, then to twenty

minutes, if you wish. Always stop if you feel frustrated but allow yourself time to observe and experience changes in your body. It can take an hour to begin to feel aroused but spending an hour will not necessarily be helpful, especially if you are just waiting for something to happen.

3. Fantasize. If you find that sexual or other fantasies arouse you, try having one while masturbating. You might fantasize that someone else is masturbating you, that you are masturbating in front of someone special, or that some other sexual or nonsexual activity is taking place.

4. Watch yourself. You can look at your own body and find that stimulating, or you can watch yourself in a mirror. There is nothing wrong with being excited by your own body and its responses.

5. Stretch your muscles. Find which ones seem to be connected to feelings of arousal. Point your toes and pull as hard as you can with your leg and buttock muscles. Arch your back and neck and stretch your torso. Push your arms out and around. You can encourage your own arousal by increasing muscle tension throughout your body.

6. Squeeze your muscles. The muscles of the buttocks, the thighs, and the anus and vagina are all involuntarily related to arousal. See if you can voluntarily get them working for you. Practice the vaginal squeeze from Chapter 5.

7. Vary the pressure and rhythm of your clitoral stimulation. If you are too gentle in your touch, you won't feel anything. If you press too hard, you may feel too much. If you are moving very fast, you may be trying too hard. If you are moving very slowly, you may not really be trying at all.

8. Change position. If you are lying on your stomach, your hand could get tired. If you are sitting on a chair, you may not be able to move in arousing ways. If nothing is happening, try standing up or bending over.

9. Use your other hand to stimulate other parts of your body, such as your nipples, neck, tummy, toes. Remember that arousal involves the whole body, not just the genitals.

10. Keep in mind that it is all right for a woman to work a little at her own arousal.

If you feel yourself crescendoing toward orgasm, by all means have one. But on the way try to note the changes your body goes through. Listen for your heartbeat, look for the "sex flush"—a reddening of the face and torso when you are aroused. Check around your vagina to see if it is wet and note the places on your body that are sexually responsive to your touch. Try to capture the recognition and enjoyment of your own arousal with pertinent, individual details.

This has been a guide for the beginner. If you are a more advanced student of self-arousal, you should be elaborating on this guide. You could do this by trying things that were suggested but which you don't normally do. Or you could try something you've thought of or heard of but never taken the time to experiment with.

Guide for men
Men are less likely than women not to know how to masturbate, but that seems to have made masturbation even more separate from "real sex." The details of arousal are the same, however, with a partner as when

alone. If you can't make love to yourself with pleasure and satisfaction, you may have trouble making love to another.

Arousal is a particularly important factor for men who climax too fast, don't climax at all, or don't get an erection. It is especially relevant to know what is arousing and what you can do to bring it about. And it is certainly easier to learn when you don't have to worry about how you appear to a partner.

Men usually masturbate by moving one hand up and down the shaft of the erect penis. You can use the whole hand or just the thumb and index finger. And, as with women, masturbation can be rubbing the genitals against something, such as clothes or a bed. How tightly the penis is gripped or rubbed and the rate of movement will vary with the man and the stage of arousal. But it is not possible to masturbate very effectively with a flaccid or limp penis. So the first step is erection.

Stroking and rubbing the glans of the penis may bring about an erection, as may touching the scrotum, perineum, and inner thighs. Sometimes gentle tugging, twirling, or pulling the penis will cause a response. The penis doesn't necessarily get hard all at once. It becomes heavier and spongier as blood flows into it. You can begin moving your hand along the shaft of the penis before it is totally erect.

There are other ways to get an erection. Some seem to come spontaneously. Although you can't really will an erection, you can certainly do things to encourage one. You can fantasize, look at pictures or books or people that arouse you. It's important to be aware of what settings, people, and activities do bring about erection.

Masturbation itself, once you have erection, calls for steady pressure up and down the penis. This may result in orgasm immediately. If this happens, don't get discouraged. Try again. You need to stretch out that arousal time so that you can recognize the changes your body undergoes between getting an erection and ejaculation.

There is a point during sexual excitement when you know that you can do nothing to keep from having an orgasm. In a few moments you will ejaculate. This point, called the moment of inevitability, occurs when the prostate gland sends the semen into the penile urethra. The second stage of ejaculation is the contracting of the muscles at the base of the penis. These contractions send the semen out of the penis. It is a process you can't stop.

You can, however, learn to anticipate the moment of inevitability and you can lengthen the time before it comes by this recognition. Being able to do this gives you more pleasure from the excitement and suspension of the aroused state itself and will also be more fun for your partner.

Anticipating the pre-ejaculatory state means being alert to the tensing of muscles, the increased pressure of engorged blood vessels in the penis and pelvic area, the faster heartbeat and shallower breathing that indicate high arousal. When you are aware of these things happening to you, stop masturbating and see if the pitch of tension will ease off a little. Then continue to that point again and let it go away again. Then if you want to come, come.

If nothing happens at all, or if you get an erection but have no other signs of arousal, limit your time with yourself to just five minutes in the beginning. It is important to keep trying. Don't push yourself to the point of feeling fed up and frustrated, but don't just give up either.

Now is the time to read over the ten arousal enhancers listed in the women's section if you haven't already. Even those of you who have no trouble becoming aroused may find that arousal is not something you are particularly able to maintain or control. Sometimes the emphasis is so much on performance and orgasm that the arousal of you or your partner is lost.

CONCLUSION
You may think it's all very mechanistic and constrained to talk about controlling arousal. And so it is. But being unable to recognize or use arousal isn't very satisfactory either. Naturally you don't want to concentrate so hard on control that nothing happens spontaneously. It's just that sometimes you have to go a little overboard in order to find the middle ground where you can enjoy yourself when you want to.

If controlling arousal is no problem for you and you don't feel you are a victim of routine, that's good. It is possible to be perfectly happy doing the things you've always done and doing them well. These suggestions are merely to give you new ideas if you need them. There is no reason to change anything if you, and your partner, are satisfied.

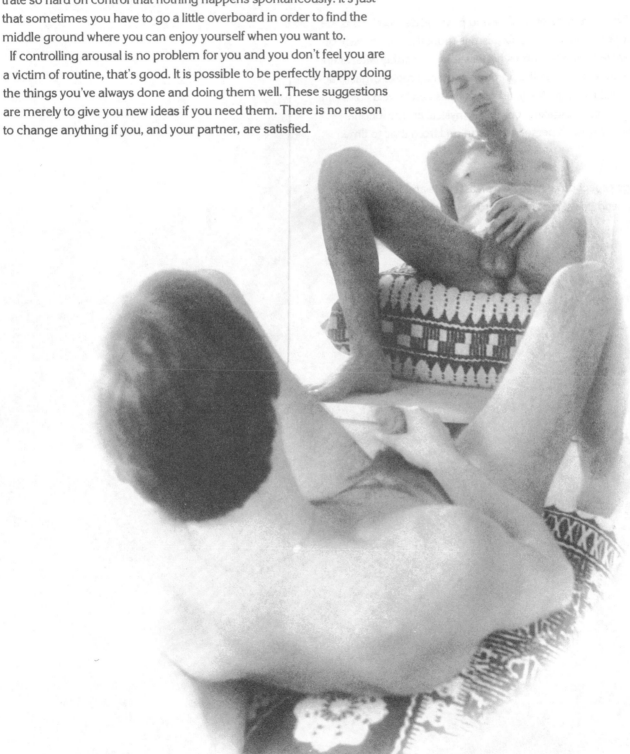

Orgasm

INTRODUCTION

"Oh," she said. "I die each time. Do you not die?"

"No. Almost. But did thee feel the earth move?"

"Yes. As I died. Put thy arm around me, please."

Ernest Hemingway, For Whom the Bell Tolls

. . . [Orgasm] is a brief episode of physical release from the vasocongestive and myotonic increment developed in response to sexual stimuli. . . .

W. H. Masters and V. E. Johnson, Human Sexual Response

Somewhere between these emotional and physical descriptions is the orgasm most people experience. Orgasm is more than the release of neuromuscular tension and somewhat less than an earthquake. Literature, from the euphemistic to the pornographic, can make orgasm appear positively cataclysmic. Medical descriptions can leave a cold, clinical aftertaste. Because orgasms combine physical and emotional responses, they vary from person to person and from time to time.

EXPECTATIONS

Human beings expect orgasm to be a pleasurable and rewarding experience. Sometimes we also expect it to be memorable, revolutionary,

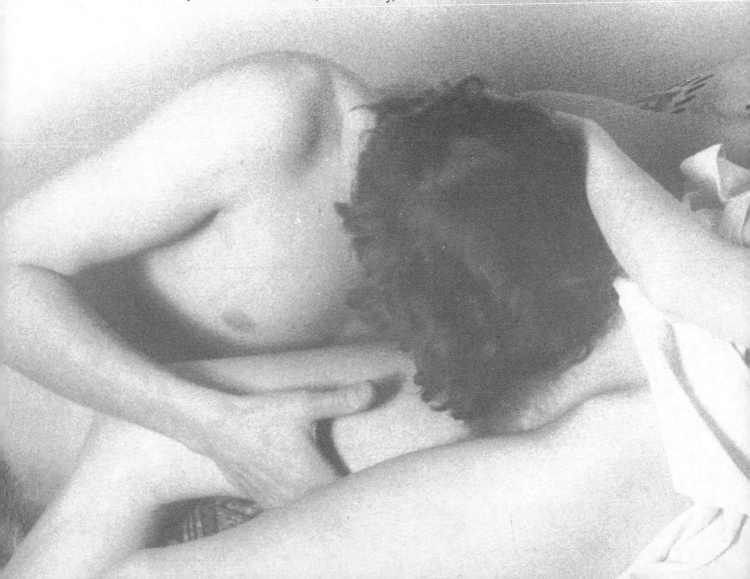

even destructive. Poets, doctors, and lexicographers have all taken a turn at describing orgasm, but there is no universally accepted definition. That's probably because it depends on individual expectations and experience. Here we'll look at some popular descriptions and discuss the expectations they convey.

Take the description of an orgasm being like a sneeze, for instance. There is a tickly premonition that it is coming, a muscular spasm when it does come, and a sense of relief afterward. Some sneezes seem centered in the nose and head, while others take over the whole body and once started can't really be stopped.

Although you might use this description for someone who has never had an orgasm, you'd have to add that orgasms are not the same as sneezes. People just don't look forward to sneezing the way they do to having an orgasm. They don't count sneezes and they usually aren't very concerned about the sneezes of others.

Another common description of orgasm is that it is a little death. Time sits still during an orgasm. Afterward, a sense of loss and possibly

timelessness is experienced. The little death idea was very prevalent in the Renaissance and it continues to be an expectation for many. Although you can go on and on having orgasms, just like sneezes, orgasm is imbued with a special sense of mortality. Each one means a little less you.

This sense of loss, though poignant and not unusual in women, is even more common among men, who, after all, do lose something each time they ejaculate. Sperm is connected to creative powers, strength, and potency. Baudelaire maintained that each orgasm meant one less poem. Athletes who perform badly are accused of having left their game in the sack. The General in the movie Dr. Strangelove kept worrying about losing his "precious bodily fluids." The whole idea of lost potency, which keeps athletes and intellectuals celibate before the big game or the big book, affects many men, and women, in mystic ways.

There is also a sense of gain from orgasm. Orgasm can bring you closer to a partner. This intimate experience of sharing with another is a high form of communication. People do expect more than physical release and pleasure out of orgasm.

Sex as the source of all energy and creativity holds orgasm as a great energizer and an invaluable aid to the creative processes. Many people say that orgasm fills them with enthusiasm for other things and gives them a feeling of competence in going about their business.

The wave theory of orgasm is a metaphorical description very close to what actually does happen physiologically. The body experiences waves of muscular contractions, centered in the genitalia and sometimes spreading through the body. In women, these contractions occur in the outer third of the vagina and in the uterus. Men have them in the penis and also through the urethra as the ejaculate moves from the prostate to the penis. They are spaced about four-fifths of a second at first and farther apart later, in both men and women. Muscles in the limbs, back, face, and torso may also contract. The feeling isn't so much like being pounded by waves as like being the waves.

Although the intensity of orgasm varies, people often build in an expectation of intensity when describing orgasm. Most people can't feel the individual contractions of their orgasms, but an intense orgasm usually means there are more contractions. However, several contractions may seem like an explosion one day and a sustained high another.

If you haven't had an orgasm for several days, you may anticipate and indeed feel a more intense orgasm than you do when it's a daily occurrence. If you have been nervous or tense, your body may respond more dramatically to orgasm than if things are going along calmly. Such psychological factors as disputes with your partner, leavetaking or homecoming, anything that makes a sexual experience special, can affect the intensity of orgasm.

Men and women have different expectations for orgasm, too, and describe them differently. Women have more variation in orgasmic patterns from one peak to a series of little peaks all run together. Men's orgasms, being concurrent with ejaculation, tend to be more defined and to follow a straight peak pattern.

Of course there are many vaguer descriptions of orgasm. It might make you flushed and sad, achey and happy. You could say it was all over with so fast that you don't know how to describe it. You might be totally unaware of what is happening around you or filled with a heightened sensual awareness. Your own orgasms may not fit any description you've heard or read about.

It's confusing to apply your expectations or experience of orgasm to a partner. If you are seized with enormous immediacy and total immersement in your body, a partner who seems to be having less response may puzzle you. Although everyone experiences increased breathing, pulse, vasocongestion, and muscle tension during orgasm, many of these symptoms are almost undetectable. You might think your partner is not having as good a time as you are, or is having a better time, if you expect his or her orgasm to be like yours.

Orgasm for you

Describe your most recent orgasm. If it was unusual in some way, say so, and describe a more typical one if you wish. Include both physical

and emotional sensations, and as many details as you can muster. If you are not orgasmic yet, describe what you expect orgasm to be. Use your journal if you prefer.

_____
_____
_____
_____

Analyzing your orgasms

If your orgasms don't live up to expectations, they may disappoint you. You could be basing your expectations on someone else's description and you might feel that orgasm just isn't what it was cracked up to be. Orgasm is purported to have all kinds of magical properties. It will change you, overwhelm you, improve your relationship, give you confidence. If these things don't happen, you are understandably unhappy and let down.

If sex just doesn't give you a charge, and you feel numb or unmoved by your orgasms, maybe you weren't very aroused. Your partner or your relationship to your partner could be to blame, especially if you are with this person just because there is no one else. Also, you may not be communicating to this partner how you like to be aroused. Perhaps you are aroused and you do care for this partner, but you get worn out trying to arouse him or her.

If you aren't well, you shouldn't be comparing your orgasms now to a time when you felt better. The same is true of age. In youth many things seem terribly exciting and intense just because they are new. As you age some of these things take on different meanings, often more significant ones. But if you project fears about aging onto your orgasms, some of the joy goes out of them.

You may find that you are reluctant to have orgasms due to your negative expectations of them. If you have experienced painful orgasms, you have an excellent reason to avoid them. See your doctor. Hormone therapy or some other medication or solution can almost always be found.

If you fear being overwhelmed by orgasm, physically or emotionally, because you have in the past, you could be reluctant to experience that again. However, the best therapy for that problem is almost always more experience. Orgasms are different. One especially powerful orgasm, either yours or your partner's, which makes you feel frightened, responsible, or unwillingly committed, can best be negated by a few less impressive ones.

Akin to this reluctance is the feeling that you look or smell or sound less than poised when having an orgasm. Start watching your partner instead of yourself. You may be too much the self-observer, performing for your own benefit and ultimate destruction.

If you feel that you are missing out because orgasm isn't all it should be, you may have to accept that it couldn't be all it is supposed to be. One of the biggest disillusionments is the feeling that sometime in the past you did have a perfect partner or a perfect orgasmic experience. You may have to check your memories and your expectations against

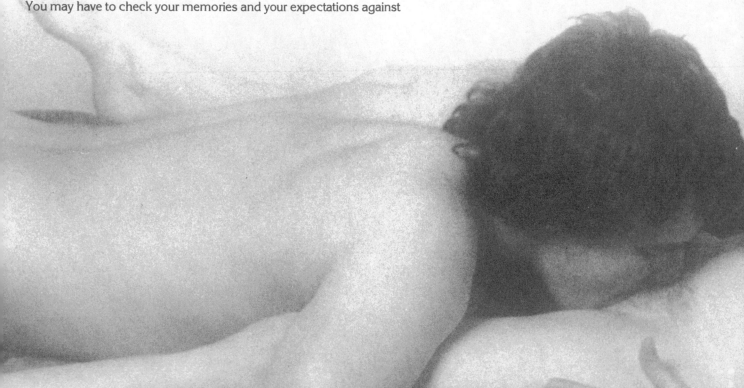

what really happened in the past. Then check exaggerated descriptions you read or hear against your own experience.

THE AFTERMATH

There is a time after orgasm which Masters and Johnson call the resolution phase of sexual response. This is the time it takes for the body to return to normal—slower heartbeat and breathing, lower blood pressure and vasocongestion, normal muscular tone, etc. This time has also been called detumescence and the afterglow.

For most women arousal subsides slowly and many can be aroused again to orgasm with just a little encouragement. This seems to be particularly true for women who have had children, since pregnancy increases the vascularity of the pelvic area and may explain why older women are more orgasmic than younger ones. Although it is both possible and normal for women to have several or multiple orgasms, there is nothing second-rate about having just one orgasm. Unfortunately, widespread awareness that women are capable of multiple orgasms has led to the mistaken notion that multiplicity is a sine qua non of femininity. Both men and women are guilty of thinking that coming all over the place is the badge of a real woman.

Men don't have a multi-orgasmic capability. For them, the "resolution" phase is more dramatic and they cannot usually get another erection for several minutes or even days. This varies in individual men, of course, and according to age, health, and state of arousal. The time between erections is called the refractory period. During this time a man cannot be aroused to another erection no matter how much he wants to be. Most refractory periods are from one half hour to several hours long even in youth, unless special conditions, such as abstinence or a new partner, prevail.

The fading of orgasm can have different individual effects. Some people feel tired and want to take a little nap. Others want to talk about the experience or the relationship. Some people like to smoke after sex—they associate smoking with pleasure and it's always done in the movies.

There are also people who want to get up and run around after sex. Orgasm buoys them up and they feel energetic, as if they could accomplish anything. This particular reaction flies in the face of the myths

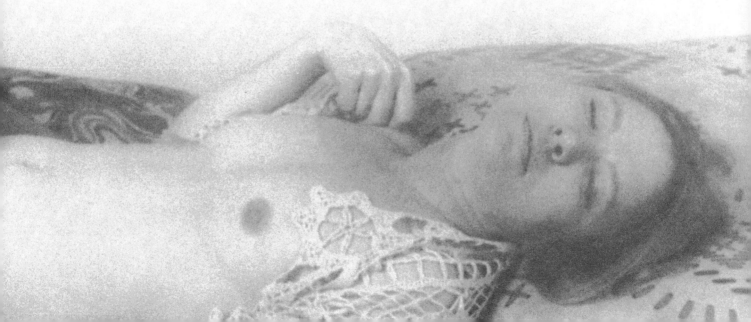

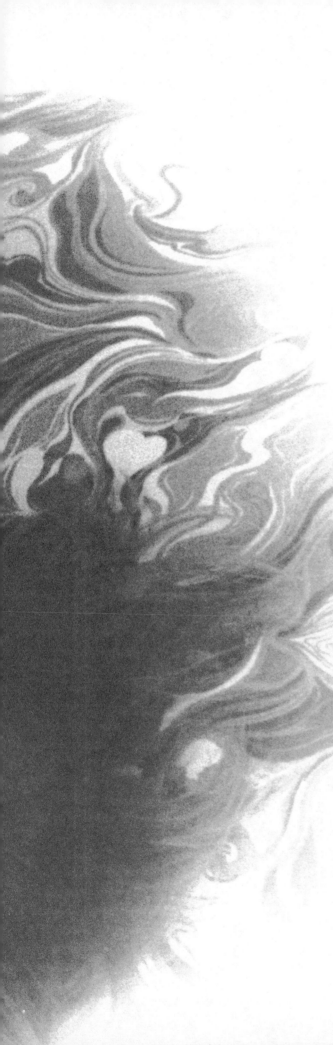

about orgasm being debilitating and may cause those who feel it, or their partners, to wonder if they had a proper orgasm.

The "golden glow syndrome" is a feeling of warmth or happiness which makes you want to just lie there and beam at the ceiling or at your partner and let time drift for a few moments. After all, orgasm is a culmination of sorts, physically anyway, and sharing it with someone you like can cast a golden glow.

Then there are the people who worry about the ejaculate. What do you do about that afterward? Is it leaking onto your grandmother's hand-made quilt? Is it ruining the decor in your new van? Yes, it's a silly problem. It is also one that people don't talk about much, including those people who long to reach for a hanky.

This conflict typifies the problems people have when they don't share the same reaction to orgasm. What happens to the nonsmoker whose lover is blowing smoke in his or her face? What happens to the multi-orgasmic woman, whose partner came long ago? What happens to the glowworm whose partner is full of energy? And how about the person who is totally spent by orgasm and has a partner who likes to chat?

It is important to recognize these differences in patterns, because if you don't acknowledge them you'll have trouble compromising, the only realistic solution. People build up resentments over unspoken, possibly even unknown, differences such as these. You can get into a bind where you are mad at your partner for always falling asleep when the partner doesn't even know that you're not asleep too. Of course, the resentment could be justified. Maybe your partner doesn't want to compromise and is falling asleep to avoid you. But don't take that for granted. Voice your own preferences.

Talking about your feelings is the first way to approach this kind of conflict. Maybe your partner doesn't know that you can't get another erection, but that you are willing to help her have another orgasm. Maybe your partner isn't aware that the smoke from her cigar turns your stomach.

Once you know what your partner likes, you may be able to change your behavior a little. It's terrific to have a surge of energy just after orgasm, but if your partner lies glowing at you, maybe you could restrain your urge to jump up, at least occasionally. The person who wants an intimate tête-à-tête just when you are on the nod is perhaps not getting your close and intimate attention any other time.

You don't have to stay together after orgasm. The person who wants to smoke could leave the room. One partner could nap while the other gets up and paints the attic. The trouble with these patterns, if they are that, is that they sometimes make one partner, or even both, feel rejected. These issues will be discussed further in upcoming chapters.

THE MYTHS

When you have all kinds of false expectations and personal interpretations of a subject like orgasm, myths naturally build up around it. Several of these will be discussed here. If you find that you share the myth, try to think when you started believing it. Then consider getting rid of it. Myths, like superstition and all misinformation, can have a powerful effect on you, especially if you picked them up at an impressionable age or in dramatic circumstances. Some suggestions for getting rid of the myths will also be offered.

The only good orgasm for a woman is a vaginal orgasm Although Freud is often blamed for this myth, the idea predates him. Vaginal orgasm might be said to support conceptual politics, since the vagina is the organ of conception. Freud and the others held that little girls have clitoral orgasms and emotionally mature women have vaginal orgasms. A frigid woman was one who could not make the transfer from the clitoris to the vagina. As the research by Masters and Johnson has shown, an orgasm is an orgasm, no matter what the site or type of stimulation. Although you don't need an orgasm to conceive, there is still a popular sentiment that "Good fucks make good babies."

Conception aside, women like to have coital orgasms just because it makes them feel closer to their partner. It is, however, often not the easiest way to reach orgasm. For some women it takes a high level of arousal and a helpful and patient partner. Increasing arousal, especially through clitoral stimulation, and using positions that increase pressure on the female genitalia, are the best ways to enhance the possibility of coital orgasm for a woman. Try these in order to see what is possible. It may be that more satisfactory and pleasurable orgasms for you will come from noncoital positions.

When a man is aroused and erect, he has to have an orgasm This is a myth perpetuated mainly by teen-age boys who want their girlfriends to let them "do it." There are veiled references to "blue balls" and testicular pain. It is true that the increased size of the testes can sometimes cause pressure that is painful. This is relieved by orgasm, but not necessarily coital orgasm. And the arousal will subside.

What is often overlooked in this regard is that women, too, can experience uncomfortable pressure if they do not reach orgasm. A woman who is highly aroused and does not have an orgasm may experience tenderness throughout the lower abdomen from the increased blood supply in that area. If this happens all the time, the woman may develop a chronic pain. This can be relieved by masturbation to orgasm if coital orgasm does not occur.

It's not a good idea to have an orgasm while menstruating On the contrary, it may be a very good idea, especially for the woman who has cramps. Orgasmic contractions of the uterus relieve cramped muscles. Of course some women don't feel like having sex at this time, due to edema (bloating), hypersensitivity in the genitalia, or general irritability.

Some women are more orgasmic during menstruation, which could be from increased vasocongestion in the pelvis. Or it may be from excitement over breaking the taboo against sex at this time or because they are not worried about getting pregnant. Lowered female hormonal levels at this time may give prominence to the male hormone testosterone, thought to have much to do with sex drive in both men and women. A woman who hasn't tried orgasm, alone or with a partner, while menstruating, might do so just to see what her reaction is.

Only men have wet dreams Well, there is certainly more evidence that men have nocturnal orgasms; but women, too, can go through a sexual response cycle in their sleep. Aroused by dreams or tangled bedclothes, both men and women become excited, possibly to orgasm and possibly without remembering anything about it. A man may wake up with an erection or semen on the sheets, a woman may feel a tingling or wetness around the vagina. A woman may not be as sure as a man that she did indeed have an orgasm unless she woke up during it or clearly remembers a dream incorporating it.

Although nocturnal orgasms are infrequent, especially after the adolescent years, they are by no means uncommon. More men than women seem to experience them and wet dreams do not account for a very high number of total orgasms. People seem most likely to have them when they haven't had sex for a while, when they read or do something arousing before falling asleep, when they are wrought up or tense. It used to be thought that there was something wrong about having wet dreams—"night pollutions," etc.—but now they are viewed as a normal, if infrequent sexual outlet. In fact, nocturnal orgasm could be seen as a healthy sign in people who are impotent or nonorgasmic when awake. It shows that there is nothing organically wrong.

You shouldn't have orgasms when you are pregnant The myth arises from a fear that orgasm will set off labor. Women who have a history of miscarrying may indeed be advised by their doctors to avoid orgasm for the first three months, but that is unusual. In the late stages of pregnancy, close to a due date, orgasm might set off labor, but not prematurely.

Women are more likely to be orgasmic during pregnancy than ever before, due to pregnancy hormones and extra pelvic vascularity. Some adjustments have to be made regarding positions for sex as the fetus develops, of course. But for a woman to go without orgasm for nine months would probably have adverse effects on her, her partner, and even her baby.

Orgasm from mechanical stimulation spoils you "Mechanical stimulation" refers to electrical devices such as an electric toothbrush or vibrator applied to the genitals. Vibrators come in the facial model available in drugstores and the various larger models which are strapped on the hand or held and used for aching or sore muscles. Because orgasms achieved through this means tend to be easier and more intense, there is a belief that they may become addictive.

Actually, vibrators can be very helpful, especially for women who are unable to reach orgasm by other means. Once a person has an orgasm by this means, she or he is more likely also to be able to have orgasms in more conventional ways. It is certainly possible that a vibrator could be used as an escape, an excuse for not trying anything more difficult or involving. Because an electrical device is impersonal, one could use it to avoid the emotional conflicts accompanying manual masturbation or sex with another person. If you do rely heavily on a vibrator, you should consider this aspect. Otherwise, occasional use can be exciting and instructional.

You shouldn't waste your orgasms—you only have so many You have an infinite number of orgasms and, although there may be reasons for not having one at any particular time, you can't exhaust your potential. Orgasm may be tiring and that, plus religious taboos on "spilt seed," is probably the source of this myth. The fatigue from orgasm is usually a positive, not a negative, experience and the body has restorative powers regarding sperm.

CONCLUSION

There are many more myths and expectations about orgasm than have been dealt with here. One of the reasons for their continued proliferation is that people don't try to talk about orgasm realistically, especially to a partner. Even though male and female orgasms are basically the same, people tend to generalize by sex instead of by individual. Men think of all female orgasms as mysterious and women think of male orgasms as urgent and easy. The only way to find out how orgasm really is for others is to talk to a friend or partner and share your own experience.

Nonorgasmic Women

INTRODUCTION

When you can't have orgasms at all, it is hard to think about any other sexual concerns. To be nonorgasmic is to be frigid, less than a real woman, inadequate. A lack of orgasm is seen out of all proportion to its real significance and worth. As with any sexual dysfunction, not having orgasms becomes an obsession.

This chapter is devoted to examining some of the reasons why you might not have orgasms, either occasionally or all the time. The most common reason women are nonorgasmic is that they do not have proper sexual stimulation. The best therapy for this is a straightforward one in which you practice the techniques and activities which are stimulating.

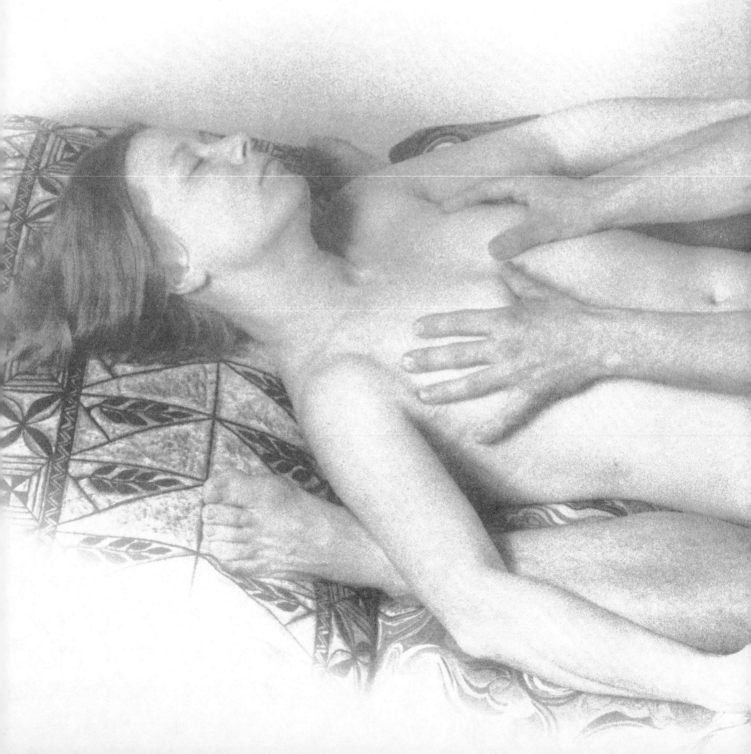

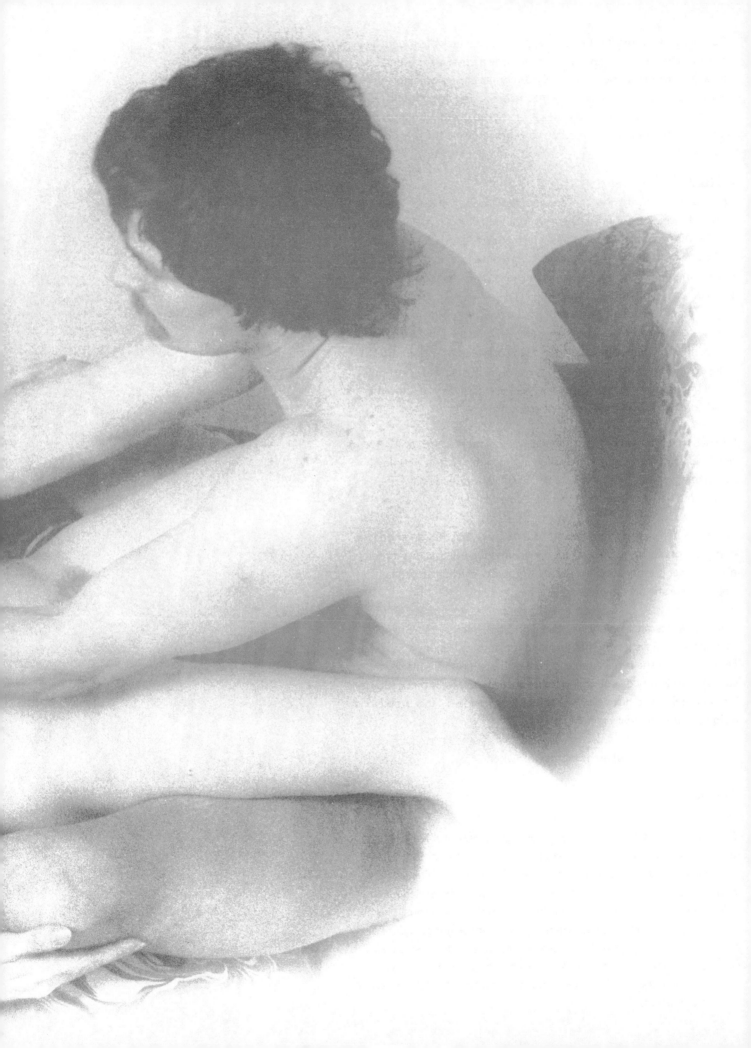

But sometimes you are unable to approach your lack of orgasm as a need for practice. You may have to overcome a physical or mental block first. If you experience painful intercourse or unpredictable orgasms, you may need to examine that before taking up a practice therapy. Since getting rid of a physical or psychological symptom does not equal becoming orgasmic, you can come back to the practical therapy later.

SEXUAL TROUBLES

There is an old saying that there are no frigid wives, just inept husbands. Although it sounds rather comforting from the female point of view, it was probably made up by some male who thought he could make any woman come. Nowadays most women like to think that they have something to do with their own orgasms and that they are not dependent on a man for sexual fulfillment.

The women described below express the most common complaints of nonorgasmic women. There are many variations on these themes. If you don't find yourself here, use the space provided or your journal to write down your own problem. The therapy is applicable at some point for all nonorgasmic women, but it is most useful when you know the conditions under which you are not orgasmic.

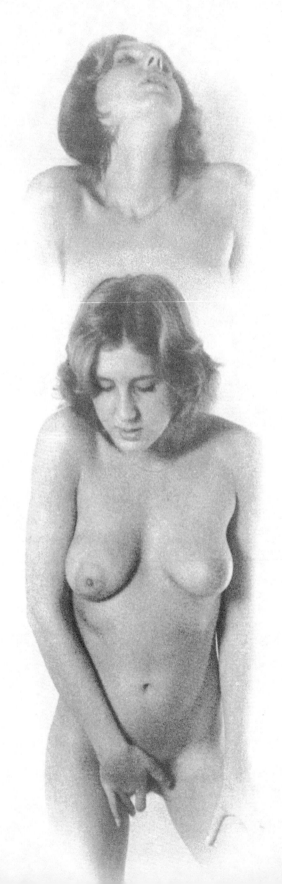

Rita has never had an orgasm in her life by any means, with any partner. She is not really sure what is meant by orgasm or how people go about having them. Her boyfriend knows that she doesn't have orgasms, but he's not sure what he could do about it.

Leslie has had occasional orgasms with partners, but they seemed to come out of nowhere. She has tried masturbating but that is unpredictable too. Her partners don't really know whether she has an orgasm or not because she always pretends she has if she hasn't.

Marcia is orgasmic in every way except through intercourse. She can masturbate, enjoys having her husband masturbate her or perform oral sex on her, but she is never able to come when his penis is inside her vagina. This is very discouraging to her because she feels that coitus is the only real way to have sex. She sometimes wonders if this problem is a sign she doesn't really love her partner.

_____ (You) are nonorgasmic when _____

You feel _____

The most common practical advice you'll get for sex problems is to relax. Anyone, from your doctor to your boyfriend to your mother, will tell you that's all you need. And it certainly won't hurt you to think about what relaxes you. Then you can apply some of those general ideas to a sexual situation. For instance, if a drink or a smoke or soft music tends to help you unwind after the big game, you use those things before or during sex. If the big game tends to relax you, you might try some kind of physical exercise before sex. People who know deep breathing or meditation find that restful. Others find that reading, television, or a nap calms them down.

All nonorgasmic women should review the chapters on arousal and physiology. You should know what your body is like and how it is sensitive to sexual stimulation. Sometimes being nonorgasmic goes back to a basic lack of knowledge about your own body and how it responds. You owe it to yourself to know as much as you can about your own patterns of arousal.

Unfortunately for those of you who feel that it is unhealthy or unsavory to masturbate, masturbation is the best practical therapy for the nonorgasmic woman who has never had an orgasm. It is only by experimenting on yourself that you become aware of what you are capable of and what kinds of touch please you. In other words, once you know what you are looking for, it is easier to find.

Rita, who has never had an orgasm, needs to feel her own body becoming aroused. She needs to work alone to have an orgasm under her own power. There are many reasons why it is hard to have an orgasm with someone present. You or your partner feels shy. The partner actually does the wrong things and if you don't know the right ones, you can't tell him (or her). And, there is always the problem that intercourse provides the least efficient stimulation for most women. Masturbation of the clitoris is the most efficient and best way to start. The confidence and experience you gain "knowing" yourself can then be with you when you are with someone else.

If, like Leslie, you are orgasmic occasionally but unpredictably, masturbation can help you, too. You may not know your arousal patterns well enough to be able, at least usually, to count on them. Leslie's orgasms when masturbating may be dependent on how long she masturbates, whether or not she's aroused when she does it, and how she feels doing it. These issues also affect intercourse. If nothing happens after five minutes, Leslie—or you—may give up. You—or Leslie—may be rather lackluster in technique. You may not touch yourself directly, may not apply the pressure you need, may disdain the aid of a vibrator, a feather, or something else that could tickle your fancy.

Leslie's random response when she is with a partner may be partially a communication problem. Once you know what you want, how do you tell or show someone else? Certainly just being with someone else is arousing, but what they do is important too. You may be very excited by having your breasts sucked, but it is possible that just any nibbling at any time won't do.

One way to teach your partner what kind of stimulation arouses you is to use what Masters and Johnson call the nondemand position for female stimulation. This is not an intercourse position. Your partner sits against a wall or the headboard of a bed with pillows behind him or her and legs outstretched. You sit between his legs with your back to his chest and your own legs crossing his at about the knees (see photograph).

You then take his hand, put yours atop it, and gently guide it around your body. You show him how and where you like to be touched, with what kind of pressure and speed. Men sometimes think that if they rub you hard and fast you'll be beside yourself with pleasure. Usually you'll be beside yourself with pain or boredom. Most women prefer gentle, steady pressure, speed, and rhythm during arousal. Otherwise, they lose interest or feel uncomfortable. Since men aren't born knowing how to touch someone else, you have to show them. You and your partner should spend at least ten minutes a day in the nondemand position getting to know you.

Another noncoital, nondemand position is one in which you can experiment with oral stimulation. You should lie on your back with a pillow under your head if you like and your knees comfortably flexed. Your partner kneels between your legs with his or her body leaning over yours, supported by his or her hands. He or she starts by kissing your hair, face, and neck. You do not kiss your partner because you need your mouth free to give encouragement and suggestions. Tell when you like something or don't, suggest he or she try the hollow of your neck or the

inside of your ear. They can move all down your body with you telling them where you'd like to be blown on, sucked, licked, nibbled, kissed. You don't have to tell in words, incidentally. You can ooooh and aaaah and move your body or their head in ways that give your message without making either of you feel uninvolved or interrupted.

During intercourse, if you get to that, you should follow the same routine. Let him follow your movements in your favorite positions. Also, show him when and how you'd like to be kissed and touched during intercourse. For example, if after a few minutes of slow rhythmic motion you feel you'd like to have your ass squeezed, you can move his hands onto your ass and demonstrate. If you want him to chew on your ear, show him how. If you want to take a break for a few moments, pull away and tell him you'd like to rest a little.

The basic ingredient in all these suggestions is that you call the shots. Many men make assumptions about what women like based on hearsay or a history of being with women who didn't tell them what they liked. Their idea of finger fucking might be to arouse you with their

finger in your vagina rather than around your clitoris. Even if they know about the eroticism of the clitoris, they may not know how and when to touch it. Similarly, they may think that the vagina is what they are supposed to eat out or go down on. You have to take a little initiative to let your partner know just what you like and when. Even a partner who is another woman doesn't know exactly how it is for you.

Getting back to our examples, Marcia, the woman who doesn't have coital orgasms, is expressing a very widespread concern of both women and their male partners. So many women have difficulty achieving coital orgasms that it seems as if other kinds of orgasms may be just as normal and desirable.

Many women pick up a preference for coital orgasm from men who feel they have to bring a woman to orgasm with their penises. This seems related to the idea that women are supposed to just lie there and the man will do everything. That attitude is as hard on the man who doesn't know what he is supposed to do, as on the woman who never feels things are going her way.

Then there is the feeling that coital orgasm will bring you closer to your partner. It may, but open and free communication in your relationship is more likely to. You may be putting some sort of mystical expectations on coital orgasms. You have to remember that you are dealing with a physiological phenomenon as well as a mystical one and recognize that it has limits.

Sexual difficulties with a particular partner can be due to a problem of his or hers, or because you bring different anatomies, experiences, and rhythms together. These difficulties have to be worked on together. If your partner loses his erection or comes too quickly, you may not have time to have an orgasm with him inside you. In that case it is important to deal with your partner's problem first. The next two chapters will cover problems men have and problems people encounter when they encounter each other.

To find out if coital orgasm is possible or even preferable for you, there are some steps you can take. You should talk this over with your partner because you will need his cooperation. If you feel shy about bringing it up, perhaps you could leave this book lying around.

Step one Increasing vaginal awareness. The vaginal tightening exercises described in Chapter 5 are very useful for increasing tension between the vagina, minor lips, and clitoris. Practice squeezing. You can also check around the rim of the vagina for spots that are more sensitive to pressure than others. And you should be sure that the vagina is lubricating before insertion of the penis.

Step two Try positions that increase pressure and stimulation on the clitoris and the sensitive points of the vaginal rim. Many women find that being on top of the partner gives them freedom to move and to push down where they want pressure. (See photograph on page 146.) The lateral position (see photograph on page 200) is also liberating.

Step three You should be the director for this show. Your partner can follow your lead on movement. You can try circular motion, up and down movement, side to side. Then if you want to stop and rest for a while, let him know.

Step four Additional stimulation or continued stimulation of your breasts or clitoris during coitus may be just what you need to maintain a high level of arousal. Show your partner what you'd like and when you'd like it. You may want a change as arousal increases or decreases.

Step five Increase the time spent in coitus. Often the reason you can't come is that you, or your partner, give up too soon. Even if you were aroused when he went inside you, it could take another twenty or thirty minutes to become that aroused again.

Step six If nothing much seems to happen and you find yourselves getting discouraged or frantic, give up. Try again another time and if, after you've given yourselves plenty of practice, you still aren't getting anywhere, forget it. You may be much happier and capable of far greater intimacy by having oral, manual, or other orgasms.

There is one other sexual trouble which is called sexual aversion. Some people, both men and women, have little interest in sex. This isn't something that just happens overnight and it doesn't mean that you have no interest in sex. Sexual aversion is a genuine and lifelong lack of much interest in sex. But you shouldn't jump to the conclusion that this is your trouble without examining possible medical or psychological reasons for your aversion. A lack of interest can mask a fear of sex, a disgust for your partner—all kinds of things. Check it out before you resolve that you just don't have much drive.

If you find that you are genuinely not very interested in sex, tell your partner. You can still show your love and acknowledge your partner's drive. Partners can feel rebuffed and suspicious if you tell them you aren't interested. They may interpret it as a dodge—and you should be very sure that they aren't right. There will be more on this in Chapter 13.

MEDICAL TROUBLES

Although generally physical problems are easier to deal with than sexual or psychological ones, women have traditionally been subjected to a great deal of skepticism from the medical profession when they complain of pain during sex. It is therefore important to pinpoint and examine carefully any physical complaint before going to a doctor. You can't count on him (or her) not to tell you it's all in your head. Most physical problems can be treated when properly diagnosed.

Claudine used to enjoy sex tremendously, but lately it's been so painful for her that she's taken to just trying to avoid it, and her husband, all the time. He doesn't really understand what is going on.

Before Claudine goes to her doctor, she should answer the following questionnaire. Knowing the answers to these questions before the doctor asks them will give her time to think over the origin and history of her problem. Some doctors are inclined to think that many physical complaints are really about something else. Although that may be the case, you should insist on a thorough exam before assuming anything.

Is the pain there all the time or only during intercourse or orgasm or both? _____

When did the pain start? (For example: with a certain partner, a delivery, an illness, a medication or contraceptive.) _____

What is the nature of the pain—burning, itching, throbbing, sharp, dull?
_____

Where is the pain—in the clitoris, lips, vagina, abdomen, anus, back, one side or the other? _____

Can you put your finger on the place where you feel the pain? _____

Has there been a discharge lately and how heavy, what color and odor is it? _____

Has there been any change in your periods in the past few months?
_____

Has anything else happened to you or changed lately that you think might be related to this pain? _____

Knowing the answers to these questions will help the doctor and it will also give you confidence in presenting your problem and asking for help. Some women would probably rather not know what is wrong with them, but most feel insulted if a doctor won't explain what the problem and its treatment are. A doctor who suggests tranquilizers or dieting or something else that doesn't seem related to the specific complaint might not be taking your trouble seriously or may not be admitting he or she doesn't know what's wrong. Insist that, although you'd enjoy being calm and slim, you don't see how it would help the pain.

Infections, which often cause burning or itching, can be treated with antibiotics in pill, cream, or suppository form. Your partner may need to be treated, too. Pains during intercourse or at other times may be a sign of endometriosis (an inflammation of the pelvic tissues), scar tissue (from surgery, childbearing, infection, abortion), or tumors and cysts (benign and malignant). These problems may be treated by medication, surgery, or a combination of both.

Women also experience pain or discomfort from allergic reactions to contraceptive, douche, or lubricating substances. If you suspect that might be your problem, try a different brand or stop the use for a few days to see if the problem disappears. If you stop using a contraceptive, stop intercourse too.

Painful intercourse or painful orgasm signals that something is wrong. It is important to seek medical care armed with knowledge about the history of the trouble. If you have reason to suspect that the pain you experience may be the result of inadequate or poor care in the past, you should seek out a specialist in obstetrics and gynecology. You can get a reference from the nearest medical school and, especially if you don't have much money, the school may be able to arrange an appointment for you gratis with one of its doctors.

Blanche is tired all the time. She has two small children, a part-time job, and a husband who travels a lot. When she and her husband do get some time to themselves, she is generally unresponsive sexually. She's worried about it because she used to find sex very relaxing and fulfilling. Now she doesn't even have that to look forward to.

It sounds as if Blanche is run-down and has no time to herself. This is a typical outcome of the rather undramatic syndrome known as Not-taking-care-of-yourself. Blanche doesn't need Geritol or a facial. She needs to have something change. Sometimes people get run-down from not eating or sleeping enough, from not getting any exercise, or from not having a minute to themselves.

Blanche should look over her day and chart what she actually does each hour. It's only by laying it out, as in the example below, that you can get a sense of where you are going wrong. Look for lost time, times your husband, your mother, your neighbor could help you out, time you could corner for yourself. Often the woman who is run-down just has no control over what happens during the day. A little planning, difficult as it may seem to start, will give you time to refresh yourself physically and emotionally so that you respond to everything, including sex, better.

	Time well-spent	Time wasted
7 am – 9 am		
9 – 11		
11 – 1 pm		
1 pm – 3		
3 – 5		
5 – 7		
7 – 9		
9 – 11		
11 pm – 7 am		

Being continually run-down, or becoming sexually unresponsive suddenly, may indicate that something more serious than inefficient use of time is involved. There are systemic diseases that do affect you sexually. There are also medications for these and other illnesses, including mental illnesses, which may affect your sexual patterns and responsiveness. If such a change is noticed, check with a doctor. Be sure to report all medications you are taking, even seemingly innocuous ones.

Two of Alice's four children were accidents. Although she loves all her children and wouldn't give any of them up, she is terrified that she will get pregnant again. She realizes she may have been careless before, but even with better birth control she's nervous. Her husband would gladly have a vasectomy in order to improve their sex life, but she's a little uneasy about that.

You may not think of a fear of pregnancy as a physical problem, but actually it can be. Alice is afraid that something will happen to her body that she doesn't want to have happen. When you are afraid of getting pregnant, you may be too nervous and preoccupied to enjoy sex. This is an extremely common and understandable fear, especially among women like Alice who are contraceptive failures, young or inexperienced women, older women who are changing partners, and women who cannot tolerate the best birth control methods.

It is possible to become paranoid about the whole issue and it looks as if Alice is getting that way. For her and her husband, sterilization probably is the best option. Other options are mutual masturbation or oral-genital sex, which are fun, satisfying, and allow the freedom to enjoy sex without worrying about pregnancy. However, if Alice and her husband prefer coitus, they should go to a doctor together to get the facts on vasectomy and tubal ligation. Even though her husband is willing to be sterilized, she might feel better having herself sterilized since she is the one who doesn't want more children.

It is certainly possible to use fear of pregnancy as a pretext in a crumbling relationship or as an excuse to deny a partner. But it is equally likely that there is real reason to be worried. It does seem wise to take advantage of the better birth control methods before digging into possible psychological explanations. Everything in the world can't be explained by psychology. Some things really are what they seem to be. The best way to combat a fear of pregnancy is to start by trying to prevent pregnancy.

Many young women are still faced with unwanted pregnancies, despite the wider availability of birth control devices, simply because they are afraid to talk to a doctor who might refuse them, or worse, tell their parents. It is now legal in many states for women under eighteen to obtain birth control devices without their parents' knowledge or consent. That's not to suggest that you should sneak off to get help if you can get it from your family. It's just that many women can't expect their parents to understand. For them the local branch of Planned Parenthood will give advice and direction. Planned Parenthood is nonprofitmaking, located all over the country, and dedicated to preventing unwanted pregnancies for women of all ages and in all situations. They teach and provide medical care and birth control, help women who are looking for abortions or sterilization, and provide counseling for women who are wondering what to do about their reproductive lives. Other organizations such as Zero Population Growth, local hot lines, and free clinics can often put you in touch with help if they don't provide it themselves. There is help out there—but you can't expect it to find you. If you like and trust your family doctor, do ask him or her for advice.

Don't forget that you can get pregnant even if you don't have an orgasm during intercourse. Some women still think that denying themselves an orgasm will protect them. It will not.

Ella and Tommy have been lovers for several months now but they have never really consummated their relationship. The problem seems to be that Ella's vagina isn't big enough for Tommy's penis. He's never had this problem before and he finds it embarrassing and confusing. Ella is confused, too. She's never loved anyone before and she doesn't know what is supposed to happen, but she is pretty sure something is wrong with her.

Ella could be suffering from vaginismus, a problem thought to be psychological in origin but physical in manifestation. Vaginismus is an involuntary spasm of the muscles around the entrance to the vagina. The spasm can be so strong that it is impossible to enter the vagina with a finger, never mind a penis of any size. This is not just an orgasmic problem, of course. Ella would be unable to get pregnant or to experience intercourse.

Vaginismus may be a reaction to a bad experience such as a rough gynecological exam, a rape, or an abortion. It can also be related to a fear of penetration or an imagined rape. Whatever the cause, it becomes beyond the woman's control and the vagina shuts up without

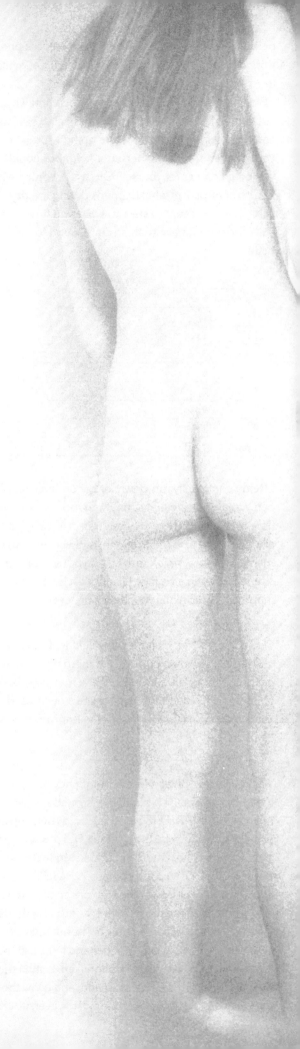

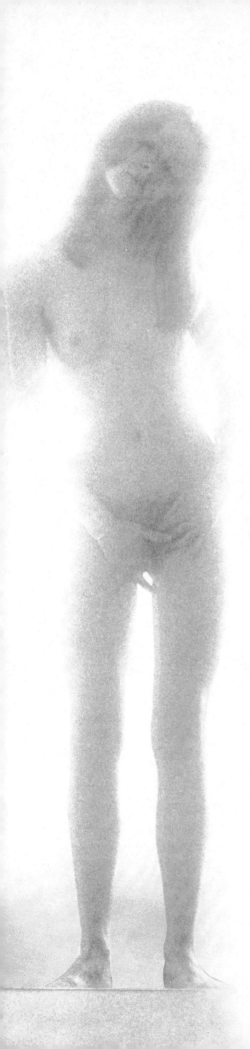

her being able consciously to prevent it. A doctor will not be able to examine her properly—the patient with vaginismus tends to move quickly to the far end of the examining table. She will not be able to insert a finger, diaphragm, penis, or Tampax into her vagina.

It is possible to think you have vaginismus when actually the problem is inadequate arousal. If you have vaginismus, your main sensations will be that your partner cannot enter you, that there is a barrier to entrance, that you cannot put anything into your vagina. A trained medical person will be able to recognize the symptom and label it; but since you can't always count on finding such a person, read through this chapter to eliminate other possible problems before treating yourself for vaginismus.

Once you are fairly sure that it is vaginismus, you can start the cure. The object of this regimen is for you to become comfortable holding something in your vagina. The most obvious and least threatening thing is your own finger.

Step one   Put the tip of your index or middle finger into your vagina. You can do this in bed or in the bathroom—some place where you can be alone. Time yourself. Hold your finger just inside for two minutes. Don't move it around, just hold it there. Then take it out. Try to do this five or six times.

Step two   Now try to move more of your finger into your vagina, all of it if possible. Hold for three minutes. You may feel some spasmodic movement of the vaginal muscles, but don't retreat. Do this five or six times.

Step three   Now try to insert two fingers into the vagina and hold them there for three minutes or longer. The object of this exercise is for you to be able to tolerate having something in your vagina for longer and longer periods of time. Back up if you feel it's not working.

Step four   Now try to substitute a Tampax for your fingers. Tampax come in sterile cylinders and that is what you use, rather than the Tampax itself. Just push the Tampax out of the container. Then put the container inside your vagina so that the muscles hold it just near the entrance. Don't move it up into the roomier part of the vagina. Leave it there for five minutes or so and then remove it. Do this five or six times.

Step five   If you feel ready to bring your partner into this, now is the time. Show your partner how to put his finger into your vagina by demonstrating how you do it. It is natural to feel a little shy about this and it may be easier to handle if you talk about the whole regimen and the problem before you start. Have him read over this section if you like.

Once you are comfortable showing your partner what to do, he can try it. Just have him hold one finger inside your vagina for a couple of minutes to start. Then you can increase the time and double the number of fingers. You might enjoy doing this together so that he uses one finger and you use one. He can then follow your lead in moving slowly around the inside of the vagina. In any case, try to practice this so that you can do it together for up to fifteen minutes with two fingers.

Step six Now you can try inserting his penis slowly and carefully after a little finger warm-up. You should be on top of him so that you can move on and off his penis to suit yourself. His penis should not be far in your vagina to start and he should not move or thrust. Under your direction, he can move farther inside and around your vagina when you are ready.

Step seven Do the above assignment but now add more movement. You should move first and then let him move a little. You can follow his movement and he yours so that you are trading back and forth, getting used to the differences in your moves. He can start doing more thrusting, but if it seems uncomfortable or scary to you, go back to no motion.

If he comes to orgasm during any of this, don't be surprised or annoyed. It is hard to slow down and take things step by step if you are not used to it. Also, his penis is more sensitive than your vagina, so this exercise will be hard on him too. If his orgasm is accompanied by hard thrusting and you feel you aren't ready for that, it may be better for him to come outside your vagina, with your help if he wants. Tell him to tell you if he feels he can't hold off any longer.

Future steps Using this basic schedule for treating vaginismus, you should be capable of intercourse in anywhere from a few days to a few weeks. You can take one step a day, every two days, or whatever seems right for you. You may find that the vaginismus never disappears completely and that you need to practice the stretching and holding exercises from time to time to keep yourself in shape.

Grace's partner always wants to try a new position of some sort, but Grace would rather not. She is responsive and orgasmic when he is on top and other positions are not very satisfying to her. Some of them are actually painful.

Grace may be built in such a way that she receives the most stimulation and pressure from the standard missionary position. In other positions her partner's penis may push painfully into her cervix or bladder. This isn't unusual and it isn't abnormal to not enjoy all possible variations. There is no reason to think that there is anything wrong with you if you aren't infinitely acrobatic. You can try various things, but if they hurt, don't do them.

Very rarely a woman may have anatomical abnormalities that make orgasm or sex difficult. Some people are born with missing or double vaginas or uteruses, clitoral adhesions, unperforated hymens, or some other irregularity of the genital tract. This is usually discovered at the time of menstruation or at the first gynecological examination, and surgery may be required.

Probably a more serious issue than the physical irregularity is the way in which it is discovered and regarded. A woman could be made to feel inadequate or inferior if her abnormality is not treated with thoughtfulness and care. If you, or a friend or relative, is the victim of unsympathetic treatment for such a medical problem, you may wish to consult several doctors.

Because clearing up a physical problem will not necessarily make you orgasmic, it may be helpful to go over the suggestions in the earlier part of this chapter on how to increase the likelihood of orgasm. If nothing happens, you should consider the possibility that you have a psychological block of some kind.

PSYCHOLOGICAL TROUBLES

Although there are no sure ways to handle psychological problems, sometimes acknowledging that they exist frees you enough to act in your own behalf in spite of them. It is true that whopping insights alone can't change behavior, but they can change attitudes which stand in the way of behavioral changes.

Abigail had a very strict upbringing. In her family, sex was not mentioned at all. Abigail not only isn't orgasmic, she has no idea what men and women do to get babies, and she's confused about the feelings she has for her boyfriend.

Sarah's father had a very special formula for sex education. His method was to demonstrate on her what she shouldn't let other men do to her. Although Sarah is now involved with a very considerate man, she is totally nonorgasmic with him.

Henrietta had a very stormy three-year affair with a female teacher during her teens. She felt she'd been seduced but she knew she was not opposed to it. She's had no lesbian liaisons since and is nonorgasmic with men.

All of these women are haunted in some way by their pasts. Feelings of guilt about sex and fear of punishment for it are not uncommon among nonorgasmic women. Women from strict, religious homes where sex was not discussed or even acknowledged are more likely than any other group of women to be nonorgasmic. Someone like Abigail has a hard time feeling right about the drives and desires she experiences toward men. As a result, an inhibitory factor takes over and she has a hard time even thinking about sex, let alone responding to the advances of a partner.

If Abigail were in therapy, the therapist would try to reassure her that the feelings she has are normal and that her parents' attitudes are the unhealthy ones. As your own therapist, whether your case fits with Abigail's or not, you sometimes have to reassure yourself that it is okay to feel what you feel and that you are not odd or strange for wanting sex.

If you were the victim of a similar kind of upbringing, use the space below to convince yourself that it is all right to be sexual. You might do this in the form of a dialogue with a parent or another authority figure who made you feel base for feeling at all. If you didn't share this experience, you can still write up a dialogue. Sometimes putting yourself in the shoes of another person makes you more tolerant and understanding of their problems. This is especially valuable if you are the partner of an Abigail.

Sarah had a more direct and difficult situation to contend with. Incest or even suggested or imagined incest is a very complicated issue. Psychoanalytic theory traces all sexual problems to old oedipal conflicts that remain unresolved. That means that before you were five you became aware of your own and your parents' sexuality. It was at this age that you decided you wanted to replace your mother and have your father all to yourself. You felt guilty about it and also afraid that your mother would punish you if she found out. If anything real happened, you assumed that it was the punishment you deserved. Even if you enjoyed it, you felt guilty. And you might still.

Sarah may feel that she deserved that kind of sex education based on submerged feelings she had had for her father long before. Whatever the unconscious motivations of either party, Sarah has to convince herself now that the feelings she had were not unusual. Everyone learns about love and relationships from their relationships with those they are closest to. If you didn't like what you learned, then you must try relearning.

For Sarah, and for anyone who had a bad past experience, it is important to purge yourself of that memory in order to start over. Of course ridding yourself of guilt and fear is easier said than done, but it might help you to write a letter here to the person who got in your way. Tell them what you think they did to you and why. Explain your own part in it and describe how you are going to regard it from here on out.

Dear _____

_____

_____

_____

_____

_____

_____

_____

Love,

_____

Someone like Sarah may also need to tell her partner about what happened to her growing up—not in order to get him to feel sorry for her or to excuse her, but to get him to help her help herself. This partner may remind Sarah of her father. She's both attracted and repulsed as a result. She needs to recognize that she could be attracted to the good in her father and not the bad. And she needs to realize that this partner is not her father. She could write him a letter telling him how he isn't.

Henrietta may not really want to be heterosexual. Perhaps that is the reason she can't feel satisfied sexually with a man. She may not be facing up to feelings of disgust or repulsion for men's bodies, for semen, for not being with a woman. This can also happen to the woman who tries to become gay for political, social, personal reasons. Sometimes it just isn't natural for you to be where you've put yourself.

To evaluate your sexual orientation, try reviewing what you like about each sex. Don't think about specific persons until you have regarded each sex as generally representative of maleness and femaleness in your eyes.

What I like about men is _____

_____

_____

What I like about women is _____

_____

_____

_____

And the negative.

What I dislike about men is _____

_____

_____

What I dislike about women is _____

_____

_____

_____

Kinsey showed years ago that very few people are strictly heterosexual or strictly homosexual; and even earlier, Freud wrote about the basic bisexuality in human nature. Henrietta, or you, could prefer women to men or vice versa and still be somewhat aroused by and sensitive to the other sex. If you think that your affinity for women, or a past affair with a woman, causes you pain and guilt in your relationship with a man, you might feel better if you talked about it rather than letting it fester.

Past experiences often don't stand in the way of anything. Many women have strict upbringings, come from obsessively religious homes, have difficult or confusing experiences growing up, and yet have no sexual problems as adults. No one knows why some people are more affected by what happens to them than others. They don't appear to be more sensitive, less intelligent, better or worse people. It's just one of the great imponderables.

That's why you should try to put past experiences behind you. Acknowledge them, give them their due, and stop reliving them. Try new things to strengthen and develop your sex life now. Then, to increase your sexual responsiveness, you can try the practical therapy for orgasm at the beginning of this chapter.

_____

Eve has never been orgasmic with her husband. She isn't particularly upset by it. She sort of figures that that's woman's lot. She occasionally masturbates to orgasm, which she enjoys, but mainly she just thinks that men need sex more than women.

_____

Eve may be missing out because of her conception of the female role. This might be said to be more of a social problem than a psychological one, but since most people are subject to having social mores become part of them, it will be discussed here.

What can you do if you feel that as a woman you should be grateful for a man's attention, a willing partner at his whim, a passive but cheerful receptacle, the all-around second vessel? Oh, you may not feel it all that lucidly or strongly, but many women have serious doubts about asserting themselves sexually for fear of appearing less feminine.

Unfortunately, perhaps, being passive and cheerful does not necessarily guarantee orgasms and sexual self-confidence. The trouble with being subject to another's desires is that they may very well differ from yours, making arousal difficult and resentment rampant. A woman who is harboring mixed feelings about always doing it when he wants it may actually be withholding orgasm unconsciously from her partner. If she sees orgasm as a kind of commitment or involvement, she may not want to be involved with someone who pays little attention to her.

The withholding of orgasm, which is not necessarily a conscious process at all, can spring from many different sources. Anger toward a partner, loss of trust or confidence, and depression can all be taken out on a partner. There are several questions to answer if you think something in you or in the relationship is responsible for your lack of orgasms.

Are you orgasmic alone? _____

Can you become aroused and interested in sex when you are with someone else? _____

Do you like this person? _____

Do you like someone else better? _____

Are you afraid of anything, such as pain, pregnancy, commitment?

_____

Would you prefer to have sex with this person under different circumstances? _____

Do you feel reluctant to ask this person for what you need? _____

Some women have trouble asking for what they need because they feel it isn't ladylike. They don't like to ask a partner to "toil" over them, even though the man may not feel that way about it. If he does, maybe there are other things he could do. It is hard for a man to maintain an erection in perpetuity, especially if nothing else is happening. You owe it to him and to yourself to communicate, verbally or non-verbally, what you want.

But consider some of the other possibilities. If you are having an extramarital affair with this man during your lunch hour, maybe you don't have time to set things straight. Even if you have time, you could feel guilty. Perhaps this person is second-best and first-best is gone. Maybe he's had a setback of some sort recently and his loss of status or dependence on you disappoints you.

Once you see that there is an anger, fear, or another barrier to your responsiveness, don't let it go at that. Knowledge is helpful, but it will be more useful if you act on what you learned. This may mean getting out of the relationship. If the feminine mystique is in your way, you might try initiating sex when you want it or showing your partner what excites you sexually. Whatever your interpretation, action is probably worth trying.

Cassandra is scared to death she will fail to have an orgasm. Then she does fail. She's tried counting backward from a thousand and self-hypnosis, but nothing works for her. She fails anyway.

The trouble with distracting yourself in order to prevent failure is that you know you are doing it so you fail at doing that too. It becomes a vicious circle, impossible to break. You're trying all the time to pretend that you don't know why you are distracting yourself. In short, you're thinking too much.

The only way to break such a cycle is to concentrate solely on what is happening to your body as it happens. Distracting inventions do work for some people sometimes. Right now, for you, they take too much energy. You need to use your brain not to harbor racing thoughts but to register sense impressions. Don't think about what happened last time or what is going to happen this time. Restrict yourself to what is happening now.

You get no space here to write down your explanations for your behavior. You aren't to think about it at all. You are to sit (or lie) down by yourself and practice arousing yourself and concentrating on each change your body goes through. You can start with a self-exam, masturbation, general arousal. And start alone. You don't need the distraction and possible self-consciousness caused by another's presence. Once you have more control, you can practice with a partner.

Narcissa has never had an orgasm and she isn't really sure that she wants to have one. She's afraid she'll look foolish.

It is possible for self-consciousness to be a problem for she who fears success as well as she who fears failure. Most people find that how they look during sex doesn't really matter, but some people can't get it out of their heads. They are watching themselves all the time just to see how really ridiculous they look.

It's true that sex can be seen as awkward or undignified. So can eating, laughing, all kinds of human activities if you choose to look at them that way. The trouble for most self-peepers is that they are not involved in what they are doing. Narcissa can use her fear of her appearance to distance herself from anything close to involvement. When you have this fear, orgasm seems like a loss of control.

In order to bring all these fears to the fore, an exercise in acting out your fear is suggested below. This is basically an orgasm role play, and you should bring to the exercise all your worst expectations. Physical contortions as well as mental distortions should be played out to the hilt. Exaggerate your expectations of doom.

Step one Start out in front of a mirror, clothed or not, as you wish. Make sure you are alone and that you can see most of yourself easily.

Step two Stretch and flex your muscles. Extend your arms, legs, neck, and screw up your face. Try to tense and then relax each set of muscles throughout your body.

Step three Now imagine that you are "overtaken" by a thundering orgasm in which your muscles twitch, your limbs are spastic, you moan and shout.

Step four Lie there a minute and reflect on how like or unlike an orgasm you think that was. Think about how it changed you or destroyed you.

Step five Now, try it again. Remember that orgasms can vary in intensity. You might try just a mild shudder or a long slow series of hiccups. Try to act out every description you've ever heard or imagined.

The object of exaggerating your reaction is to see what really does happen to you when you tense all your muscles and then let go. You will survive. Sometimes meeting fear head-on is the best way to deal with it. If you play out all your silly expectations, the real thing can't surprise you.

If you feel inhibited not only by you watching you, but also by your partner watching you, you could do this together. Some partners only seem to get excited when they see that you are. When you realize that they are watching you, you lose all enthusiasm and become self-conscious again. Perhaps talking to them about how you feel and then doing the orgasm role play together would reduce this anxiety somewhat. Better yet, you can try exchanging roles.

CONCLUSION

It may be difficult to decide exactly what your problem is, given all the possibilities and the fact that most people are composites of the examples here. If you cannot figure out who you are, rely on the practical solutions suggested in the beginning of this chapter to bring you around. With patience and practice, they will work for you. It is difficult to make these changes and you cannot expect immediate success. Give yourself plenty of time. If nothing seems to be working, forget the whole bit for a while and return to this chapter later. Be sure to use your journal to record your difficulties as well as your successes. Journal therapy works.

Also, your partner is very important in your process of change. Talk to him about what you feel you need and how he can help. Sometimes, regrettably, the partner has an investment in your not changing. If you become orgasmic suddenly, you may threaten him and find that your relationship changes. This doesn't happen very often, but you should be aware that a partner may feel left out, inadequate, or insecure if you change unexpectedly. Be wary and considerate, and let him, or her, share your success.

Impotent Men

INTRODUCTION

Impotence is probably even more devastating to a man's self-esteem than being nonorgasmic is to a woman's. Men's ideas of manhood and masculinity often depend on a very delicate mechanism called "getting it up." To be impotent isn't just a blow to your sex life. It's a blow to your confidence and competence in all areas of life.

Moreover, even one experience of impotence can be the beginning of the end if you can't accept not having an erection every once in a while as perfectly normal. At any one time probably half the adult men in this society are experiencing or have experienced impotence to some degree.

To what degree is a critical question. Generally impotence means not having an erection. But that includes such variations as not having a firm enough erection for intercourse or masturbation, not having an erection with a partner, or not ejaculating. Impotence may be due to physical problems, but it is more likely to be caused by anxiety. This is especially true when one instance of impotence leads to more and more experiences of failure. The expectation of failure is itself a very common source of failure.

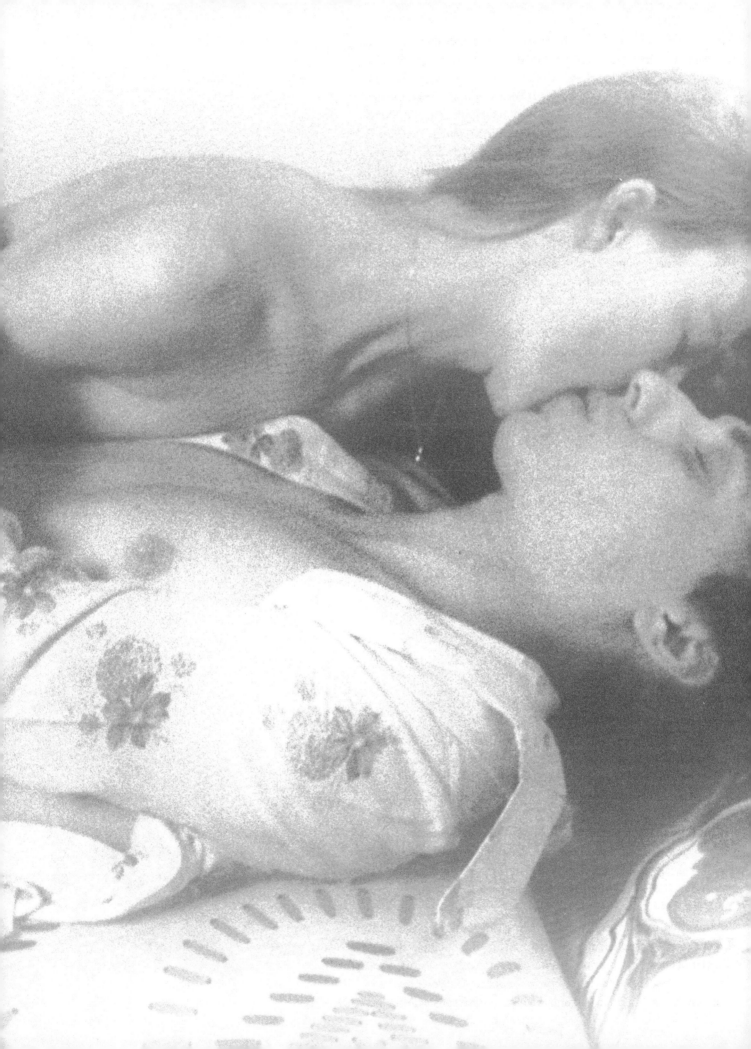

Anxiety also comes from the performance demands that you put on yourself. No matter how unreal or unnecessary priapic expectations really are, many men feel they ought to be able to perform under all conditions. It's been popular lately to blame women for men's impotence—the cherchez la femme explanation for male sexual dysfunction. It is true that demands from partners can absolutely ruin you. But the demands you put on yourself are likely to get you first. If you are worried about what a partner thinks of you or whether you can still please her or him, you may find yourself wildly exaggerating your expectations in new or insecure situations.

In this chapter we'll start with practical ways you can begin treating your impotence, no matter what its source or duration. Later, we'll look at some of the psychological or physical blocks to potency which you can examine at the same time that you are taking some active, practical steps to get beyond your difficulties.

SOME PRACTICAL SUGGESTIONS FOR THE IMPOTENT MAN

Acknowledging to yourself that you are impotent is a very important part of this self-therapy. The popular wisdom is that you are impotent because you think too much about it. It becomes a self-fulfilling prophecy. The trouble with trying to put it out of your mind is that it's always there anyway, hovering on the edge of your consciousness.

If you have ever had an experience of impotence, or if you are having one now, write out a description of it here. Start with when it first happened, when it happens now, and include with whom it happens and at what point in sex play or arousal. That is, do you get an erection that disappears at some point, or do you just not get one at all? Do you get an erection alone but not with a partner? Write down everything about your problem that you think is important.

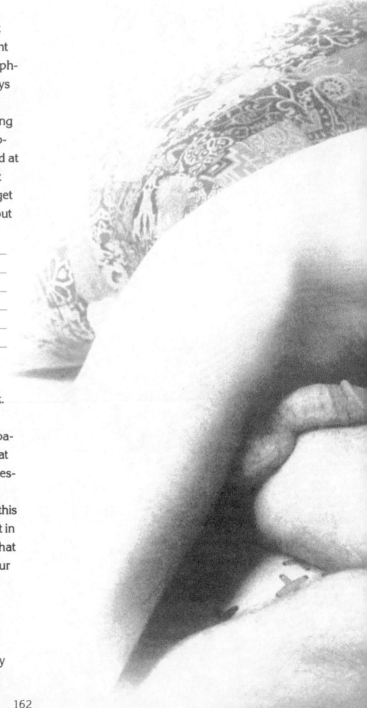

_____

_____

_____

_____

_____

_____

Is there anyone you would show this description to? Some of you wouldn't show it to anyone. Some would like to rip it out of the book. Others would only show it to someone they consider "qualified" to handle such a business, like a psychiatrist or a urologist. Some probably didn't write anything down. These actions indicate the feeling that you are not qualified to help yourself, which, as you'll see, is not necessarily true.

The only outside source who could be genuinely helpful to you at this point is your partner, if you have one. She or he can play a large part in helping you help yourself. But you have to impress upon a partner that you indeed have a problem, that it requires self-centeredness on your part, and self-sacrifice on theirs.

Although most partners are more than willing to help, you should know that many could feel used since you are demanding a service which puts them in a compromising situation. You must stress the seriousness of your impotence and how appreciative you'll be if they will turn their attention to you and put off their own satisfaction for a

time. The end results should be more satisfying to you both anyway. You might even offer to do something sexual or nonsexual in return.

A partner may think that you are using impotence as a way to seduce them or to make them feel sorry for you. Unfortunately for the truly impotent man, these are not uncommon ploys. A partner who has been used in this way (especially by you) in the past is naturally going to be suspicious of a self-confessed impotent man. The best way to counter this is to anticipate it and address it right off.

Some partners may feel inadequate and insecure themselves about your impotence. They think it may be their fault you are impotent with them. If they were sexier, more experienced, more loving, and so on, you wouldn't be impotent. To approach them with a request for help may make them feel even more as if they are doing something wrong.

You have to point out that it is your problem and you who needs the help. Both men and women can often find fault with partners when it comes to sexual difficulties. Annoyingly enough, however, affixing blame does absolutely nothing to alleviate problems. It's wiser for each partner to take on the responsibility for change and to forget about blame.

Very few men are absolutely impotent. Even if you can't get erections when you want to, you may get them spontaneously. You may have one when you wake up, while watching or reading something, after physical exertion of some kind. Use the space below to note down when, where, and with whom you do have erections.

_____

_____

_____

The occurrence of these spontaneous erections shows that the erectile reflex is not impaired. If you have never had, or no longer have, erections of any kind, you may wish to read over the psychological and physical sections of this chapter before you start on these practical suggestions. It's possible that your problem is not just a matter of re-learning.

The suggestions which follow are for a daily regimen. Don't skip ahead if the beginning steps seem too slow. Rushing to perform may be part of your problem. Take it all at a gradual, relaxed pace, setting up a regular time for yourself to practice. Set the period for practice, too —maybe fifteen minutes at a time. Stop at the end of the allotted time, no matter what is happening. Just because you feel aroused at the end of your session doesn't mean you won't feel aroused again tomorrow.

Suggestion one You're going to take away that pressure to perform by concentrating for a few days on what pleases and arouses you sexually, short of erection or ejaculation. You can begin by being comfortable and relaxed, playing some music, taking a shower, setting up some private time and space for yourself.

Suggestion two Today you can start on the things that do arouse you. Maybe you'd like your partner to do something for you. She could give you a pedicure or pose for you. Perhaps you'd prefer to be alone, nude, reading something erotic or fantasizing away. Enact these and other suggestions with your partner's help (if you have a partner and wish for her or his help).

Suggestion three Now you can examine your body in the nude, if you haven't already. Pay special attention to your limp penis. If it isn't limp now, wait until it is. Part of your problem may be that you aren't really comfortable with or proud of your penis except when it's erect. You need to look at it and let someone else look at it flaccid. Maybe you haven't been with your partner enough in a nongenital but still sexual climate. You may be projecting your own doubts about your penis onto your partner. Women don't find limp penises shocking or undesirable. If you don't have a partner to be limp with, imagine such a situation and test your feelings about it.

Suggestion four The next step is trying to arouse yourself a little by touching, or having your partner touch, your genitals. The goal here is not coitus or ejaculation, so if you do feel a little swelling or heaviness or even erection of your penis, just let it subside. Continue the touching and sex play. If your penis stirs again, take a look at it and let the feeling ebb away. Describe aloud to yourself or to a partner what this heaviness or erection looks and feels like.

Suggestion four and a half If you never get an erection during this exercise, continue anyway. It takes time and patience to feel comfortable, especially if someone else is with you. If you feel that your partner is making you self-conscious, ask her or him to go into another room for a while while you play alone. You can, of course, be self-conscious without a partner just because you are watching yourself so intently and expectantly. If you feel this is a problem, why don't you give yourself a thorough self-examination and watch yourself in a mirror until you've seen all there is to see?

Suggestion four and three-quarters Another way to handle self-consciousness is to concentrate on your partner for a while. If you don't have a partner, you can fantasize what you might do that would excite you if someone were there. Touch her or him where you want to (not where they want you to or where you think they want you to). Kiss where you want to kiss. Try arousing her or him in a way that arouses you. You may find that you can arouse and please someone without using your penis at all.

Suggestion five If you do get an erection several times and let it go away, you can ejaculate if you wish. But not inside your partner. The important thing now is sex—arousal, erection, even ejaculation—without intercourse.

Suggestion six If you have an erection and a partner and you feel fairly comfortable with both, you can try putting your penis just inside the vagina or mouth. Ask your partner to guide your penis in. This may be easiest if she or he is on top. (See photograph.) If not, try being on top yourself. Don't thrust, move, or rush. Just stay there calmly and then pull out. You may lose your erection right away or ejaculate right away but don't worry about that. Return to noncoital-arousing activities or just spend some time together talking.

Suggestion seven After several experiences of resting in the vagina or mouth, you can ask your partner to move around a little, according to your directions. Then ask her or him to stop while you move. Trade off like this until you are both comfortable and you are able to maintain your erection or semi-erection for several minutes. You can ejaculate then if you wish.

Suggestion seven and a half If you find that you cannot ejaculate once inside the vagina or mouth, pull out and practice more arousal activities, or come outside. Gradually move closer to the vagina or mouth or anus over your next few sessions until you can come just inside and then all inside.

Suggestion seven and three-quarters If you find that you are losing your erection just before or just inside your partner, there are a couple of things to try. First of all, your partner can gently push your limp or semi-erect penis inside and just hold it there. If she is not aroused, she may want to use some saliva or a lubricant to make this easier. Then she or he can try some tentative movements under your direction. If you do not become erect, pull out and try other activities for a while. Then try again. This exercise will teach you to tolerate the vagina or mouth and reduce your sensitivity to it. Next, your partner can give you extra stimulation while you are inside. She or he can reach around to tickle your balls, perineum, anus, and to hold onto the base of your penis if you like that.

Suggestion eight As you can see, this is a regimen designed gradually to increase your acceptance of your situation, your appreciation of your own responses, and your tolerance for a partner. You are the best person to set the limits and the pace. You must never forget that this is all for you, not for your partner. If you ever feel discouraged, stop everything and come back to it later. Short sessions are always better than long ones anyway.

If you don't have a regular partner and find that your problem only exists when you are with someone, you can use many of these suggestions even if the other person doesn't know the therapy. For instance, you can certainly admit to your impotence, reveal it, and concentrate on what pleases you about this partner. It may please her or him, too. You'll find that your hand and your mouth, which are much more under your control than your penis, can be more than satisfying to her while taking the pressure off you.

It is important when working on a problem like this that you keep at it. These suggestions are a place to start, but they offer no instant potency. Give yourself plenty of time and lots of encouragement.

It's always possible with things sexual that there are other issues to be dealt with while you are relearning how to be responsive. Read over the next two sections to be sure there isn't more for you to be alert to. Sometimes working on arousal in the ways suggested is enough no matter what other issues are involved. And clearing up those other issues doesn't necessarily make you responsive. But you can work on both at the same time.

PSYCHOLOGICAL ISSUES

Men seem to have just as many—if not more—psychosexual problems as women. Many of them are very similar to women's, especially in terms of upbringing and past experiences. The two most typical situations which lead to impotence, however, are unique to men and are combinations of symptoms which all come together at once.

Rory got drunk one night and couldn't get an erection. It was the first time anything like that had happened to him and he was mortified. He worried about being impotent and then found he was.

Alcohol is particularly destructive to the erectile reflex and it is not uncommon for a man to first experience impotence after he has overin-

dulged. If you don't connect the alcohol and the impotence, you might start thinking, as Rory did, that something similar would happen again. The alcohol, plus the fear of failure, plus the continued use of alcohol, combine to make normal sexual functioning unlikely.

This isn't going to happen after one drink, but excessive regular consumption can have such results. Rory probably thinks a little alcohol will relax him. That's where he goes wrong. Other men may go wrong by trying a new partner. If they don't drink, they may be all right but they would attribute their success to the wrong thing. This could lead to breaking up a marriage or relationship and then having the same thing happen all over again.

Obviously, the best therapy for this syndrome is to cut out the alcohol and then start using the suggestions given earlier to regain confidence and sensitivity. If you find that it is difficult to stop drinking, there may be another problem as well. Men who know that alcohol is dangerous to their sexual health but drink anyway may be trying to fail.

Harry had always had a problem of coming too fast. Part of the reason he married Shari was because she didn't seem to notice. Lately they've had a couple of big fights in which Shari brought up Harry's lack of staying power. Although they still have sex regularly, Harry has been impotent on several occasions.

According to Masters and Johnson, it is not uncommon for men with a history of coming too fast to become impotent. This does not mean that men who come too fast are destined to become impotent. It just means that sometimes, in some people, years of being unable to control ejaculation builds up to a total lack of response.

It sounds as if several things are going on with Harry and Shari, however. For one thing, Shari may have always resented Harry for being so fast. Even though he thought she didn't mind, she may have. He could have been unconsciously aware and afraid of this. Although he managed on a conscious level to believe that everything was all right, he could actually be feeling inadequate.

Shari might actually enjoy sex with Harry and be mad at him about something else. His premature ejaculation may not really upset her, but she knows it is his weak spot and when she's upset she uses what she has. Or, she could have always wished that they could have better coital sex but been afraid to talk to him about it because he might leave her, he might be hurt, and she might ruin what they do have.

It sounds as if this couple really hasn't talked much to each other. There is no doubt that it is hard to talk about sex, but it can be the most important thing to talk about. Very often one partner hesitates to bring the subject up for fear of hurting or alienating the other. Usually this means that that person is afraid of being hurt or alienated. Examine feelings of reluctance about approaching a problem with a partner. It may be your own feelings you are afraid of.

Harry and Shari do need to talk about the course of their sexual experience together. They need to think about what each brought to the relationship and then how they each changed and developed in that relationship, particularly in terms of their sexual needs. If you share this kind of history of false starts and noncommunication, you might try writing an analysis below of what you think happened from your point of view and then from your partner's point of view. When and if you feel like it, you can ask your partner to do the same. Even if you don't compare notes right away, this exercise will start you both thinking about how to right what went wrong.

For me, sex was always _____

_____

_____

_____

During my relationship with _____, sex became _____

_____

_____

For _____, sex was _____

_____

_____

During _____'s relationship with me, sex became _____

_____

_____

Histories of sexual problems go back farther than just the present relationship. In the following examples, all these men had something happen to them as youngsters or adolescents which may be related, in part, to their current impotence.

Tom's brother took him to a prostitute when he was fifteen. Tom was the last in line, after his brother and a couple of cronies. By the time his turn came, Tom's erection was gone. He has had trouble getting an erection with a partner ever since.

Many men report a bad first experience as the beginning of their feelings of sexual inadequacy. In fact, it's almost a cliché to have run into an impatient prostitute. Other clichés are the very demanding first partner and the partner who is afraid of you, of pregnancy, or of commitment. Unsettling experiences like these sometimes combine with fears of failure or inadequacy to make each subsequent encounter a test.

What men tend to forget when these obsessive fears take over is that women are insecure too. They are probably wondering if you think they are all right. The size of your penis is of much more concern to you than to them. They're thinking about the size of their vagina or breasts or whether they should have brushed their teeth. No matter when this all started for you, it's not unique to you or to your sex.

Just to see how foolish you've been, try making a list here of all the things a partner might feel in a sexual situation with you. What does she think you are thinking of her? What might turn you off or on about her, or him? What might this person's fears about him- or herself be?

_____   _____

_____   _____

_____   _____

_____   _____

Carry some thoughts about the other person into sexual situations and concentrate on reassuring them. You may lose some of your own fear by realizing you aren't alone in feeling unsure.

Tim had a very loving mother, very loving. His father was killed when he was four and his mother and he slept in the same bed until he was fifteen. Although nothing untoward ever happened, his mother was always kissing and fondling him. He's now engaged to a lovely woman with whom he's never been able to keep an erection. She assures him it will be okay once they are married.

It's natural for a child to feel responsible for anything that happens. So when his father died, Tim may have felt that it was his fault. Since that is the age children start making an identification with their parent of the same sex, as well as the time they become aware of the sexuality of themselves and their parents, the loss of a parent then may have sexual repercussions. The end of a relationship with either parent can make it harder to develop other relationships later on.

It seems possible that Tim's mother may have made him into a substitute for her husband in some way. The displays of affection may have been symbols of her need to possess him. She may not have had any incestuous designs on him at all, but he isn't so sure. He decides at some point that the only way to escape her power over him is to make sure that she can't have his penis. Unfortunately, no one else can have it either.

Even if you completely discount oedipal conflicts and the importance of parental relationships as models for later on, you can see that Tim's anxiety about his past is in his way. If you grew up in a family where there was strife of some kind, you may feel that you are still trying to settle the conflicts that that engendered. Instead of rueing your past, why don't you meet it head-on? Tell your mother or father or sister what you think they could have done to make your life easier. Write them a letter, which you'll never show them, but which gives you a chance to vent a little spleen.

Dear _____,
  Why the hell did you _____
_____
_____
_____?
  What I really needed was _____
_____
_____
_____

          Love (?),

                    _____

Now, of course, this little exercise isn't going to wash all your anger and distress away. But recognizing and owning up to your feelings can be the beginning of being able to give them up. Your partner, who, after all, is not your mother, can help you. Direct your attention toward the current relationship and go through the suggestions given in the beginning of this chapter together. It's a good place to start over.

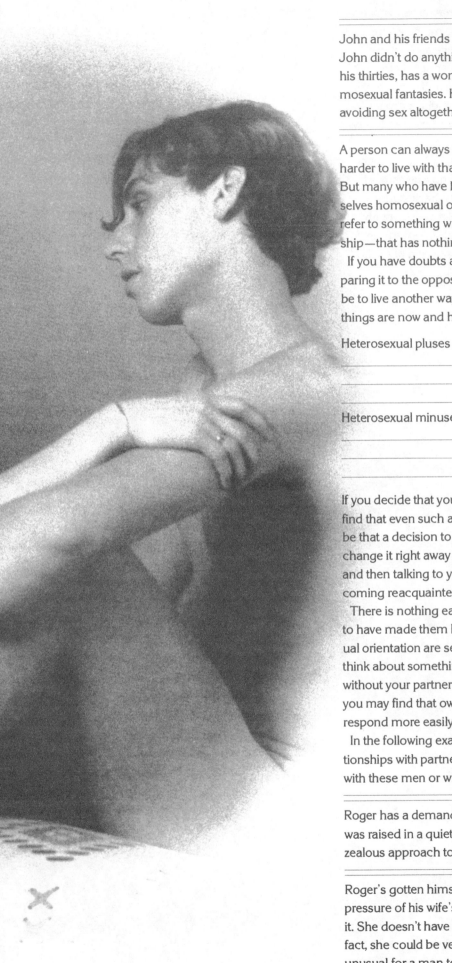

John and his friends used to do a lot of messing around in junior high. John didn't do anything, but he did let himself be done to. Now he's in his thirties, has a wonderful family, and is constantly entertaining homosexual fantasies. He's been impotent with his wife and has taken to avoiding sex altogether.

A person can always make a choice of sexual orientation that he finds harder to live with than he expected. John may really wish to be gay. But many who have homosexual experiences in youth imagine themselves homosexual out of guilt. The need to use this guilt may really refer to something wrong in the present—in a job, a marriage, a friendship—that has nothing to do with sexual preference.

If you have doubts about your present sexual commitment, try comparing it to the opposite commitment. You can consider how it would be to live another way. You can make a comparison here between how things are now and how they might be if you pursued your fantasies.

Heterosexual pluses	Homosexual pluses
_____	_____
_____	_____
_____	_____
Heterosexual minuses	**Homosexual minuses**
_____	_____
_____	_____
_____	_____

If you decide that you want to continue being straight (or gay), you may find that even such a decision doesn't change your impotence. It might be that a decision to get out of your present relationship wouldn't change it right away either. But talking to yourself about your feelings, and then talking to your partner if you can, may make it easier to try becoming reacquainted with your own sexual responses.

There is nothing easy about decisions like these and you can't expect to have made them by the time you finish this page. Questions of sexual orientation are serious and long-ranging. Give yourself a break and think about something else for a while. Come back to this with and without your partner. You may never know for sure who you are. But you may find that owning up to what you don't know will liberate you to respond more easily sexually.

In the following examples there seems to be something in the relationships with partners that brings out the impotence. See if you identify with these men or with some of their problems.

Roger has a demanding, experienced wife. He, a virgin until he met her, was raised in a quiet, religious home which didn't prepare him for her zealous approach to sex. He is often impotent.

Roger's gotten himself in a difficult situation. He is clearly feeling the pressure of his wife's expectations and doesn't know what to do about it. She doesn't have to be unsympathetic or mean for him to feel bad. In fact, she could be very understanding and he'd still feel awful. It's not unusual for a man to be upset by a "helpful" or overly solicitous partner. Sympathy just makes him feel his inadequacy and failure more.

Roger has to insist that his wife back off a little so that he can concentrate on Roger. If you have a partner like Roger's, you might ask her to read this section. She has to stifle her needs for a while and put her mind and his into arousing and encouraging him in nongenital, nondemand sexual play. He has to regain his confidence and some sense of his own potential alone and then with her. They should approach intercourse very slowly, allowing plenty of time for other sexual activities which give them pleasure.

We also know that Roger had a religious background. That might not mean a thing, depending on the type of religion and how his family interpreted it. Some people from religious or repressive backgrounds consciously or unconsciously see the female genitalia as evil or dirty. If you suspect you have some of these feelings, mutual self-exams are in order. You should look at your partner's genitals closely and often, and have her look at yours.

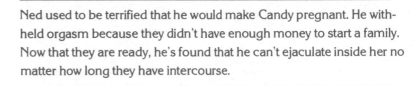

Ned used to be terrified that he would make Candy pregnant. He withheld orgasm because they didn't have enough money to start a family. Now that they are ready, he's found that he can't ejaculate inside her no matter how long they have intercourse.

Ned has evidently made himself impotent from trying to prevent pregnancy. This form of impotence, also called ejaculatory incompetence or retarded ejaculation, is actually quite rare. But it isn't rare for men, as well as women, to be affected in some sexual way by a fear of pregnancy and a lack of confidence in or access to birth control. Men can also have this impotence as the result of a traumatic incident during ejaculation, restrictive religious beliefs, or disliking their partner.

There certainly could be relationship or even oedipal issues here. Ned may not actually feel committed enough to Candy to want to consummate their marriage. He could be afraid Candy will abandon him if he loses control. The fact that he is taking all the responsibility for birth control, or feels that he must, raises some questions. Also, not to ejaculate could be related to castration fears from childhood. The young boy fears that his father will chop off his penis for lusting after his mother. By not ejaculating the boy leaves no evidence that he is aroused by his mother.

Whatever the symbolic or real fears and doubts Ned has, the realistic approach, after you've talked to yourself about it, is to talk to your partner. If you then decide you will work together on your problem, you can start at the beginning of this chapter. One of the most important steps for the man who can't come inside his partner is to come outside her. It is important to have some kind of orgasm with your partner, whether you just show her or she helps you.

Carlos does not really think of himself as being impotent, but every so often with a new partner he finds to his chagrin that he is. Usually he'll have an erection all through the movie and then back at her place his enthusiasm has dwindled away.

Carlos may like the idea of being with certain partners better than he likes the real experience. He could find that, although he likes the woman, he really isn't attracted to her up close. Physical attraction is an important part of arousal and it isn't always there just because you think it should be. Also, Carlos may feel guilty about this relationship. Or, he might think he should be able to perform at all times, even with someone he doesn't know or care about.

A man may be impotent with a new partner simply because he gets overly excited and anxious to please. Both men and women experience great expectations that they can't live up to. Carlos could be afraid of being rejected and just to guarantee that he isn't, he sneaks out. It's possible to fear acceptance too. Maybe the partner will consider this a commitment. Being impotent avoids that.

Impotence can be used to make a partner feel sorry for you or excuse you for not liking them. You might not even be aware that somewhere in the back of your mind you feel a need to protect yourself this way. Impotence of this sort could be a sign of unwillingness to take risks or get involved with other people.

Another problem any man may have with a partner is that she or he has a problem too. A particularly demanding partner may have some need to put you down that has nothing to do with your sexual adequacy. A woman who has vaginismus or an unperforated hymen or who is never aroused could lead to you becoming dysfunctional yourself. A partner who is not receiving enough stimulation during intercourse could drag it out so long that you lose your erection from tedium.

Conrad is getting along in years now and he's not surprised to find that impotence is with him more and more. His doctor told him nothing could be done about it.

It's been pointed out by many professionals that men are unbelievably susceptible to any advice concerning their potency. So if the doctor had told Conrad he was impotent because he masturbated as a little boy or because he hadn't paid his doctor's bills, Conrad might have believed that too. Sometimes men actually give up on becoming potent again just because they receive some misinformation.

The doctor could have been more helpful to Conrad by thoroughly examining him and then explaining to him that although it takes longer to have an erection and to ejaculate when you are older, you are still perfectly capable of enjoying a potent old age. You may not feel the desire for sex as often as you did when younger, but if you have had a regular sex life, you will probably continue to have one.

There is another angle on this, which you may want to consider. Men of all ages who hold back feelings, especially hostile feelings, occasionally have their anger show up sexually. What does Conrad have to be upset about? One possibility is anger about aging. It's not unusual to feel mad at the world because you have to leave it. Other possibilities concern feelings about your spouse, boss, life, and self.

Concerns other than those discussed always have the potential of showing up as sexual difficulties. Use the methods of self-questioning described here to examine yourself. Then talk to your partner if possible and turn together to the practical suggestions for changing yourself no matter how you got that way.

PHYSICAL PROBLEMS

Conrad, above, demonstrated one of the most rampant physical misconceptions men have about potency. Getting older does not mean that you are not able to enjoy sex. It does mean that some parts of your sex life will be different and, of course, if you are not in good health at any age, your sex life may be affected.

Although physical problems are not as common for men as for women, they can be very real and should always be treated seriously. Check with a medical school or the medical association in your area for the name of a urologist to treat you. If you don't feel you are getting the care you need, see another one.

Stan has been depressed lately. He's had some reverses in business, his children seem particularly troublesome, and, to make things worse, he's become impotent with his wife and with his mistress both. The pills the doctor gave him do calm him down, but he's still impotent.

The medication that Stan is taking for the depression may be affecting the erectile reflex. Possibly Stan hasn't told the doctor about his impotence. It's often hard to admit that impotence is a problem. In order to be sure that any medication being used isn't inadvertently wrong, Stan should tell the doctor his whole story.

There is some evidence that when people are depressed, the testosterone level in their system dips. Since testosterone is related to male sexuality and to sex drive, it is possible that this would influence potency. Experiments with testosterone supplements aren't really conclusive yet, but there may be an appropriate hormone therapy that would be helpful to Stan.

Sam has had some burning and itching during urination and even ejaculation. He has no discharge but he has never had this trouble before and he has been with the same partner for several months.

Sam could have an infection of the urethra or of the prostate. Even though he's been with the same partner, has the partner been with anyone other than him? Venereal disease is a possibility, but there are also other infections which can be transmitted between partners. Sam should try to describe when the pain occurs, just before or just after ejaculation, and what its history is, so that he can tell the doctor as much as possible. His partner may need treatment too.

Sam could also be allergic to a contraceptive or douche that his partner is using. To test this out, he could use a condom to see if the symptoms are still with him. Also, she could try a different brand to see if he still has the same reaction. It's important to do something because burning and itching aren't normal.

Intercourse has been painful for Les the last few times. He doesn't know why and he can't really even describe the pain.

Pain like this should be pinpointed as much as possible before the trip to the doctor. If you can't tell exactly where it hurts, try to remember when it started and under what circumstances. Perhaps you can say whether or not it hurts inside the abdomen or outside around the genitalia. For instance, if the penis hurts, you may be suffering from a hypersensitivity of the penile glans, a tight foreskin, or poor hygiene. Medications, surgery, or better hygiene might be helpful.

Pain inside the scrotal sac or testes could be from growths or inflammations. This early sign of possible trouble should be treated soon. Pelvic pain could stem from a change in the prostate gland or the bladder, or even from the position of intercourse. Priapism—a sustained erection with no accompanying desire or release—causes similar pain. This is a most unusual and painful condition and one little understood. As with any of these problems, however, consult a physician.

Anatomical irregularities and injuries can affect arousal and sexual functioning. Sometimes surgery to correct these and other conditions causes problems of nerve damage which affect the erectile response or damage to the blood supply of the penis. These are rare occurrences but you should ask the doctor about the risks in any surgery to the pelvic or genital area.

Frank has been impotent with great regularity in the past few weeks. He can't understand it. Everything has been going swimmingly for him lately. He's prosperous, he's just got himself a new wife, he has no problems.

Maybe having no problems is Frank's problem. He could be run-down from trying to stay in the swim. Sometimes people just don't know the effort it takes them to adjust to fresh conditions such as a new marriage, baby, or job. Frank might need to check out all those dull things like rest and diet and exercise to see that he is keeping fit.

If overdoing doesn't seem to fit you and you still have trouble getting an erection, it might be wise to have a complete physical. There are diseases—of the nervous or circulatory systems, the spinal cord, the kidneys or liver—which may show up first as a loss of erectile reflex. It's not worth not checking up on.

These are not the only possible physical problems that could affect sexual response. Certainly trying to make your body do something when you don't really feel like it or are exhausted is likely to lead to failure. The impotent man should check with a urologist to be sure that there are no physical problems. This clears the air to concentrate on addressing possible psychological problems and trying some relearning exercises.

If you are always secretly hoping that your problem is physical, you may not be applying yourself to solving your problems in other ways. Overcoming a physical problem will not necessarily make you potent overnight, especially if you have been impotent for some time. It takes time and perseverance.

CONCLUSION

There is no clear profile of the impotent man and no one answer about what to do for impotency. There is much we don't know about how the mind and the chemistry of the body affect sexual response. But we do know that fear of failure and obsessive self-consciousness are the most common barriers to recovering normal responsiveness. In order to get out of your head and into your body, you have to be an active and interested participant in your own arousal.

Once you decide to try the practical suggestions offered earlier, you have to think mainly about yourself. Your vulnerability for, or fear of, women may defeat you. Most partners are going to be concerned and helpful, but some will try to sabotage a dysfunctional partner, possibly because they like a dysfunctional partner. Unreal as that sounds, you have to realize that your potency could be a genuine threat. Your partner may fear that you'll start running around. She may fear that you'll become dependent on her if she helps you. She may not want to have your child. Don't look for such trouble, but don't be blind to it either. You can help yourself and your partner if you are alert, active, and keep trying.

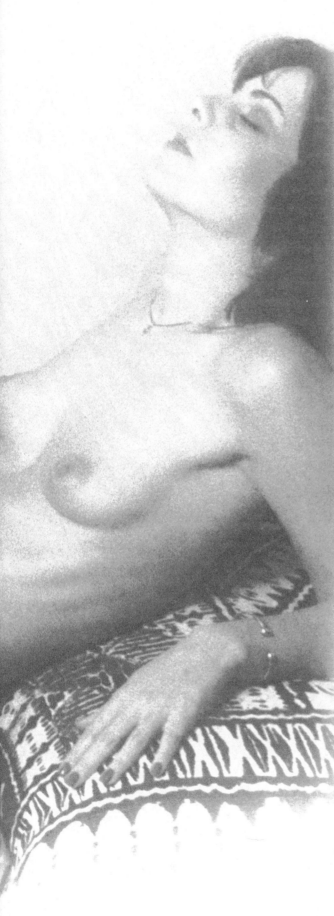

Being Together Without Falling Apart

INTRODUCTION

Everyone in the world has trouble with sex sometimes. Often the problem centers on a little matter called control. There you are with somone you care about and suddenly you seem to be out of control. You expect to be perfectly orgasmic and potent and compatible with every imaginable partner. All you have to do is what comes naturally. But in this real world, there is no such thing as a natural-born lover.

Although you might allow that natural-born athletes and accountants and cooks have to practice, the idea that anyone would have to practice sex is embarrassing. Furthermore, analyzing sex can be repugnant to those who wish to see sex, and love, as mysterious or mystical. Some people mistakenly expect their affection and love for one another to carry them through the bad times. When that doesn't work they start wondering if it is really love at all. They are unwilling to talk for fear of suggesting that they don't love each other, that they are rejecting the other, or that they are themselves inadequate.

This chapter is about substituting confidence and control for mystery and incompetence. Here you will get to know what happens to you when you are with someone else. You will find out what fears, anxieties, old habits, and expectations get in your way when you make love.

BEYOND THE BIG O

We've spent the last three chapters talking about orgasm. Now, in order to put orgasm into proper perspective and to see that there is more to sex than orchestrating orgasm, you are going to do some sensate focus exercises. These are specific activities developed by Masters and Johnson for couples who have forgotten or never learned arousal sensations pleasing to both partners. In the chapter on arousal we touched on the ways you can arouse yourself. Now put that experience to work for you by learning about someone else—what is pleasant or not for her, what is arousing for him.

Just as important as learning what your partner likes is learning what you like about your partner. Take turns exploring and pleasing each other and yourselves in these exercises. Find out where you want to touch your partner, what parts of his or her body particularly fascinate or delight you. When you are being explored, don't try to influence your partner with directions or requests. Wait until they know what they like, then tell or show what you like.

You are not to have intercourse during these exercises. They don't lead to the Big O—they are complete unto themselves. Not having intercourse for two weeks will seem impossible to some of you, a godsend to others. You shouldn't feel that orgasm by some means other than intercourse isn't possible. It's intercourse that's off limits, not orgasm.

These exercises are presented as a programmed schedule covering two weeks. Don't go too fast. Some of you will cover the material more slowly and it can all be extended and integrated into later lovemaking. Learn well for future reference.

First week: Monday Begin by spending about ten minutes at a time lying or sitting next to your partner fully clothed. You are not going to take off your clothes, you're going to use them. One at a time you'll be exploring each other and giving a description of what you find. The one who starts tells what he or she sees, feels, smells, and thinks. The other does not respond in words, but an occasional smile or giggle is okay.

As the explorer start with something small, like a hand. Describe what it looks like, how it feels and smells. You can wax rhapsodic or you can be very clinical.

Is it soft? _____ rough? _____

What is the shape? _____ color? _____

Is it a healthy, cared-for hand? _____

A nervous hand? _____

How does it fit into your hand? _____

Does it smell of soap or grease or onions? _____

Tuesday Today start with an ear. Is it clean, pierced, hairy? Now go on to the hair, the neck, an arm, a leg, a foot. Don't do the whole body in any one session. Spend at least ten minutes at a time but no more than thirty. Space your sessions at least two hours apart, but don't go without a session for more than twenty-four hours.

Wednesday Now pay some attention to your partner's clothes. Don't take them off. Describe how the body feels through the clothes and how the clothes complement the hair or eyes or build. You may want to dress up for this. Some materials are sensuous, some are stiff, some retain the scent of perfume or smoke. Become a detailed reporter using all your senses.

Thursday Now try all that you've learned in the nude. If you feel shy, start in the dark and rely on your senses of touch and smell. Tomorrow you can add a soft light or even a flashlight. When that seems comfortable, graduate to a stronger light and describe what you see. Look for tan marks and musculature. Count ribs and freckles. Is one hip bigger than the other, one breast? Don't examine or touch the nipples or genitals right now. They are off limits until you are familiar with everything else. You can use this space to itemize what you have found.

_____

_____

_____

_____

Friday Extend yesterday's assignment. Maybe some part of you that you never noticed pleases your partner immensely—a soft or hairy place, a mole, an odor. If he or she likes something you really dislike having touched or even noticed, think about why that might be and tell your partner if you can. Be considerate of each other's feelings but try also to share and learn more about each other.

If these sessions aren't pleasant for you or if you can't seem to get around to doing them, ask yourselves what is threatening about such a regimen. If one of you is reluctant, don't automatically assume that one

is at fault. An overly zealous or insistent companion can inhibit his or her partner. Don't pressure each other but try to stretch out to one another. If you are using work, kids, or your busy social life as excuses, be suspicious. You could be resisting getting together. It's all right to be a little timid, frightened, or eager. Keep trying.

Saturday and Sunday Now have a lovely weekend. Expand the time you spend together. Extend your exploration and pleasure until you feel familiar and comfortable with each other's bodies. Start touching your partner's genitals as a natural part of your general exploration. Don't just concentrate on the genitals in any one session. Include them in your quest to find out what pleases this partner and yourself, but do not try intentionally to arouse each other.

You may wish to use some kind of lubrication when touching each other. Oils, creams, certain foods, and saliva or natural lubrication from the vagina for the female genitalia especially may be fun for you. Because it is greaseless and nonirritating a sterile jelly, available in drugstores, is nice for the genitals. Experiment with other things you have around the house.

Some people are reluctant to use creams because they think they're messy. Of course some are messy, especially if too much is used. But occasionally the creams are equated with the "mess" of making love. To some people the perspiration, lubrication, and semen are disgusting. This inability to accept and enjoy reality may be connected to storybook people who don't have problems and don't sweat either.

Second week: Monday Have you two been doing the assignments in the same place at the same time every day? Today try changing the scene a little as you practice including and continuing the genital exploration from the weekend. Try a rug or blanket instead of a sheet, a chair or couch instead of a bed, the kitchen instead of the living room, and so on.

Tuesday Now that you know this body, you can start to have some fun with it. Find out what you can do to make this body happy. Where does it want to be scratched, stroked, massaged, tickled? Give it a bath, a shampoo, a pedicure. Blow on it, sit on it, lick it, curl up next to it. Try using creams and oils or even Béarnaise sauce. Then let this body please your body.

Remember to take your pleasure from the giving as well as the receiving. Describe here what you like to do to your partner and what your partner likes to do to you.

Me giving _____

Partner giving _____

If either you or your partner feels uncomfortable at this or any other point, back up a ways. Some signs of nervousness are excessive ticklishness, giggling, unwillingness to continue, a general tightening throughout the body. If you sense that your partner is uneasy, or if you are yourself, just stop for the day.

Wednesday The instructions stressed that you were not to intentionally arouse your partner. If one of you becomes aroused, let the excitement go away and return again. If the partner inadvertently has an orgasm, that's all right, but don't stop there. Continue the body exploration, learning how his or her body responds to different stimulation after orgasm.

Thursday Concentrate on arousal exercises today with the intention of learning what changes this other body goes through during arousal and orgasm. Some people are very sensitive after orgasm and do not want to have their genitals touched. Others like continued stimulation. Some might like another kind of care, such as being kissed or talked to. Find out as much as you can about this person's arousal and orgasmic patterns and preferences.

Friday, Saturday, and Sunday This is your three-day weekend. Review all that you have learned and try to put it all together over these three

days. Do a clothed exploration, then a nude one, try pleasing and being pleased, arousing and amusing each other. Concentrate your whole body on this assignment.

You can have intercourse now if you want to, but you don't have to. If you find you are just concentrating on orgasm, stop immediately. Return to the less demanding activities. You may find that mutual masturbation or some of the earlier sensate focus exercises would be better now.

Although this program was described as a progression, any of the exercises can be complete in itself. There is no reason why sex can't just mean being together doing something intimate you both enjoy. If intercourse and orgasm are your only goals, you may be missing the other things it takes to build comfort, trust, and understanding between people. And those are things you really cannot do without.

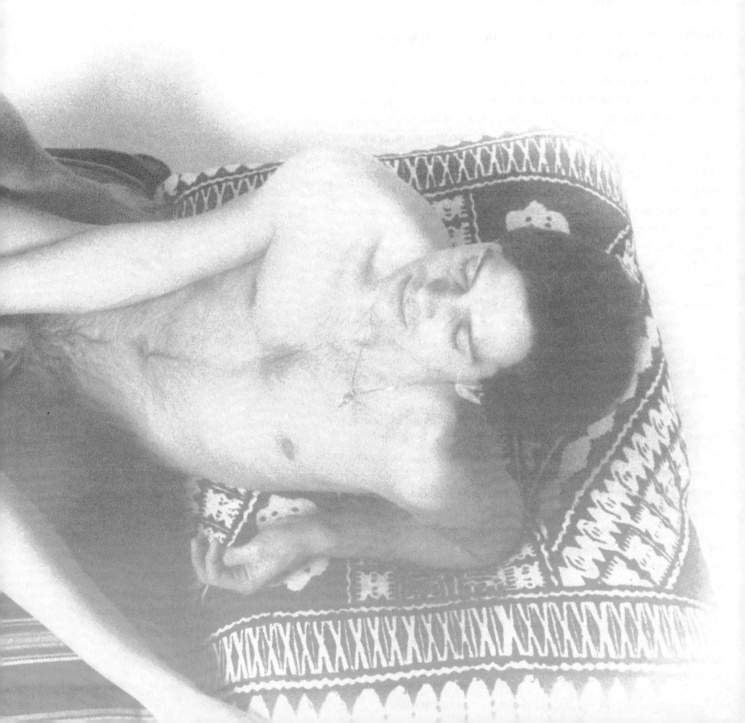

FALLING APART

Even though you did those daily assignments faithfully and enjoyed them, they alone cannot be the answer to long-standing, specific control problems many people have when they are with a partner. You can fall apart worrying about them or not facing up to them. They are:

Coming too fast This means you have orgasm before you want to. It may happen when you are alone, but it is a problem primarily when you are with someone else.

Not coming fast enough You cannot have an orgasm as soon as you'd like. You feel self-conscious and uncomfortable about it when you are with someone.

Coming together You want to come at the same time as your partner, but you seldom or never do.

Coming apart You don't want to come at the same time as your partner, but you usually do.

All these timing problems cause distress and embarrassment, but if you are physically healthy and willing to spend a little time on it, you can help yourself. First, though, you must recognize and acknowledge your particular timing problem. This may mean abandoning some of the methods you've used to cover up the fact that you have a problem.

People cover up sexual timing difficulties in many ways. Some ignore that anything is wrong, hoping it will go away. Others turn to questionable treatment, such as drugs, alcohol, acupuncture, hypnosis, abstinence, or forcing themselves to perform more and more impossible sexual feats. Or they may disguise the sexual problem by becoming very tired or worried or drunk before or in the middle of a sexual encounter.

Some people will feign disinterest in sex so they don't have to face their feelings of inadequacy. Others will use excuses such as not having an understanding wife or having had a bad experience in the past that make them unable to enjoy sex now. That may be perfectly true, but why are those explanations being dredged up now? A sympathy ploy may be an excuse not to improve or change.

Probably one of the most common covering-up techniques is faking orgasm. Men can and do fake just as well as women, at least during intercourse. A man who comes too fast might have an orgasm early on and not draw attention to it only to fake one a little later on. Or if he can't come when he feels he should, he'll pretend he already did. A man can fool his partner quite easily by groaning a little and doing some powerful thrusting. A woman cannot, contrary to popular myth, feel the semen splashing inside her vagina. And as for the orgasm itself, her own lubrication and rhythm may be such as to make her unsure whether her partner has come or not. Since men take different times to detumesce, there is no telling for sure, especially with a new partner.

A woman who cannot come as fast as she feels she should, or as fast as she thinks her partner expects her to, will do much the same thing. And a woman who thinks she comes too quickly will ignore her real orgasm in order to have a fake one later. A lot of movement embellished by little noises will turn the trick. The spasms of orgasm aren't usually detectable by the man anyway, but tightening the vaginal muscles can make him think that something big is happening.

It isn't entirely unnatural to cover up or fake sometimes. But if it is a regular pattern, maybe even to the point of not recognizing it, you are in trouble. Honestly know yourself or you won't be able to change. The following statements are to be answered true or false:

I have pretended I was interested in sex when I wasn't.   _____

I think I'm too slow.   _____

I think my partner thinks I'm too slow.   _____

I just get too excited when I'm with my partner.   _____

I often fake orgasm.   _____

I sometimes lose interest though my partner is aroused.   _____

If I can't come at the same time, I feel real disappointed.   _____

I sometimes think my partner fakes orgasm.   _____

I've said I've had too much to drink when I didn't.   _____

I know I have a problem but I'd prefer not to think about it.   _____

I feel I should have an orgasm in order to please my partner.   _____

I've said it didn't hurt when it hurt like hell.   _____

I think my partner has a problem but I don't know how to help.   _____

Having a husband and kids is a hassle when it comes to sex.   _____

My partner ought to read this book. Has he or she ever got problems.   _____

I'm afraid to have sex with someone new for fear they'll think I'm not good enough.   _____

I sometimes fake answers on tests in order to look good.   _____

Add up the number of times you answered True. If the total is three or more, it is time for you to stop covering up.

COMING TOO FAST—MEN

This is one of the most agonizing of conditions. You don't know why it happens or how to control it. You have tried biting your lip, holding your breath, even using drugs or desensitizing creams to keep from coming, but it happens anyway. You feel inadequate and foolish. Somehow this problem makes you feel immature and unworthy and, more than anything else, furious at yourself. You avoid being with anyone for fear that it will happen. Even the clinical name for it, premature ejaculation, seems to indicate that you are a kid trying to make it in a world of natural-born lovers.

Well, those same clinicians who gave it that ghastly name have found that it is the most curable of afflictions. There really is something you can do about it. You can actually find the control you seek if you are willing to try to settle down, take your time, and stop watching yourself. Read on—slowly.

What is too fast?

Too fast can be in your shorts. It can be when you are kissing. It can be during oral sex, that is, when your partner is kissing, licking, or sucking your penis as part of foreplay. It can be just outside the vagina. It can be as soon as you are safely in the vagina. It can be after five minutes of holding your breath in anxious terror hoping you won't come. It can be coming before your partner wants you to. It can be after ten minutes of frenetic thrusting. It can be after trying three different positions but wanting to try a fourth. It can be after thirty minutes of staring into your partner's eyes while joined and motionless. It can be anything that is not what you and your partner want. And it is something almost every man has experienced.

When does it happen?
When was the first time it happened to you?
How old were you? _____
Who were you with? _____ What were the circumstances?
_____
_____
_____
How did your partner react? _____
_____
_____
How did you feel? _____
_____
_____

These questions are to start you thinking about whether coming too fast is something you learned. You may come too fast now because of something that happened in your early sex history. For example, your

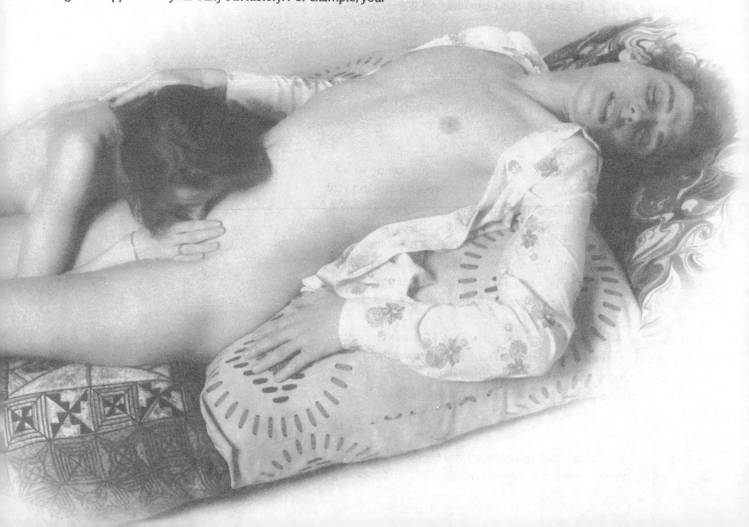

mother could have walked in on you while you were masturbating; your girlfriend's parents could have come home early and caught you two messing around on the sofa; you might have expected to be interrupted by roommates, children, or in-laws; you could have been summarily dismissed by a busy prostitute; your partner could have been reluctant or you could have been afraid of being rejected; you could have been afraid of getting someone pregnant; and so on. Any of these experiences could condition you to get it over with before something like this happened.

If you did learn you can unlearn, as long as you aren't still affected by these issues. If you think they still get in the way you could go to a motel, start earlier, send the kids to camp, use better birth control, not be with a partner who doesn't like you, and so on.

When does it happen now?

With possessive partners? _____

With your regular partner? _____

With new partners? _____

With reluctant partners? _____

When you are tired or drunk or have indigestion? _____

Here we're looking for your own pattern of coming too fast. For instance, if it happens only with new partners, are your partners always new? It's hard to adapt to one person, never mind a steady stream. You could be seeking a partner with whom you'll fail; or maybe you are making sex hard for yourself by performing when you are not physically or mentally prepared.

If you come too fast regularly with your regular partner, ask yourself about the relationship itself. Do you like this person? Do you want to be with her or him? You could feel hostile toward, dependent upon, or unhappy with this person for reasons beyond your sexual relationship. However, it is possible to have more orgasmic control before settling all the underlying conflicts—given that you want to work on that control with this person.

What can you do?

Step one Slow down. A not uncommon characteristic of a man who comes too fast is that he is a man in a hurry. Try to be reflective and careful in examining yourself. It may take some time to be able to do this. You cannot expect to change overnight just because you read a book. Part of slowing down is appreciating that it takes time to slow down. You could start by reading more slowly. You're probably ready right now to skip a few lines in hopes of finding "the answer." If so, you just missed the answer.

This whole section is outlined in steps. Some may be giant steps for you and others will seem very small, but all lead to the control you want. Set a realistic pace for yourself in which you allow time for reconnoitering but not for lagging. Select the time and the frequency for taking these steps, such as morning and evening sessions every day or lunch-hour sessions every other day. You can take as many or as few steps per session as you feel best for you at the time. Jot down your proposed schedule here.

_____

_____

Step two Write a detailed description of just exactly what does happen to you physically when you ejaculate. Your description should include the setting, the stimulation, and the physical signs. For example, it might be in bed with your aroused wife at 11:06. She could be doing things to you or you could be doing things to her that excited you. Record your position and what you are thinking or fantasizing about.

_____

_____

Step three Your moment of inevitability, that point where you know you are going to come and can do nothing to prevent it, is particularly important to be able to anticipate. You may wish to review the chapter on orgasm before you begin. Some men who come too fast aren't aware of anything preceding their orgasm, but if you concentrate you will begin to notice some of the following:

Erection _____
Rapid breathing _____
Tightening of scrotal sac _____
Contraction of anal sphincter _____
Racing thoughts _____
Swelling throughout the genitals _____
Flushed feeling _____
General body tensing _____
Other _____

If you still can't feel anything happening, come again.

Step four Now that you know when you are going to come, you can practice not coming. You have to change something between the time you recognize that you are getting close to the moment of inevitability and that moment itself.

If you are having erotic fantasies that are too arousing, change your concentration. If you are moving, slow down. If you are moving slowly, stop. If you aren't moving at all, move. Change what you are doing to your partner or ask her to stop what she's doing to you. Concentrate on your own body and what it is doing. If you are inside the vagina, pull out. Do not reenter until you feel your testes drop a little, indicating that the crisis has passed. Anything you do is better than just letting yourself come too fast.

Step five One fear you may have is that your partner won't want to do this, that she will get bored or impatient. It does take real sympathy and patience on the part of the woman or other man, and you should talk this over before you start the program. One way some couples work this out is for the woman to have an orgasm through oral or manual stimulation before you get started. Remember that short sessions are better than long ones. If you have a partner and see that your problem only occurs during intercourse, you may find that a change in position will help you. Any position which reduces friction on the penis is better for you. Standing may be good because it not only reduces friction, but is strenuous—giving you something else to worry about. Try it.

Rear entry positions, "doggie style," where you enter your partner from behind, tend to lower friction because you usually cannot get in too far. You can do this standing or sitting, or you can do it by being on

top of your partner when she is lying face down. Do not try standard missionary position with her facing you when you are on top. That is the worst position for you.

Probably the very best position for you is to have your partner on top. It can be inhibiting if you haven't done it, but that may help inhibit orgasm. See what you think.

Step six The penile squeeze is a very effective method of retarding ejaculation. It was first used by James Semans, a urologist, in 1956 and was later developed by Masters and Johnson. It is used by almost every sex therapist and it has been demonstrated over and over again to work.

Squeezing the tip or the base of the penis for a few seconds just before the moment of inevitability will inhibit the ejaculatory reflex. This squeeze can be applied by you or your partner whenever you want to delay orgasm. It is easy and it does not hurt. Here is how to do it.

Hold your erect penis with your thumb on the frenulum and your first two fingers on top as in the photograph at left. This is a little awkward at first but you'll see that it puts pressure where needed. Grasp the tip quite firmly around the ridge and press hard for a few seconds. You'll need to practice this grip until it feels like an almost natural thing to do. You'll find that you can squeeze quite hard without hurting yourself. If you are near the moment of inevitability when you squeeze you will feel a subsiding, possibly accompanied by a flush or tingling. If your orgasm is already under way, do not continue to squeeze. Just relax and enjoy coming. Try to squeeze earlier next time. Practice by yourself as shown. Don't expect anything to happen right away. You won't learn this in a day, but keep practicing and you'll begin to see how it works.

Step seven When you have started to gain some confidence in the squeeze, teach it to your partner. She may be afraid of hurting you, so let her watch you do it before she tries. Practice having her do it as soon as you have an erection, even if you don't feel that you are anywhere close to orgasm. It's better to squeeze too early rather than too late. Remember that her hand will be reversed. Practice until she feels as comfortable as you do.

Step eight How long since you've had a day off from sex? Maybe this is the day for it. Don't do, talk, or think sex for the next twenty-three hours.

Step nine Try doing some of the sensate focus exercises, with your partner squeezing you every few minutes or less as you need it. Practice being able to signal your need for a squeeze with a word or a gesture.

Step ten Now you can try intercourse, but do not have an orgasm. That is, put your penis inside the vagina or anus for a moment and then take it out. Condition yourself to tolerate being there. Don't stay very long at first. Have your partner squeeze each time you take your penis out, so both of you can learn what is involved. This is possible when you are on top of your partner, but remember that is not a good position for you anyway. It is best if she is on top. She can slide on and off your penis to apply the squeeze on signal.

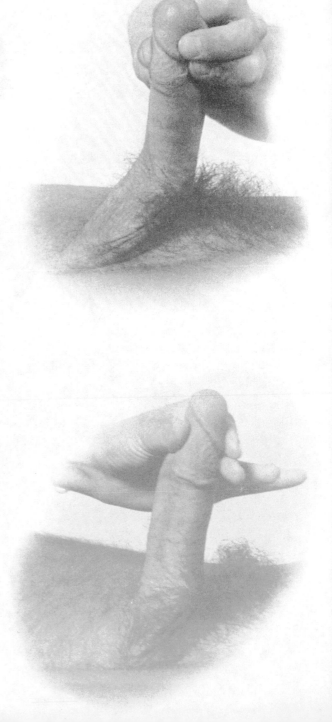

Step eleven Continue practicing tolerance. Try to pull out and receive a squeeze at least five times before coming to orgasm.

Step twelve Try intercourse to ejaculation now if you haven't already, but don't abandon the squeeze. You may find that you need it less and less often over the next few weeks or months, but don't be hesitant to use it whenever you want to. You can always return to it.

Step thirteen Some couples prefer to use the squeeze at the base of the penis rather than at the tip. This has the advantage of being applicable during intercourse but it doesn't work as well for all people. You have to grasp the penis as far down as possible. Give it a try sometime.

The penile squeeze technique is extremely effective, but it will be awkward and embarrassing for both you and your partner in the beginning. Expect that and go ahead anyway. No matter how silly it seems at first, once it starts working it doesn't seem silly at all.

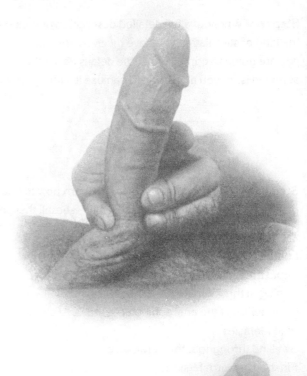

COMING TOO FAST—WOMEN

It's common for the man to come too fast; the woman with the same problem, a much rarer one, does not get much sympathy. Since it is more likely that women will have the opposite problem, the woman who comes quickly is envied or even made fun of. Just because it is unusual does not mean that it isn't a real concern. The woman who comes too fast may feel she is somehow easy or odd.

What is too fast?

Too fast depends on the situation and the partner. But it can mean having an orgasm while thinking about it. It can mean having an orgasm while being aroused or while arousing someone else. It can mean coming just as the penis enters the vagina. It can be after ten minutes of trying twelve unsatisfactory positions. And it can be coming before your partner, or you, really wants.

When does it happen?

Follow the outline for the men (page 190) to see if your early experiences taught you to get sex over with in a hurry. Update your history by checking to see if you are still concerned about the baby waking up, being "caught," being rejected, and so on. Consider the effects of such feelings as wanting to reject this partner, being too dependent or demanding, and other underlying issues you think are involved. Use the space below to outline what you think is important for you to change.

What can you do?

Step one Plan out a realistic pace and schedule for yourself to follow. Do these steps slowly and carefully. There is no rush and you are competing with no one.

195

Step two Write out a full detailed description of your orgasms. Include the kind of stimulation you have received, the point at which you know you are going to come, and some details about the setting. This description is for you alone or you can use it with a partner.

_____
_____
_____
_____

Step three Use the checklist below to learn how to anticipate your orgasms. You should be able to predict the stimuli that encourage orgasm.

Lubrication _____
Rapid breathing _____
Aching in the vagina _____
Contraction of the anal sphincter _____
Wild fantasies _____
Swelling throughout the pelvic area _____
Flushed or warm feeling _____
Muscular tension _____
Other _____

Step four Using the sensate focus exercises if you are with your partner, extend yourself to sustain arousal. Try to come to a high state of arousal and then let it fade away and return. Concentrate on your partner, on the physical sensations you feel, on fantasy, and so on. Change your rhythm, stop what you are doing, or start something else. Try to always be ahead of your orgasm so that you let it come when you want it to rather than being overwhelmed by it.

Step five Positions that lessen pressure on your clitoris and restrict your mobility are best. Try the rear entry positions described above. By all means don't get on top. The best position for you is the missionary position, with the man on top and your legs extended parallel to his.

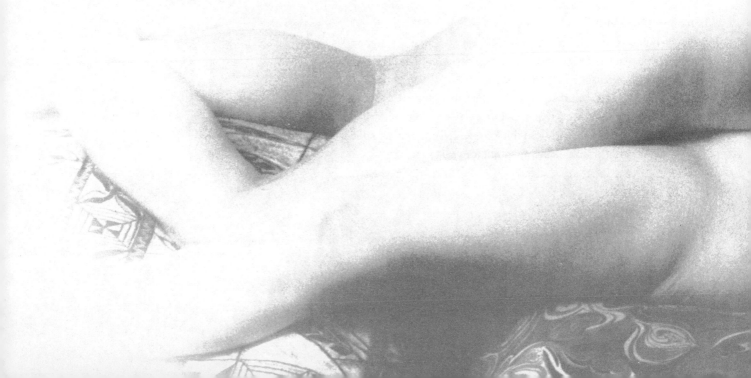

Step six Many women can have more than one orgasm if properly stimulated. Is this true of you? If so, one solution to your problem is to have an orgasm right away and then have another later on.

With a little time and practice you, too, can slow down.

NOT COMING FAST ENOUGH—WOMEN

This can be a devastating problem because many women fear that they are inadequate or uncaring if they cannot respond as fast as a man. The idea that men and women have different orgasms and get them in different ways isn't discussed very much. Men and women can both reach orgasm in three to four minutes, or less, when masturbating, but women often take longer through intercourse for an understandable reason. The intensity of stimulation is considerably less. The clitoris, not the vagina, is the sexual nerve center for a woman. During intercourse, the clitoris receives indirect stimulation from the movement of the penis against the outer vaginal lips and/or from the pressure of the partner's body.

What's fast enough?

Fast enough is before you or your partner starts getting restless. You might be restless because you are worried about what he thinks or you're affected by his restlessness. He may be restless because he expects you to be just like him. Or he may not know anything about orgasm for women, including how long it takes and how he could help. If you suspect the latter, you may want to give him a copy of this book.

Maybe you have some ideas about how long you should take. Try to think about where you got those ideas and when. You may be able to

have a better time if you allow yourself less rigid expectations. Coming fast enough is as much a control issue as coming too fast. Realistic expectations and knowledge of yourself and your partner are needed. Knowing what is involved in using that information is next.

Why does it happen?
Answer these questions as truthfully as you can.

Does it happen because it always has? _____

Does it happen because you aren't sure of this person? _____

Does it happen because your partner doesn't do the right things for you? _____

Does it happen because you're not in the mood? _____

Does it happen because you are worrying about it? _____

If you can say why it happens by answering these questions, maybe there is something you could do about it. Think about how it would be different if you were aroused, could talk to this partner, could express your own needs.

What can you do?

Step one Set a schedule for yourself to go through these steps and put it down here.

_____

Step two Make a list of the fantasies and other stimuli that arouse you. You may feel some are too bizarre or silly to mention. You don't have to tell them to anyone. Just write them down here or in your journal for yourself.

_____

_____

Step three It is essential that you be in the mood for sex when you have it. It is possible that you have been blocking that mood and it's also possible that you have been trying to respond when your partner wanted you to, rather than when you really wanted to. Don't torture yourself by trying to have sex when you don't feel like it. If you find that you are lying there making grocery lists or waiting for the phone to ring, maybe you didn't want to be there in the first place.

Step four Concentrate on the things that arouse you during the sensate focus exercises. Write them down here.

_____

_____

_____

Step five Spend some time teaching your partner what is exciting to you. Direct clitoral stimulation is the most arousing activity for many women, but some men don't know how to do it. Take your partner's hand and gently guide it over your vulva. Show him the kind of motion, pressure, and touch you like. He will know when you are really aroused because the clitoris will seem to disappear and the area around it will become very slippery. It may take fifteen or twenty minutes to reach this stage. Kinsey found many years ago that for women who had had twenty minutes or more of foreplay, only about 8 percent did not reach orgasm during intercourse. Times have changed but that time has not.

Some women are very sensitive around the nipples, the neck, or another special personal erogenous zone. Show your partner what you want.

Step six Manual and oral stimulation are very arousing to many women. And positions which put the most pressure on the clitoris and allow freedom of movement are also exciting. Two particularly delicious ones are woman on top and the lateral position (photograph below). When you are on top, facing your partner, you have the freedom to move your hips and to position your legs in such a way as to give yourself maximum clitoral stimulation. You can kneel astride your partner or you can stretch your legs down between or beside his.

The lateral position is not strictly side by side, but it does have the advantage of not putting too much weight on either partner. Start with the woman on top. The man bends his right leg to the side and the woman shifts onto his leg. Then she bends her right leg and wraps it around his torso. Both left legs are extended straight down.

Incidentally, your partner should know if he doesn't already that hard thrusting, or bamming as it is delicately called, is not the only way to bring a woman to orgasm. Some women prefer slow, circular motions occasionally interrupted by teasing changes in rhythm.

Step seven There are other things you can do to increase stimulation during intercourse. Try the vaginal exercises from Chapter 5 (page 91). Other muscles can be called into action, too. Stretching your legs and back or squeezing and pushing down with the abdominal and perineal muscles may interest you.

Don't forget that almost all women take longer to reach orgasm through intercourse than men do. You should not be comparing yourself to anyone. You should enjoy yourself your own way.

NOT COMING FAST ENOUGH—MEN

It's very deflating to be a man who cannot come instantaneously if he wants to. Although it can be a pleasure for your partner, you could be very worried about it. It threatens your ideal of manliness and potency to be slow, especially if you are slower than you used to be. You may start feeling inadequate, which can be as harmful as the problem itself.

What's fast enough?

Fast enough for a man is much the same as for a woman. It is being able to have an orgasm when you feel you should. You may have unreal expectations for yourself and you can certainly be influenced by what your partner thinks—or what you think your partner thinks. Fast enough is before you begin getting self-conscious.

Why does it happen?

Quiz yourself.

Does it happen because you have some misgivings about the partner?

_____

Does it happen because it always has? _____

Does it happen because your partner won't do anything to arouse you?

_____

Does it happen because you are desensitized by drugs or condoms?

_____

Does it happen because you're not as young as you were? _____

Does it happen because you're thinking about it? _____

Sometimes it happens because you or your partner are not aware that men, especially as they get older, do not come as fast as when they were younger. It's not that you don't come, it's just that you slow down. This is very common and not at all a reflection on your masculinity. After all, you probably don't run as fast as you did either.

If you find condoms desensitizing, maybe you haven't been using good ones. You get what you pay for in condoms. If you drink or use drugs, you should ask yourself why you might have wanted to fail at intercourse.

Maybe you haven't explained to your partner, or admitted to yourself, that you really cannot and do not want to have sex three times a day. Good grief, what does she think you are anyway? What do you think you are? Maybe you're trying to live up to standards that are not right for you.

What can you do?

Step one Write down a schedule you can stick to—not for intercourse but for taking these steps. Put it in your journal.

_____
_____
_____
_____
_____
_____

Step two Make a list of what does arouse you and contrast it to what does not:

Arousing	Not arousing
Morning	Evening
On sofa	Under covers
Elaine	Helen
Kissing	Oral sex

and so on.

Step three Don't have sex unless you want to, or, at least, don't force yourself to orgasm. You can get and give a great amount of pleasure doing the sensate focus exercises and you won't have to come at all.

Step four Concentrate on some things that arouse you, such as fantasy, erotic sensations, being fit, your partner. Make a list of them here.

_____

_____

_____

Step five Try telling your partner what you like and share your list with her if you wish. Show her how to stimulate you by guiding her hand. The glans of the penis, the testicles, and the anus usually respond to various kinds of touching, licking, or pressure. Show her.

Step six If you've learned that there are physical things you can do for yourself, such as the tightening of certain muscles, do them.

Step seven Experiment with the positions that give you the most friction and freedom of movement and use those that are most comfortable. It won't help you to have to strain to maintain a position. The lateral position, described in the previous section, is highly recommended. Also, being on top will give you more stimulation.

If you are a man who has always been active sexually, there is no reason why you cannot continue to be. Allow yourself plenty of time. As you get older it takes a little longer to get an erection and it takes a little longer to ejaculate. Accept that and enjoy yourself.

COMING TOGETHER

Having an orgasm at the same time as your partner is a much-publicized ideal goal of sexual relations. Popular literature and old marriage manuals depict it as the only true expression of love. Many people feel they have missed something if it hasn't happened to them. As a form of utter togetherness, however, it is not always the ultimate experience. For one thing, achieving it is not easy for every twosome, let alone threesome or foursome, because it requires synchronizing patterns that may be quite different. And yet again, it puts all the emphasis on orgasm.

Why do it then?

You may want to try, either because you've heard about it or you've experienced it in the past and found it particularly satisfying. Whether you've experienced it or not, it may have great symbolic significance for you as a sign of total completion. If you feel that trying to come together puts unnecessary or unnatural pressure on you or your partner, perhaps you'd have more fun coming apart.

What can you do?

Step one Think about your own and your partner's individual patterns of arousal and orgasm. Determine if one or both of you should change and discuss how it could be done. You can't very well tango while he's doing the hustle. Record your styles here.

Me   My Partner

_____   _____
_____   _____
_____   _____
_____   _____

It may seem stagey and artificial to sit around talking about how out of phase you are. But some of you would rather endure a dull or unsatisfactory routine than talk about changing it. Sometimes you have to rely on contrivances in order to get beyond the old habits or fears that prevent you from enjoying yourselves.

Step two Don't dwell on the singularity of your responses. Try to figure out the positions and stimuli that might bring you closer together. In other words, use what you know about each other to look for some practical solutions. You don't have to rely on penile-vaginal intercourse either. It is possible to come together through mutual masturbation, and oral-genital or anal intercourse.

Just to warm up, what would you recommend for these people:

The Joneses He's been trying to keep up with her for years. She usually comes just as he is really getting excited. He can't come for another five or six minutes.

What do you suggest for them? _____

_____

Gloria No matter who she is with—and she has been around—it takes her a long time to have an orgasm. Some men wait for her; some don't.

What should she do? _____

_____

Dick and Jane Dick made a million dollars before he was thirty but he still can't "make" his wife. It is all over for him in two shakes and she comes more or less on her own.

What would you tell them to try? _____

_____

The Does There is something awfully anonymous about their lovemaking. One-two-three and it is all over. They don't know if they're coming or going.

Well, what do you say? _____

_____

Rob Rob can last forever but nobody ever seems to care.

Maybe Rob should _____

_____

Tom and Jerry For years and years they've been making love in the same old way. Twenty minutes of foreplay, twenty minutes of union culminating in mutual orgasm, and twenty minutes of cat-napping afterward. No quick tricks on the kitchen floor, no mistakes, and no variety.

How could they spice things up? _____

_____

Step three Now what are you two going to try to make coming together more likely? Use these lines to jot down your ideas.

_____

_____

_____

COMING APART

Coming apart here means coming apart voluntarily. It means knowing what both you and your partner like and how you can achieve it. Coming apart may mean having your orgasm a little before or a little after your partner. It may mean that one partner does not have an orgasm at all. There is no optimal duration for sex. The ideal condition is that both partners be reasonably happy and satisfied.

If you've never thought of coming apart as a plus, you may be unable to regard it with pleasure. It is possible that for you it always meant missing the big-time, all-meaningful mutual climax. Some people are afraid to think of coming apart as a positive experience.

If you've always come apart because you had no choice in the matter, coming apart could just carry overtones of failure for you. But if you have now gained some control which gives you a choice, you might want to try it.

Many people do not want to have their partner see them having an orgasm. They are afraid they look ridiculous. One thing about coming together is that you don't really watch your partner very closely. Therefore you are spared the embarrassment or pride that makes you want to be heard but not seen.

Earlier we spoke of coming apart involuntarily, being unable to control orgasm. Now we are talking about each partner being free to follow his natural rhythm and to enjoy his partner's orgasm as much as his own. This gives any couple flexibility, something that may have been lacking in your sex life for some time due to fear, habit, inexperience, and not knowing what to do. Many people find that coming apart is the easy and natural way to be together.

CONCLUSION

No doubt much of this sounds hopelessly self-conscious and here we are suggesting that self-consciousness is part of your problem. The trouble is that you've been stuck with your self-consciousness, unable to use it. Only by carrying some of your own watchfulness to extremes will you be able to float back to a middle ground where you can watch yourself when you need to and forget yourself the rest of the time.

Learning about yourself when you are with another person is necessary if you are to truly know yourself. It also gives you some sensitivity to the problems someone may have with you. You've probably already noticed that it's been hard to talk to your partner about some of the things in this chapter. That's what we'll work on in the next chapter. Communicating your needs now that you know them.

Knowing your patterns, how they might have developed and how they might be changed, should help make sex a pleasure rather than a time of anxiety and confusion. If ever you feel a loss of confidence, don't hesitate to go back to a point that was easier for you. As a matter of fact, if this paragraph seems overly optimistic, read this chapter again.

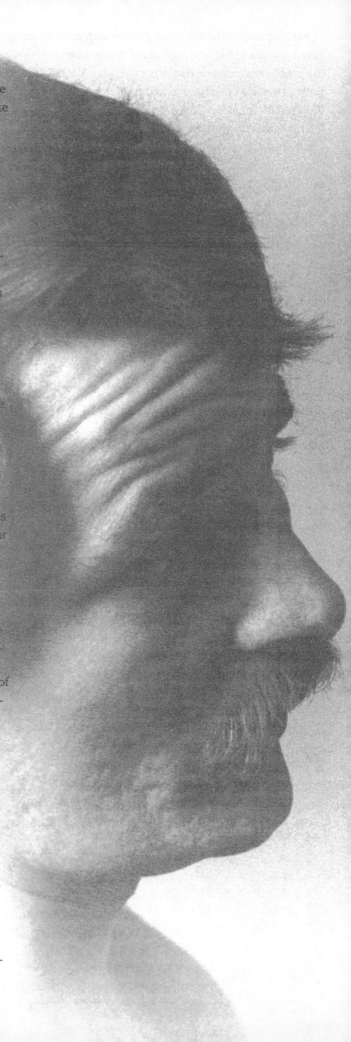

Words, Words, Words

INTRODUCTION

Throughout this book you've had instructions to talk to yourself. You've been implored to ask yourself questions, write yourself notes, and make lists for yourself. As you know, this type of self-examination is itself a therapeutic technique. But now you may be wondering how you are going to talk to another person about sex. There have already been suggestions to talk to your partner. These may have struck you as terrific if only your partner wanted to talk to you, if only you knew how, if only you could find the words.

There has been much emphasis in the past few years on how much people communicate non-verbally. You show by gesture, facial expression, and how you move your body what you feel and want. You tell a partner many things by smiling, hugging, moving toward or away from her or him. Sometimes you "say" things in body language that you aren't even aware you feel. It is certainly useful to be able to read your own and other's unconscious expressions by being alert to non-verbal behavior. But it is hard to know for sure whether you are getting a come-hither look or just an expression of polite interest. In this highly verbal society, only words come anywhere close to communicating the range and depth of human emotion and perception.

Before you can start talking about sex, you have to overcome that widespread feeling that sex is something people don't talk about. Words take away the special sacred quality that sex is supposed to have; if you talk about it, you take the mystery and romance out of it. You are supposed to know intuitively what your partner feels and needs and, if your partner really loves you, he or she will instinctively read your feelings. Besides, words freeze thoughts and emotions that you may later regret having expressed.

These popular myths about not talking explain why there is so much ignorance and fear about sexual functioning. At least 20 percent of all sex problems could be cleared up if people felt free to talk to a partner, a friend, a doctor about their sexual feelings. But even those who don't have specific problems can benefit from sex talk. Never to share your elation and curiosity about sex is never to realize that sex, itself a form of communication, can be enhanced by the give-and-take of verbal communication.

To refuse to talk, for whatever reason, "tells" your partner something you really have to take responsibility for. It might mean that you are afraid to talk because of what you or they might say. Many people put up with almost intolerable situations because they don't know how to change or are afraid to open themselves to a shift in their relationship. Other people really don't want to talk to their partners. Feeling that there is nothing to say or that talking won't help may mean that you don't think the relationship can be salvaged.

Even though words may not seem precise or accurate enough to express what you really want to say, they show a partner that you care enough to try. Otherwise, your partner doesn't know whether you are harboring romantic notions about words spoiling the mood or you really just don't care enough about them to want to communicate anything. Talking about sex with a partner, or with anyone, takes a willingness to reveal yourself. It is admittedly difficult at times but it is a

difficulty you share with just about everyone. That's why this chapter is about how to practice talking.

FINDING A SEXUAL VOCABULARY

One big reason that sex is hard to talk about is that sexual words have so many connotations. Although this makes them fun to use and adds zest to everyday language, it can be confusing when you have something to say specifically about sex. Because many sex words are also taboo words and are used contemptuously—fuck off, fuck yourself—many people have negative associations to them beyond the biological ones. Some people prefer euphemisms like "making love" or "sleeping with," and medical terms like "intercourse" and "coitus," rather than a taboo, if accurate, word like "fuck."

Naturally, who you are talking to will influence your choice of language. Most people don't talk to their friends in the same way they talk to their children or parents. You use words that identify you with your age, your class, even your politics. And you may not use words that, though accurate, would identify you with a group you're not comfortable in.

A sexual lexicon

So your first job is to find some words. Listed below are all kinds of sexual words and some synonyms. There is space for you to add synonyms and categories. If you are using a journal instead of writing in this book, write out all the words. Either way, circle the words you like and underline the ones you don't like.

You can use a dictionary, friends, or lovers, for more synonyms. Write in any words from your private sexual vocabulary if you have one. If you come up with more than five extra synonyms for any expression, send your entries to the author, care of The Dial Press.

Intercourse, fucking, balling, coitus, screwing, going all the way, banging, getting laid, having sex, sleeping with, making love, _____

Dove, pipe, organ, penis, dick, prick, peter, rod, machine, dong,

_____

Honey pot, vagina, hole, box, frog's mouth, herring pot, lotus bud,

_____

Snatch, vulva, seashell, tail, pussy, bush, pudendum, beaver, cunt, bearded clam, poontang, _____

Derrière, can, ass, backside, buns, _____

Asshole, anus, back door, bung hole, shithole, rectum, _____

Balls, nuts, testes, testicles, family jewels, _____

Boobs, tits, titties, breasts, headlights, melons, knockers, tickets,

_____

Little man in a boat, clitoris, chicken's tongue, hornet, pearl, tender button, _____

Semen, come, scum, cream, ejaculate, jizzum, _____

Honey, clam juice, juice, vaginal lubrication, groin gravy, _____

Getting wet, turning on tap, lubricating, juicing up, aroused,

_____

Getting a hard-on, aroused, standing up, turning on, getting stiff,

_____

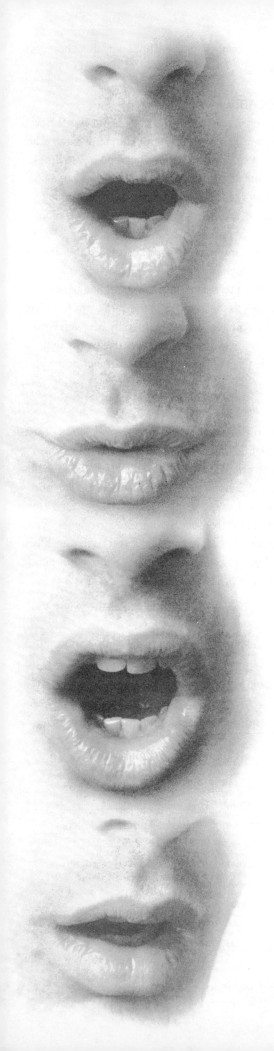

Climax, come, orgasm, shoot off, get rocks off, _____

Beat off, masturbate, fiddle around, jack off, jerk off, beat meat, whack off, abuse self, commit solitary sin, _____

Giving head, cocksucking, blowing, sucking off, going down on, fellating, oral sex, genital kiss, blow job, _____

Going down on, eating out, cunnilingus, genital kiss, oral sex, muff diving, tongue job, _____

Anal intercourse, cornhole, butt fuck, _____

Cheating, extramarital affair, taking a lover, getting even, being unfaithful, broadening your horizons, open marriage, _____

Spouse, lover, husband, wife, old man, old lady, boyfriend, girlfriend, woman, associate, chick, partner, piece of ass, meat, _____

Dating, seeing, going with, sleeping with, going steady with, having an affair with, having a relationship with, _____

My daughter's boyfriend, the man my daughter is sleeping with, my man-in-law, my lover-out-law, _____

_____

Although these lists are by no means exhaustive and many of the expressions are used interchangeably, your circles and underlinings should give you some ideas about your sexual vocabulary. If you either didn't circle any words or circled all of them, you should probably go over the lists again. It's hard to learn a language without having some feelings about words, especially taboo words. To like or dislike all of them may indicate an inclination to take the easy way out of this exercise. Even examining a couple of your reactions can show you how inextricably words are linked to attitudes.

Take the overall picture, for example. Did you tend to favor medical terms, raunchy expressions, unfamiliar words, euphemisms, words someone you know uses? If you find that a lot of medical words turned up, think about why you might be comfortable with them. Perhaps you are a doctor, maybe those were the words you first learned, possibly you want to distance yourself from the subject by using cool, professional language. You might be amused by raunchy expressions or you might feel that sex itself is raunchy. Unfamiliar words can be attractive because they carry no negative connotations for you or because they don't really seem to refer to sex. Euphemisms may make sex seem beautiful or far away. Words that friends use may be words you'd like to use or feel comfortable using.

The words you underlined because you didn't like them may be words that people you don't like use. They may be expressions that derogate sex in your eyes. They may seem silly, inaccurate, too masculine or feminine for you, too technical. You may have unpleasant memories from when and how you learned them. If you are doing this exercise honestly, you'll be able to find plenty of words that set your teeth on edge, at least in certain contexts.

For the purposes of this book you'll need a big enough vocabulary to express your feelings and questions about sex to a friend, a relative, or a partner. You shouldn't have to use words you don't like—unless you've managed to cut off all possibility of communication by rejecting all words. In that case, you ought to ask what you are trying to protect yourself from.

To get comfortable using the words you need, and hearing yourself say them, say them aloud to yourself. Try to use them in sentences. Say them to a mirror. If you have a tape recorder, use that too. Try shouting

the words, whispering them, and saying them in different ways to see what coloring you can and want to give them.

The words you say are only part of communicating. You also have to be able to hear the words other people use. If you close your ears to those words, you may not hear others' need to talk, their feelings about you and the words you use, nor their anxieties and pleasures. Try listening to how other people use or decline to use sexual words and how the people around them, including you, react. Observe what kind of language is most prevalent in a group of men, of teenagers, of older people. Listen to the allusions to sex on radio or TV talk shows and note the audience's and your own reaction.

Then try becoming aware of how people react to your use of sexual language. Even if you never actually talk about sex, consider how you refer to your body or to someone else's. Think about how you talk about or to your gynecologist, how you tell a dirty joke, how you describe someone else's sex life. Try dropping sexual words in a conversation that has some sexual component and see how you feel doing it and how other people hear it. See if you use sexual words to impress others, seduce others, shock others, put others off. Becoming aware of how you and others use and hear sexual language will prepare you for starting a sexual conversation with someone you want to talk to.

STARTING A SEXUAL CONVERSATION

It's fun to talk about sex. It can be psychologically thrilling, intimately funny, infinitely rewarding, and sexually exciting. Unfortunately, many people think that if they are going to talk about sex, they must have a problem. It's true that if you don't talk all the time, "having a talk" probably means trouble. So here are some ideas about how to get the ball rolling without making a big deal out of it.

Step one The best way to slide into a sexual discussion without calling attention to it is to pick up on something in the general conversation. Listen for openings. You'll find that discussions about movies, advertisements, jobs, other people, even politics, often have a sexual component.

Step two Use these openings by stepping in with the personal pronoun, "I think . . ." "I feel . . ." Your ability to turn the conversation personal will encourage others to do so. Offer a part of yourself, give a personal opinion.

Step three Use past experiences to illustrate points or to develop themes. You don't have to reveal your whole sex history in one crushing blow. It's easier for you and for others to start talking about the past than about the present. Once a level of trust has been established, you can move into more current interests.

Step four Never ask someone a question you wouldn't be willing to answer yourself. And don't ask questions you either know or suspect they aren't ready to answer.

Step five Stick your neck out. Say things about yourself even when you don't know how they will react. Don't do it to upset them or show off or

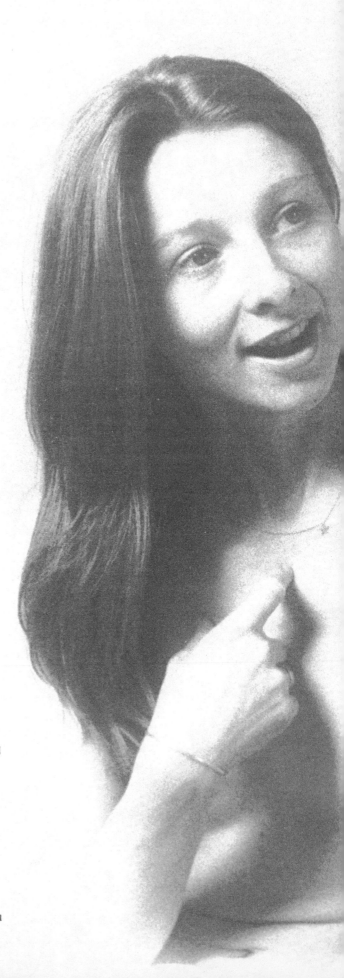

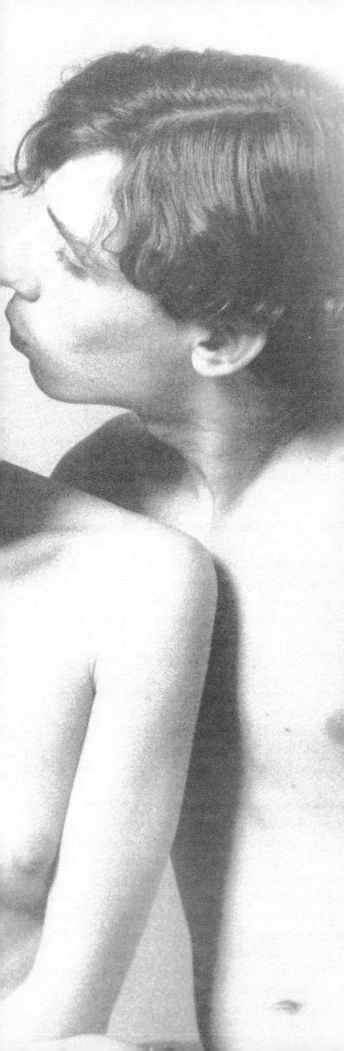

end the conversation. Do it to scare yourself a little, to get away from safe ground, to test your ability to communicate spontaneously.

Step six Try talking about sex while you are doing it. Tell the other person that you like what he or she is doing or what you are doing. Ask your partners what they like to do or to have done.

PRACTICING SEXUAL COMMUNICATION

Although the preceding suggestions will get you started, the following ones will take you farther. These are controlled, centered exercises in hearing and talking. They are fun to do and you'll be amazed at what they teach you not only about communicating, but about sexual attitudes. You will need someone to do these with. You can choose a partner, a friend, a relative—someone you feel comfortable with. You'll also need a timer, some time, and some privacy.

VERBAL GYMNASTICS, 1. You are going to start off by talking about talking. Set your timer for ten minutes. Start with sexual language. Compare your vocabularies, even your lists from above, and tell each other what you like and don't like to hear spoken. Tell each other who it is easy or hard to talk to and why. You can spend another 10 minutes at this if you want to.

This exercise gives you a chance to start communicating about something that is a little removed from your relationship, your problems, your sex life. At the same time, it is current (if you've been reading the book) and something you share. It will give you an example of how a relatively unthreatening subject can be personal and meaningful.

VERBAL GYMNASTICS, 2. To experience just how important listening is, you are both going to talk at once. Take a topic from the attitude chapter, pages 46–69, and decide who is going to speak for it and who against it. You are going to trade positions, so it doesn't matter how you lead off. Set your timer for three minutes. Don't listen to the other person and don't stop explaining all the virtues of your position. When the time is up, set the timer for another three minutes, trade sides, and go to it without taking time out to discuss the first part.

This exercise gives you a chance to see how it feels to get no response to what you are saying. You may not have been able to finish the exercise. One of you may have been able to go on talking while the other couldn't. The way this exercise worked out may reflect that one of you always dominates the other verbally. It may show you how much you depend on having someone listen to what you are saying. It may show you that you feel freer to express yourself when the other one isn't listening. All of these possibilities relate to how you communicate in real situations.

Of course, part of your reaction to this assignment will depend on how you feel about the topic. Talk over how you each felt playing each role. You may have been more or less fluent defending one position than you were defending the other. Discuss why you think that might be. Sometimes it is easier to talk about things remote from you than those you feel strongly about.

213

VERBAL GYMNASTICS, 3. You can use the same topic or a new one for this exercise. You are going to say a few words about the topic to your friend or partner. They are not to interrupt or say anything until you finish. Then they repeat what you said, or the gist of it. If they are wrong, correct them. When they have repeated your statement to your satisfaction, they give you a statement. You repeat it to their satisfaction before responding to it with your next statement. Try to do this back and forth at least five or six times. You can then do it with another topic. You don't need to time this.

This exercise can show you how important it is to really listen and how easy it is to misunderstand. You may find that you never get it right the first time. This could be from thinking about what you are going to say next, one of the main blocks to effective listening. It can also be from feeling that the other person isn't listening to you right. That is, she or he isn't looking at you, giving you non-verbal encouragement or little nods. How you are being listened to affects what you say.

Now, think about the topic itself. You could have been surprised or pleased by something you said or heard. You may have felt like arguing at some point. You may have found yourself trying to dissuade or agree with the other person. Go over the exchange to see what each of you learned that you may not have known before. A structure like this can make it easier to reveal attitudes than a conventional conversation would.

VERBAL GYMNASTICS, 4. This time you aren't going to follow up on the other person's remarks. You each get five minutes to talk about anything you want. You can talk about several different things, or you needn't say anything at all. Then your friend or partner talks for five minutes. As listeners, you should be as empathetic and supportive as possible without speaking. Even if you don't like what is being said or don't agree with it, try to be an understanding listener. When it is your turn to talk, you can talk about anything that is on your mind.

Here is the opportunity to bring up problems, discontents, and questions within a set framework. Now you can see what concerns you both have, whether they are related, and how the other feels about them. You'll also find out whether or not it is possible for you to be a good listener, from your partner's point of view. And you'll know how well she or he can listen. It is hard to talk for five minutes, especially in the beginning, but after a while you should try to build it up to fifteen and then thirty minutes. Learning to talk about yourself is communication.

By this time you may be champing to talk about these topics without the constraints of these verbal gymnastic structures. Go ahead and talk, but don't give these exercises up entirely. They can be very helpful if at any time you feel you and a partner are not communicating very well.

Because talking without formal guidelines may be difficult to do even after you've had the experience of these exercises, you might want to set up a time for chat with your regular partner. You could arrange to spend fifteen minutes a day when you first get up, before you go to bed, when you get home from work, or on your way to work, just talking. Try to pursue subjects that are hard for you, rather than just reporting what happened during the day. With practice, you can learn to be both trusting and trustworthy in exchanging confidences and feelings.

If you do not have a friend or partner with whom to practice these suggestions, you can do quite a bit by acting out in writing and in person your feelings about some of the subjects raised here. Choosing a topic and expressing your feelings, even to yourself, will give you a start toward communicating when you get a chance to do so.

Being able to say things to another person that you've never or rarely discussed and hearing his or her own revelations can be a very liberating experience. But it won't make you ready immediately to put aside years of harboring certain attitudes and styles of talking (or not talking). What it will do is free you to talk more, to examine with the help of another why you feel the way you do. Once you have more of a sense that it is all right to feel both good and bad about sex, you will have more confidence to deal with the conflicts that arise when your attitudes differ from those of a partner.

Words, of course, have a sexual application beyond their use to communicate feelings. They can also be instruments of seduction and arousal. Some people become deliciously witty or suggestive in their speech when there is someone around to seduce. Others become stupid or wordless around people they are sexually interested in. Some are aroused by partners who talk dirty, give directions, or offer a running commentary on how they feel during sex. Others are turned off by talk during sex. These preferences may be another topic of conversation with your friend.

Some refinements of sexual communication

In doing the exercises, following the steps, and initiating intimate tête-à-têtes of your own, keep a couple of things in mind. First of all, both you and your partner should be on guard to see that one person isn't overwhelming the other. There are several ways to overwhelm. One is by sheer force of fluency combined with an inability to listen. Another is by the amount of self-disclosure. Some people actually distance themselves by giving what seems like a lot of personal feeling that is really not touching them at all. Others overwhelm with tears, silence, anger, or depression, which cut off the conversation.

Also, you and your partner should respect each other's privacy. You will be better able to trust and be trusted if you both agree that everything said is confidential, not to be bandied about and not to be brought up to use against the other. If either of you doesn't want to talk about something, come back to it later. If you don't feel ready to reveal certain things, you can work together to get ready.

Don't forget that language will still get in your way occasionally. Because your resistance to certain words or phrases may be a resistance to what they stand for, talking about attitudes and feelings when practicing communication is a very good way to find out where your blocks and fears are. By expressing yourself and hearing what another has to say, you will learn where you are and why you might be there. Sometimes just saying these things will make you aware that they are really not frightening at all, especially when shared.

Some extensions of sexual communication

Many people who are together really don't know each other at all. Al-

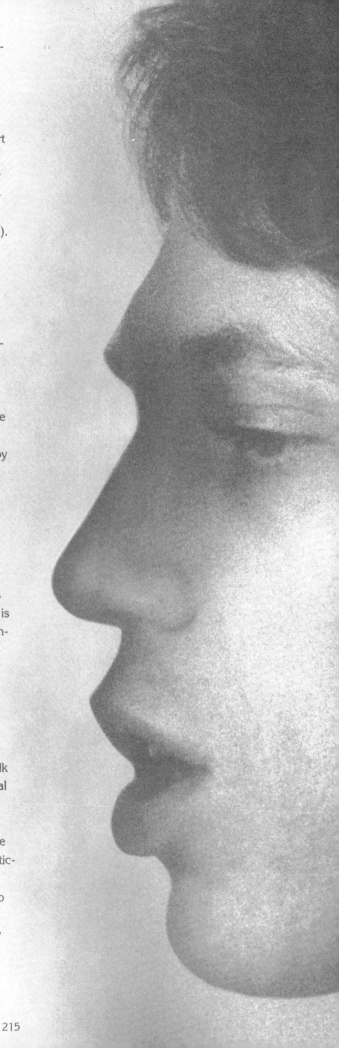

though this is naturally true of new relationships, it is also true of long-standing ones. People who start out not talking find it harder and more artificial to start talking as time goes on. Some couples stop talking after a while because they get no pleasure out of it, possibly due to problems in the relationship that they don't know how to talk about. Others slip into routines that really don't allow for discussions of changing feelings and new ideas.

The questions below are examples of some things you might like to know about a partner. If you've been communicating all along, you probably know the answers to many of them. If you don't know the answers, you might try to find them now.

What sexual positions does your partner like?

When does your partner like to have sex?

Does your partner like to have the lights on?

Does your lover like to fuck under the covers?

Does your partner like to ball with clothes on?

What does your partner think about swinging?

Does your partner like to talk while making love?

Does your partner like to be clean for screwing?

Does your partner like you to be clean?

Does your spouse like oral sex?

Does your partner like to be watched?

How often does your partner like to have sex?

What do your partners think of your kisses?

What does your partner think of the smell and taste of your genital juices?

Does your partner like to squeeze your pimples?

What kind of a body rub does your partner like?

Does your partner like quickies?

Who does your lover think should come first?

Who does your spouse think should tell the kids about sex?

Does your partner think you are perverse?

Is your partner anally erotic?

Does your partner like an energetic sexual encounter?

What does your partner think about abortion?

What would your partner think if you were unfaithful?

How would your partner expect you to act if she or he were unfaithful?

Does your partner think you are too conservative?

What does your partner think about affection in public?

What does your partner think about dirty jokes?

Has your partner kissed another of the same sex sexually?

What does your partner think about heterosexuality?

What does your partner think about pornography?

What does your partner think about the size of your cock/tits?

What does your partner think of this book?

What does your partner think of you?

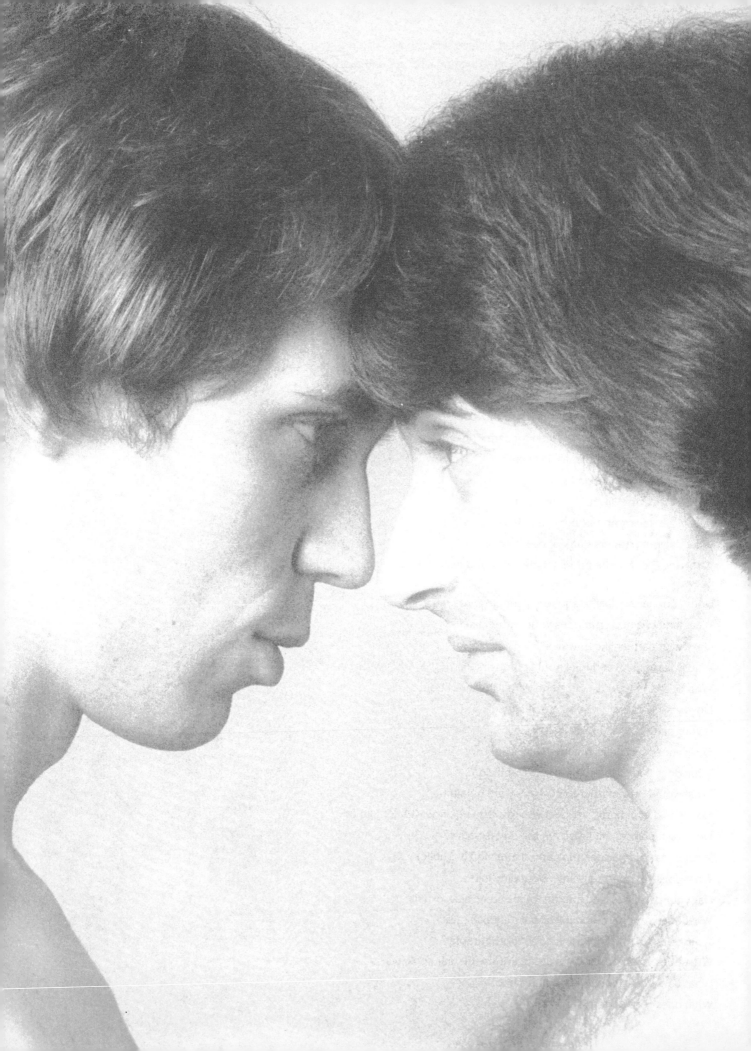

CONCLUSION

If you find that you can't talk about many of the issues raised here, maybe you are expecting too much of yourself or your partner. It takes time and practice to learn to trust another and yourself enough to communicate. You won't achieve it just by reading through this book.

Being able to communicate about sex can be a tremendous boon. It takes you away from those interior monologues that fill you with fear and uncertainty about how normal you are. Words can't explain everything, but talking about these taboo subjects can open you up to a more intimate relationship with another person. It is also a way to defuse the hush-hush, profane, and uncomfortable feelings you may have about sex.

If you have the opportunity, it can be very rewarding to open your discussions up to a circle of friends. You and your partner or friend might bring up topics you'd both like to know more about when others are present. The more you can share and compare sexual attitudes, feelings, and language, the more you'll realize how common and acceptable your own feelings are.

Connective Bargaining

INTRODUCTION

Communicating with a partner about sexual feelings won't necessarily make it a cinch to get along. Sharing and exchanging attitudes can't mitigate the fact that those may be different attitudes; and examining your different needs won't make such needs magically the same. Even people who are in strong, fulfilling relationships have different drives for sex, just as they do for success or sleep. Those differences have to be mediated whenever they become so central for the people involved that the relationship is stopped short.

Conflicts of sexual interest arise between couples no matter what their experience, age, sex, or background. These kinds of issues are not so much trouble for single people for several reasons. First and foremost, new or casual affairs tend to be so exciting that different drives and attitudes are glossed over in the rush to get to know someone sexually. Then, too, a problem with one partner doesn't seem too serious if you have other partners you care for just as much. Also, it isn't necessary for you to try to work things out when you have nothing at stake. A casual or passing relationship doesn't provide much impetus to change.

Even if you aren't in a relationship now, however, you should be aware of the kinds of issues that can arise and what can be done to alleviate them. You may be in such a situation one day, or you may wish to review your past to see if the reasons you couldn't get along with a past partner have anything to do with your expectations that he or she would have the same responses as you.

If your relationship is with two or more people, or with a person of the same sex, you'll have the same problems. Any people involved sexually occasionally have trouble with their different drives. Although such differences are perfectly tolerable much of the time, when you can't talk about them or change them they get in your way.

"Drive" in this chapter really constitutes a variety of elements that make you want to have sex—including a need for communication with a partner, a need for release or relaxation, a desire to escape or be dependent. Even the "drive" for food has multiple facets people might disagree on. You or your partner might want to eat on the run or sitting down, when you first get up or not until noon, in bed or in the kitchen.

One of you might like lima beans, cheeseburgers or licorice even though the other doesn't. There's more to "drive" than hunger.

The difference between sexual drive and the drive for food or money, for example, is that you can usually talk about, even yell about, eating habits and buying patterns a lot easier than you can talk about sexual hunger or spending yourself sexually. Talking in itself isn't an automatic cure, but it is a beginning. And it sets the stage for acting in the new or different ways you've discussed.

The goal here is to treat sex as natural and sexual differences as less than signs of inadequacy, restlessness, rigidity, or moral turpitude. Sexual behavior can be all those things. But before you look for what is going on behind the scenes, look at what is going on in front of your eyes. It is natural but misleading to generalize from your own experience. People are different and sexual pleasures are often beyond the range of any one person's experience.

Now we'll look at some people who are having trouble getting along because they don't recognize or accept their legitimate differences. As your own sex therapist, take the role of each participant and examine what your own feelings and suggestions might be in their places. Even if you have no experience remotely like theirs, try to put yourself into the situation. You can learn how to help yourself by what you learn about helping others. At the end of each case history is a chance for you to work on a case that is similar to the one presented.

CASE HISTORY A

Helen and Tommy have been living together several years. When they get home from work Helen always likes sex before dinner. Tommy is hungry when he gets home and he'd like to have sex later or on weekends. In the beginning he went along with Helen but more and more lately he's been holding out. Helen is complaining that he's just not interested in her. Is she right?

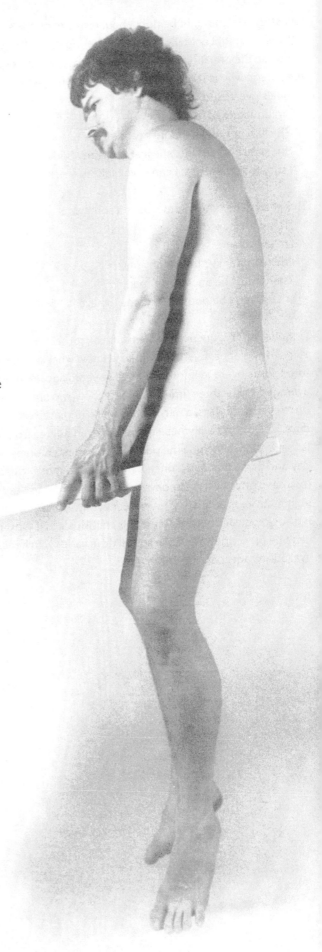

His story Helen might be right about him, but on the surface it looks as if the issue might actually be one of differing drives that weren't apparent when their relationship was new. Here are some examples of what the person who is less interested in sex than his partner has to say:

"She's oversexed."

"I'm undersexed."

"She'll wear me out before my time."

"She doesn't want me, she just wants my body."

"I should respond but I can't even fake it."

Her story The other partner sees it somewhat differently:

"He's undersexed."

"I'm oversexed."

"I'm not attractive to him any more."

"There must be another woman."

"I need it and he doesn't want me to have it."

Negotiating Frequency problems are extremely common in relationships at all stages. Everyone wants to know what is normal. Kinsey ventured some average figures twenty-five years ago. People under thirty averaged coitus three times a week, at thirty two times a week, at forty once every four days, at fifty once a week, and at sixty once every twelve days. The trouble with these figures, or even figures from other studies, is that averages include the people who had intercourse three times a day and those that had it once a month. Even those who do average intercourse once every four days could do it by having sex twice on every eighth day or four times every sixteenth day. Averages may be interesting sociologically but they aren't for individuals to live by. Frequency can't be prescribed, because sexual drive varies with health, stress, availability, age, partner, and so on.

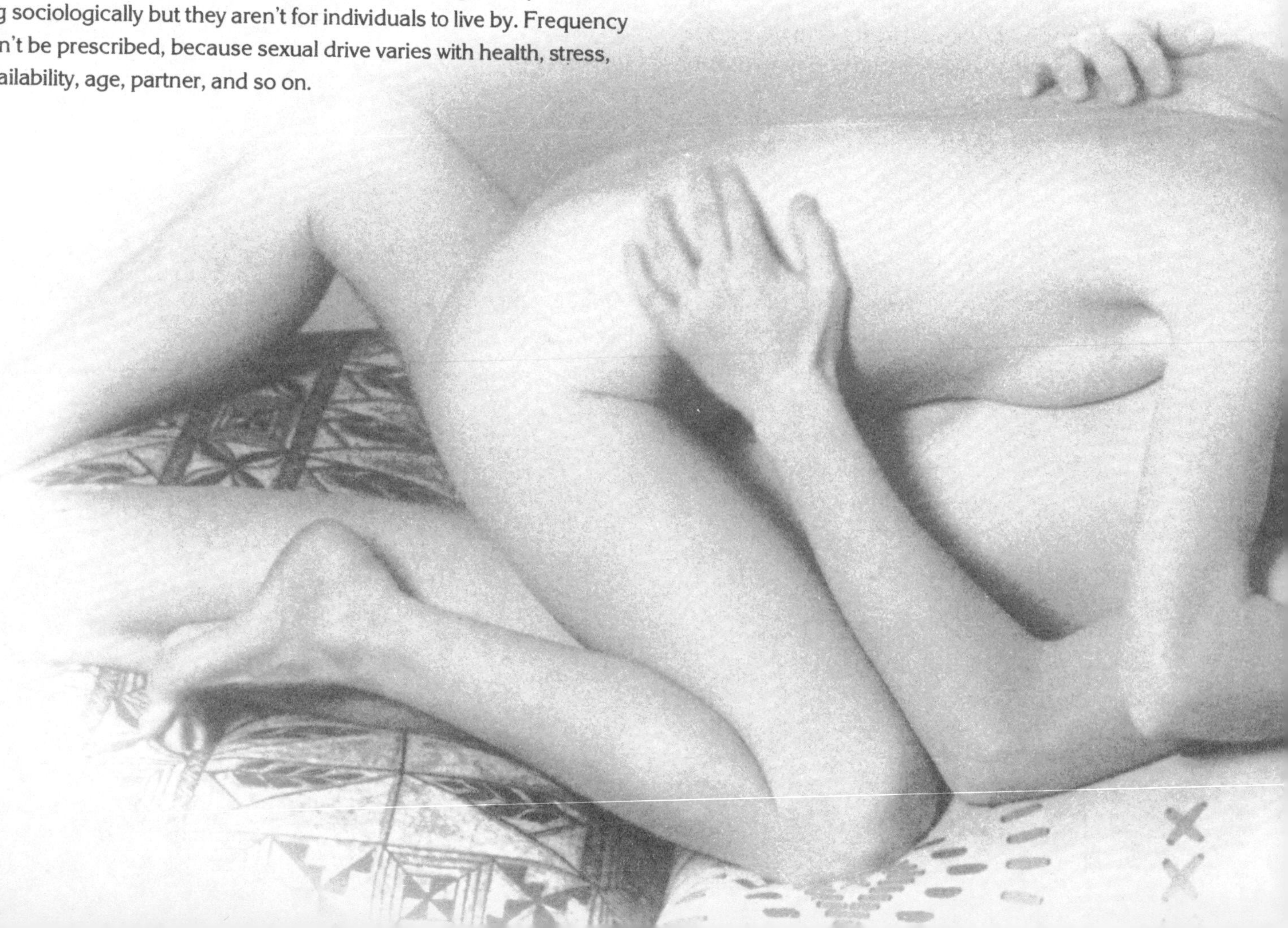

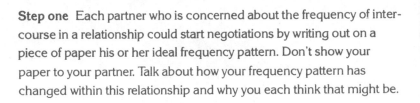

Step one Each partner who is concerned about the frequency of intercourse in a relationship could start negotiations by writing out on a piece of paper his or her ideal frequency pattern. Don't show your paper to your partner. Talk about how your frequency pattern has changed within this relationship and why you each think that might be.

Step two Without revealing your ideal pattern (which is just for your own reference), attempt to reverse roles with your partner concerning your present pattern. If you are the one who wants sex less, take the position of wanting it more, and vice versa. Try to explore the feelings of inadequacy, dependency, and anger your partner may have toward you. Ask your partner to examine your position by playing your role.

Step three Sometimes knowing how your partner feels and learning that his or her position is justified will make it easier to accept a change in frequency patterns. One kind of a change is a compromise in which each partner retains rights and gives in to some of the other's rights. It may be that one partner would agree to weekday sex if it were in a different room or position each day. One partner might give up some weekday sex in exchange for more oral sex on weekends. You can be creative as well as fair in striking a bargain. If you can't arrange something fair within the sexual realm, you can trade off other favors for sex.

Comments This compromise solution may seem like an awfully economic view of sexual relations, but it could be the best way for you two to reach a compromise. If you ask your partner to do something he or she doesn't want to do, you ought to be prepared to do something extra or out of the ordinary yourself. This is a simple kind of solution you probably use every day with other less loaded issues.

  If, in your discussions, role reversals, and attempts at compromise, you find that you can't reach agreement about anything, back off for a while. Bring the subject up later for discussion. It is possible that you are acting out in your sexual lives problems that really aren't sexual at all. But you needn't jump to that conclusion until you have sincerely tried to resolve a possible difference in drive.

CASE A-1

Let's go back to Case A and reverse it. Here or in your journal write out what would or could happen if the man wanted sex before dinner and the woman wanted to wait until the weekend. Chart what the feelings on both sides might be and how these people could negotiate about the problem. Although the reasons will be very similar to those expressed in the original case, you may find that changing the sexes brings up more pertinent or controversial feelings for you. If you'd prefer to use a frequency problem of your own instead of a simple reversal, do so. Just to get you started, here are some opening remarks:

His story Here is a chance for you to add some reasons you might want sex more than your partner:
  "We only do it when she wants to now."
  "Sex helps me wind down after a hard day on the road."
  "_____"
  "_____"

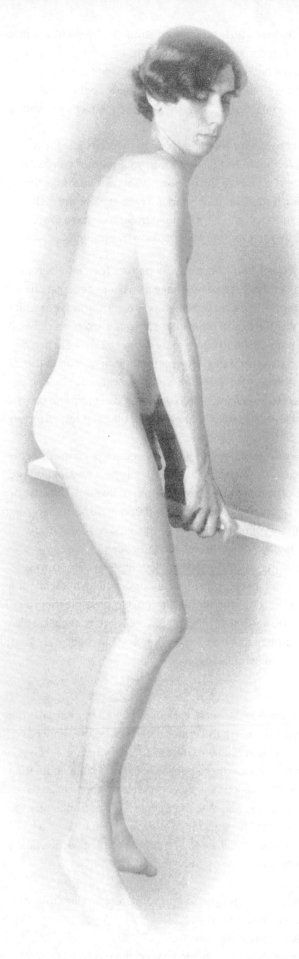

Her story Use your own experience or imagination to fill in here.

"We always have sex when he wants to."

"Even if I have a big lunch I'm hungry when I get home from work."

"_____"

"_____"

Negotiating For this part, go over the steps outlined in the original Case A to see if they can be used or modified for this slightly different situation. Also, refer to the quotations for new material that needs negotiating. Use your journal or the space below to work this case out.

_____

_____

_____

CASE HISTORY B

Tina and Thomas have been going together for several months. Everything about their relationship is fine except that Thomas would like Tina to suck his penis now and then. He's pushed her head suggestively netherward, but she always artfully dodges his penis. He cares too much for her to force her, so he brought up the subject of oral sex over breakfast. It became clear that she didn't want to do it. She apologized. Can any more be done?

His story The first concern here is to find out why he wants her to do it. Below are some typical things men who like fellatio say about it:

"It's different than intercourse. It feels warmer and you have the direct pressure of the tongue and lips and even teeth."

"Giving a guy head is really a sign of caring."

"It really makes me feel good to have a woman working on me like that."

"I like it because it gives me a feeling that my penis is okay. If a partner likes it despite its size and smell, I don't have to be ashamed of it."

"If a woman will do that I feel she's kind of dirty or hungry and I guess I like that kind of woman."

Her story As you might have guessed, she sees it differently:

"I find that the taste, the smell, and the texture of semen really make me nauseous."

"I wouldn't mind so much if they didn't always want you to swallow it."

"The thrusting makes me gag and that scares me."

"Frankly, I don't really know how to do it."

"If I really loved the guy, I probably would."

"I feel humiliated doing that—like I'm a prostitute."

"What's in it for me? Just boredom, that's all."

"It's just not normal."

Negotiating Clearly, there are strong sentiments on both sides of this dilemma. Kinsey found that the longer people were together or the more experienced they were, the more likely they were to try to enjoy oral sex. But many people saw it then and see it now as a perversion. In most states there are still laws against sex acts that rule out the possibility of conception—even though underpopulation is no problem here and the Church is supposed to be separate from the state. Even what consenting adults do in private may be illegal. Although the laws against oral sex aren't invoked very often, they do reinforce the notion that there is something inherently evil about a very widespread practice.

In the quotations above attention is mainly on the physical and symbolic aspects of fellatio, which are what you come down to once you recognize that it isn't uncommon. The symbolic issues of dominance and subservience may lie behind the praise of sensations or the complaint about smell, but it is easiest to deal directly with the physical aspects first. Sometimes this is the best way to reach the symbolic issues as well.

Step one Both partners should examine what is really involved in fellatio with a mind to knowing what they are actually asking for or turning down. For example:

A man can:

1. Start slowly by letting the woman find a comfortable position, her own pace, and style.

2. Guide her verbally and non-verbally before and during oral sex so that she'll know what she is doing right.

3. Spruce up your penis with a little soap and water beforehand.

4. Any kind of thrusting or demanding motions may scare your partner, make it hard for her or him to breathe, cause their mouth and lips to get numb, make them lose interest. Let yourself be aggressed upon.

5. If your partner doesn't want you to come in their mouth, pull out before you do. Sometimes a partner is afraid you'll come despite your best intentions, so give yourself a margin of error until you both have confidence in you.

6. Don't ask your partner to do something you wouldn't do yourself. If you'd like her to taste or swallow your semen, be sure you've tried it yourself.

A woman (or another man) can:

1. Start out by looking at, touching, washing, kissing, licking his penis before you put it in your mouth.

2. A comfortable position for you may be kneeling between his spread legs while he is lying down. This will give you room to move as you wish and to pull away if you need a little break.

3. Don't try to take the whole penis in your mouth. Concentrate on stimulating the frenulum and tip with your tongue. Use your lips and an up-and-down motion around the shaft. You can also touch his balls and perineum with your fingers.

4. Get directions from him but set a pace and motion that is comfortable and stimulating to you, too.

5. If you want to take his semen in your mouth but you don't like the taste, texture, or smell, you could fill your mouth with something you do like, such as ice cream, honey, cream of wheat—anything soft and mushy that will slide around in your mouth.

6. If you'd like to have your partner come in your mouth, but you don't want to swallow the semen, you can always spit it out. Incidentally, swallowing semen won't hurt you, but if you'd rather not, don't.

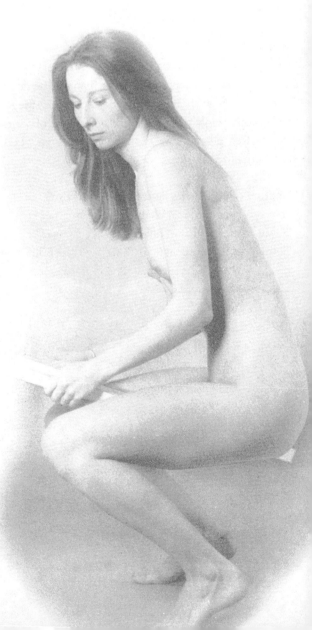

Step two If you feel that there are still issues of power unresolved by trying oral sex, you can try some role reversals to explore your partner's feelings of humiliation, adulation, importance, or boredom during oral sex. For instance, if your partner feels put down by oral sex, tell him or her why you agree. Even if the position seems untenable to you, try to maintain it. That is the best way to empathize with another person.

Step three If trying oral sex and reversing roles still leaves something desired, see if any kind of compromise can be made between you. The man could decide he didn't really like it all that much or the woman could find that it really could be exciting for her, but it is also possible to settle for something in between. She could say she likes sucking the penis but only occasionally. He could offer to give her oral sex, if she likes it, whenever she gives it to him. If she doesn't like oral sex herself, she might prefer a night out in exchange. And so on.

Comments These experiments and bargains all presuppose a willingness on the part of both partners to share their feelings, to accept each other, and to try to work out a way to keep any sexual difference from being something you can't negotiate. If you feel at any time that one or both of you is being pushed into a corner, forget the whole thing for a while.

CASE B-1

Now try on your own to negotiate the reverse of this case. This time assume the woman wants to fellate the man and he doesn't want her to. Think of things each might say, what techniques they could try, how reversing roles might help them, and what kinds of bargains they could arrange. Rely on your own experience or feelings when you can. To start, here are a few ideas:

Her story Women who like to give oral sex say,
  "I'm very orally erotic. Fellatio arouses me."
  "Other men I've known have really liked it."
  "It makes me feel so virile to swallow all those little sperm."
_____
_____

His story And men who don't like it say,

"I'm afraid she'll bite me."

"That's not something I want from a woman I'd like to marry."

"It's embarrassing."

Negotiating Now describe here or in your journal what you would do or recommend that they do in order to reach an understanding.

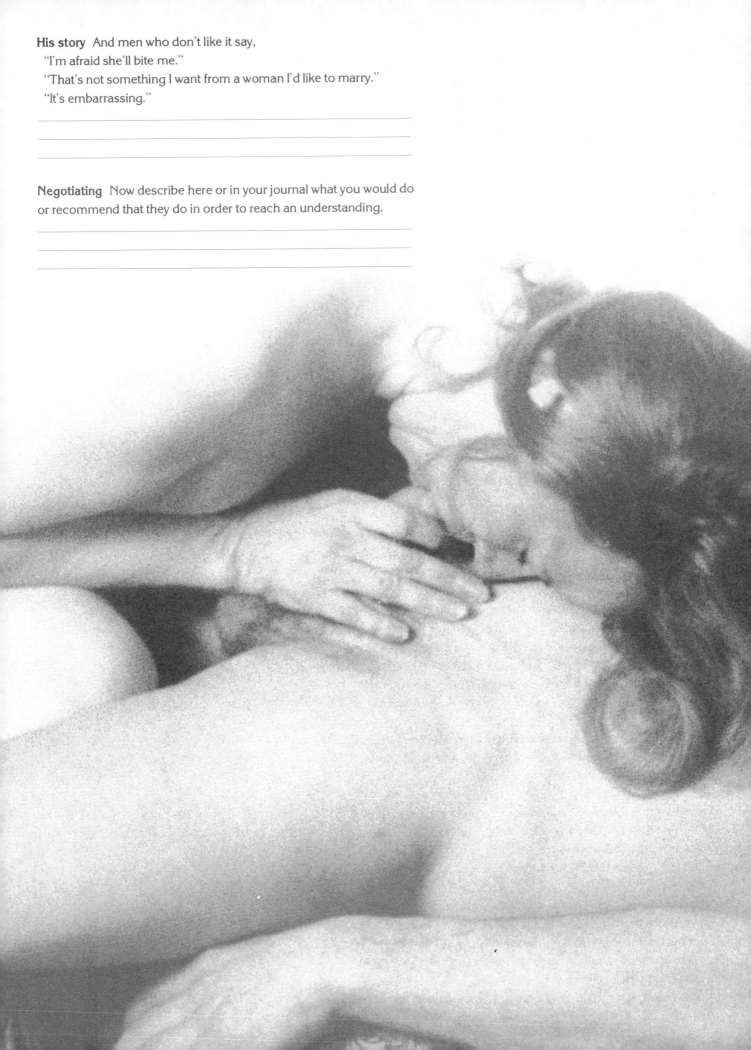

CASE HISTORY C

Mandy and Norman have been married for two years. One day Norman walks in on Mandy masturbating. Norman is absolutely horrified. Mandy says that every now and then the desire to masturbate comes over her and she didn't see any reason to make a big deal out of it. He wonders why she didn't tell him. Is there any way for them to see eye to eye?

Her story Consider some of the reasons a woman might not think that masturbation is a rebuff to her partner:

"I've always masturbated. I guess I started when I was about eight and I still like it."

"I find masturbation a good way to relax."

"Masturbation seems like a good idea when your partner is busy or isn't interested in sex."

"I need more sex than my partner and masturbation is easy."

"I just like the sensation. It's different from intercourse."

"I like the feeling that I can do it for myself and I don't have to be dependent on a man."

His story Here are some thoughts men express when they find out their partner masturbates:

"Aren't I enough for her?"

"She's abnormal. Women don't have to masturbate the way men do."

"I wonder if she'd let me watch."

"I don't masturbate any more, so why should she?"

"I wouldn't mind so much if she'd told me."

"If I'd known she was horny, I'd have been happy to oblige her."

"If you can't trust her at home, can you trust her anywhere?"

Negotiating Communicating about sexual feelings and attitudes makes you less surprised or hurt by something like this. Norman feels left out and robbed of his husbandly role. He may like the idea that Mandy is dependent on him for sexual pleasure and feel inadequate if she "has to" masturbate. But for her, masturbation may be natural and not at all a sign that she loves him less or enjoys sex with him less.

Step one Norman needs to be reassured that Mandy cares for him and she needs to know that he can accept her. They have to talk over whether sex between them is satisfactory.

Step two Reversing roles now can give each partner a chance to identify with the needs and experiences of the other. They have to evaluate such ideas as masturbation is disloyal, fun, or abnormal. They have to try to find things in each other's positions to respect.

Step three In changing roles, either partner could decide that the other had a strong case worth going along with. Mandy might decide that whenever she felt interested in masturbation she'd invite Norman to join her or to watch her. Norman might decide that he'd just leave Mandy alone and knock before entering her room. They could also decide that she would masturbate only when he was out of town or that he

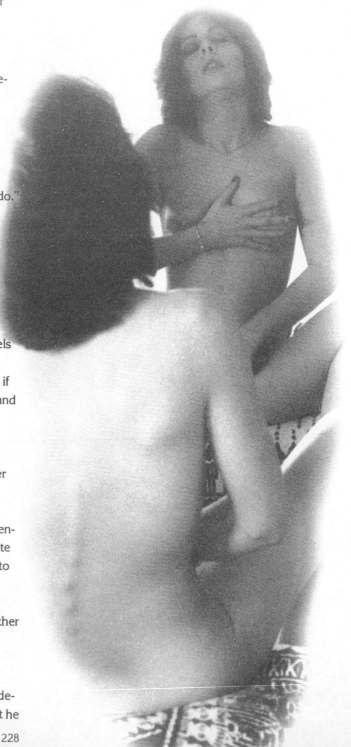

would masturbate too. Norman might decide to forget it. In that case, perhaps Mandy would do something for him.

Comments People have different dependency needs in relationships and these manifest themselves in different ways. You have to be sensitive to these changing needs in your partner. Since women reach their peak of sexual drive generally much later in life than men do, you can't expect your partner to always feel the same way about sex.

CASE C-1

How might things have been different if Mandy had walked in on Norman? Here or in your journal write out some of the feelings each may have had in this situation. If you think that the feelings and possible negotiations would have been very much the same the other way around, take the same case and assume that Norman wasn't at all shocked and that Mandy was terribly embarrassed and consumed with guilt. Tell how Norman might go about convincing her that he felt her masturbation was all right or how Mandy might decide not to continue.

His story _____
_____
_____
_____

Her story _____
_____
_____
_____

Negotiating _____
_____
_____
_____

CASE HISTORY D

Suzanne wants Charles to perform cunnilingus on her. All she's read or heard about oral sex makes her think that the gentle stimulation of a tongue would be more arousing than anything else. Charles isn't very interested.

His story Men have different reactions to going down on a woman. For example:

"Where I come from they call that 'being queer' on women."

"It's so dirty down there."

"It wears me out."

"What's in it for me?"

"I don't care for the taste."

"I can't breathe."

"Are you supposed to put your tongue in the vagina or should you use a vibrator or something?"

"It's not normal."

"The trouble is that she gets so wet and sloppy if I do that before we have intercourse, that I can't feel anything when we do get together."

Her story The woman who likes oral sex sees things differently:

"It feels so much more commanding than intercourse."

"I come in about two minutes that way and I take about twenty any other way."

"It's the best birth control method I know."

"I felt funny and self-conscious the first time, but now I just lose myself in it."

"If a partner will do that, he really cares."

"Wowwweeeeeee!"

"It makes me tingle all over."

"I feel freer when my partner goes down on me because he can't see my face."

Negotiating Once again there are physical and symbolic reasons behind both the interest and lack of interest in cunnilingus. In negotiating, it's best to start with the physical issues raised on both sides.

Step one As you learned in Case B, there are simple things you can do to make oral sex more enjoyable. The woman can let the man find a comfortable position and set a pace enjoyable for both. She can guide him with her voice and her hands to the clitoris and sensitive area around the lips. Some men don't realize that the vagina isn't particularly responsive. She can also be sure that she is clean and that she doesn't move or stay in a position that is difficult for him. And she can sample her own vaginal fluids and menstrual flow.

A man can look to see where he is going, find a good position for himself, ask for directions, and start slowly. If he gets tired, he can use a little manual stimulation for a while and then return to oral stimulation. If he doesn't feel ready to continue through orgasm, he can build up to that. A female partner can follow the same procedure.

Step two The partners can reverse roles to examine how it feels to be the other person. A partner who feels that women's bodies are dirty may have had an experience or history that gave credence to this prejudice. A partner who thinks that men are only interested in their own pleasure may not be giving anyone a chance to know what her pleasures are.

Step three If the man still needs persuading, maybe there is something the woman could do for him that would even things up. If he really finds cunnilingus impossible, maybe he shouldn't expect fellatio. Maybe after experimentation and communication this couple will decide oral sex is, or is not, for them.

Comments There is a general assumption abroad that no one likes to give oral sex and everyone likes to get it. That is not true at all, even though it may hold for some people. You really do have to find out how your partner feels, try to put yourself in his or her place, test the experience of oral sex for yourselves, and try to come up with a compromise or bargain that will satisfy you both.

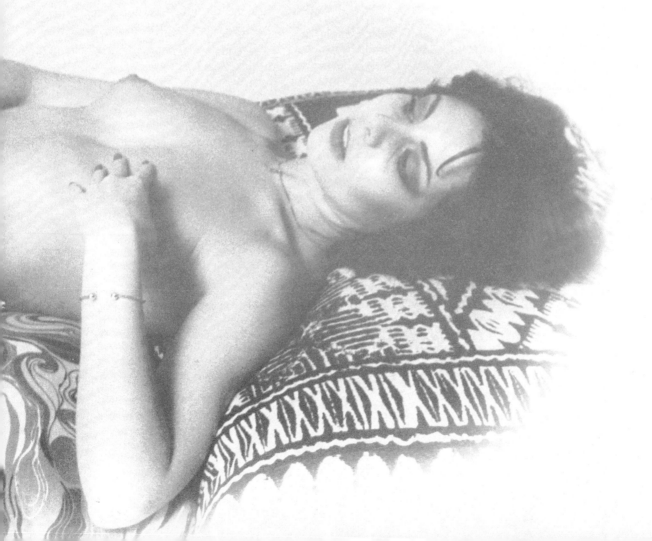

CASE D-1

To turn this story about, assume that Charles wants to try oral sex on Suzanne and she is reluctant.

Her story

"I don't like always being done to."
"I feel silly and remote with him on me like that."

_____

_____

_____

His story

"If she'd let me do it, she'd open a whole new world to herself."
"It makes me feel free."

_____

_____

_____

Negotiating In working out what these people can do to explore their conflicts of interest, put yourself in both their places and see what you could do.

_____

_____

_____

CASE HISTORY E

Carrie likes to have sex with the lights on and Ned would prefer to make love in the dark. This is a constant problem for them and generally they trade off, lights on one time and off the next. That way neither of them is ever happy at the same time. Is this necessary?

Her story This kind of compromise might be best, but not without some attention to the reasons behind their preferences:

"I like to see what's going on, where I am, who I'm with. It makes sex more real for me."
"I'm aroused by the sight of our nude bodies."
"I always had a light on in my room growing up and I just feel more comfortable that way."
"I like to watch my partner's face."

His story

"It's hard to fantasize with the lights on."
"It's touch that really arouses me. I get distracted with the lights on."
"It's more romantic in the dark."
"I feel shy with the lights on."

Negotiating These kinds of small potatoes probably cause more trouble than the bigger, more dramatic differences couples have because they can be constant annoyances. Although such differences may cover up real power struggles, you can first take them at face value and see if you can't give them their due. Some people assume that there aren't reasons for such preferences except orneriness, but that isn't necessarily true.

Step one Talk to your partner about your feelings. One who is turned on visually may never have thought that someone could be aroused by smell, and vice versa. It's that old thing of thinking that everyone—especially someone you love and who loves you—is going to like exactly the things you do, want the things you do, need the things you do.

Step two Reverse roles to see if you can articulate your partner's preference in your own words. Maybe he or she isn't so odd, after all.

Step three Some compromises besides lights on and off might be dim lights, red lights, or flashlights. But you might decide that on and off wasn't such a bad idea at that.

Comments Although traditionally it has been men who are more stimulated by visual images, women can be too. A lot of what arouses you comes from your conditioning and what you have experienced before. Since people can always change, you may want to try something new.

CASE E-1
Instead of using lights this time, consider the same dilemma over some other common petty annoyance. For instance, one partner wants to be nude, the other doesn't. One partner wants to be under the covers, the other doesn't. Both partners really prefer to be on top. Take something that is or has been of concern to you.

Your story

_____
_____
_____

Your partner's story

_____
_____
_____

Negotiating _____

_____
_____
_____

CASE HISTORY F
Lillian and Syd haven't been together long, but already Syd wants to try anal intercourse. She can't see why he wants that. He tells her he isn't gay, he isn't unhappy with her in any way, he just wants to try it. What's to be done?

His story It's always possible that there is nothing to be done, but first, listen to this,

"Let's face it, the anus is smaller than the vagina and it feels snugger, gives you more friction."

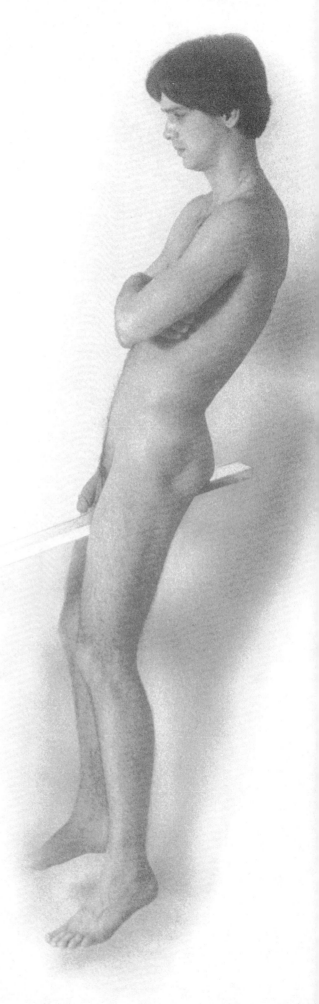

233

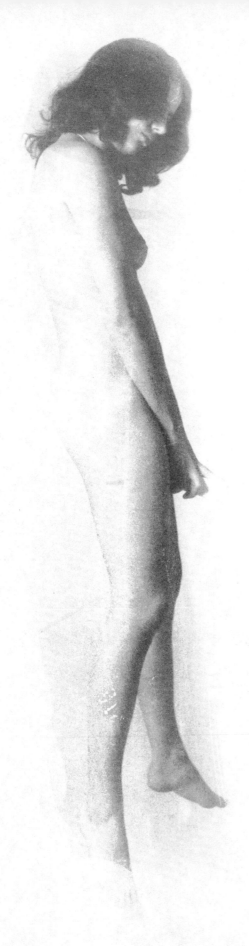

"The anus is kind of scratchy compared to the vagina and I think I like that little element of discomfort."

"I like the idea that she'll let me."

"I've known some women who really got off on that."

Her story Lillian really hasn't considered anal sex seriously before and neither have these women:

"I think you can get diseases that way."

"It will hurt."

"It's a filthy and unnatural practice."

"He wants to make me feel like a dog."

Negotiating Some people think that anal sex is a strictly homosexual practice, which it is not at all. In fact, many homosexuals find it as unappealing as heterosexuals do. But some people are more anally erotic than others. This is evidently due to more (and more sensitive) nerve endings in the anus and to conditioning. Some people find defecation and enemas more stimulating than other people do. It is true that contractions of the anal sphincter are common during sexual arousal, and orgasm and anal sex may increase that arousal in some people.

Step one There are some things you can do to make anal sex more appealing and easier. The man can be sure his partner is comfortable and that both the anus and the penis are well lubricated with sterile jelly. If the anus is tight, he can hold a finger in it until the anal sphincter relaxes (which may take several tries). He can enter the anus very slowly under directions from the partner. If the partner is uncomfortable, he can stop or pull out until and if she or he feels ready to try again. If you are going to move from the anus into the vagina, you should wash your penis thoroughly. It is easy to transmit disease going that way.

  A woman, or another man, can apply the lubricant and suggest comfortable positions. Some partners prefer entry from the front because that gives more stimulation to what is up front. You should never pretend it doesn't hurt if it does. Let your partner know what you are feeling. If it seems impossible, don't continue. The anal sphincter will usually relax in a few moments, but if it doesn't, don't continue.

Step two Reverse roles to experience, as much as possible, what anal sex is like for each of you.

Step three The fair exchange for trying anal sex may be another kind of sex, doing the dishes, whatever you feel is right.

Comments Although anal sex may be uncomfortable if rushed or forced, it needn't be if the active partner is careful and gentle and the more passive partner is sexually aroused. If it doesn't seem arousing or comfortable, maybe it isn't for you.

CASE F-1

It is possible that a man would like some kind of anal stimulation from a woman partner. Imagine a case in which he would and the woman would be unwilling to do it. It is also possible that the woman wants anal sex and he is reluctant to try it. You might want to write out that case.

His story

_____
_____
_____

Her story

_____
_____
_____

Negotiating _____
_____
_____
_____

CASE HISTORY G

Melissa and Theresa are in their thirties. They found each other five years ago and have lived in harmony ever since. Lately, however, Theresa has expressed an interest in Melaney, a woman they both know who is free right now. Theresa would like to initiate a threeway relationship for a while and see how it would work out. Melissa is hurt and wary. What do you think?

Melissa's story   Melissa is in the familiar role of the person in any relationship who is content with things as they are and would like to keep them that way,
 "If my partner wants more, I'm not enough."
 "This is my partner's way of replacing me."
 "I don't want to hear about her affairs."
 "I think I'll have an affair myself."
 "I absolutely can't handle it—it's her or me."
 "I guess I should be glad she wants me in on it, too."
 "I think affairs are a lot of trouble."
 "I think they're dangerous."

Theresa's story   Many people would assume that Theresa is discontented with Melissa, else she wouldn't want to run around. That could be, but Theresa doesn't necessarily think so.
 "I have a primary relationship but I like casual sex."
 "I don't think that just because you are 'married' you aren't attracted to other people any more."
 "Sex isn't all there is to love."
 "If my partner will join me in this, I won't feel guilty doing it."
 "I guess I'm not really monogamous."
 "I just want to try it."

Negotiating It's not easy to negotiate what may be the most volatile sexual conflict of all. No matter what your political or moral stand on extracurricular activities, the actual event may give rise to unexpected

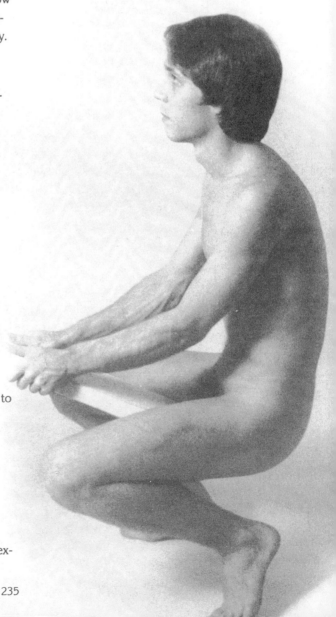

235

jealousies, inexplicable entanglements, and unforeseen feelings of loss, inadequacy, or anxiety. It would be fatuous to pretend that there is an easy solution to this age-old dilemma. Still, there are some preventive measures you can take.

Step one If you haven't talked to your partner about fidelity, do so now. You can't prevent an attraction from happening and you can't really make it happen, but you can have an idea what the consequences of taking action might be for your relationship.

It may appear that the homosexual life style is freer in this regard, but gay women have been raised, usually, to expect long-lasting relationships just like other women. And homosexual males also have longings to be dependent on just one other and to experience the trust and sharing implicit in a marriage. No matter what the primary relationship, including that of a group, outside sexual encounters can threaten that relationship. All persons concerned should know how before it happens.

There is also a general assumption that men can handle affairs and women can't, and that such institutionalized activities as swinging even everything out. Discuss with your partner how true these things are in your experience or how realistic they appear to be to you.

Step two If you pretty much agree on this issue, you may not have roles to reverse, but you might try anyway. Things do change. If you find it hard to get into a for or against role, experiment with a nonsexual friendship or business relationship that you don't share with your partner. Examine the feelings of rivalry that might arouse.

Step three Some compromises or bargains that could be made are to have an "open" relationship, not to tell each other about affairs, to share extra relationships or not to have them. If you can't really reach agreement about affairs, you may be able to decide to talk more about it.

Comments Your patience, understanding, and willingness to put yourself in your partner's place can make the consequences of infidelity more predictable.

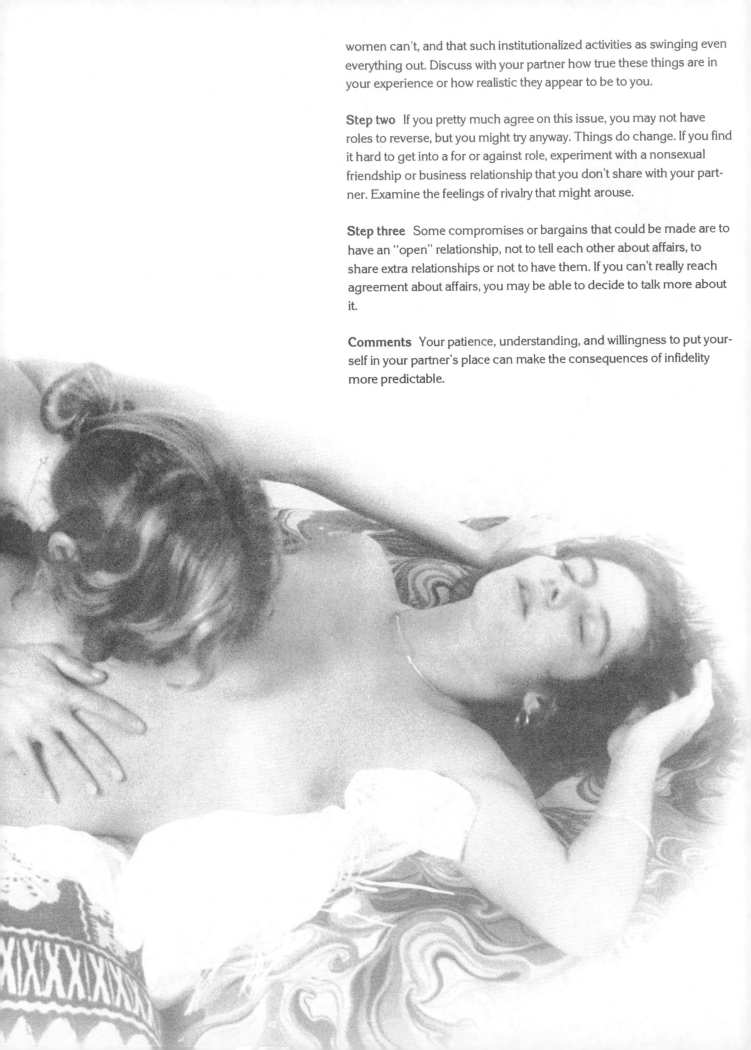

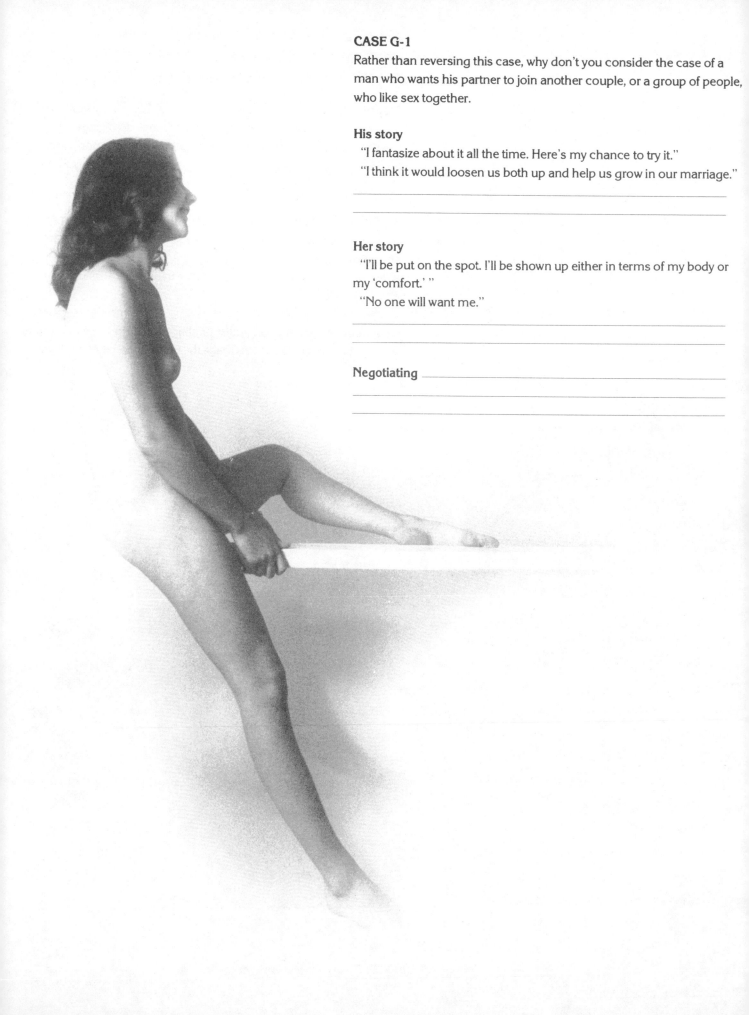

CASE G-1

Rather than reversing this case, why don't you consider the case of a man who wants his partner to join another couple, or a group of people, who like sex together.

His story

"I fantasize about it all the time. Here's my chance to try it."

"I think it would loosen us both up and help us grow in our marriage."

_____

_____

Her story

"I'll be put on the spot. I'll be shown up either in terms of my body or my 'comfort.' "

"No one will want me."

_____

_____

Negotiating _____

_____

_____

CONCLUSION

By testing yourselves and trying to accept that people have different needs, tastes, and drives, you may be able to take the conflict out of these and other differences you and your partner have. It is not uncommon for people to feel uncertain and uneasy about sexual behaviors and desires, including petty and seemingly minor ones.

If your differences appear to be irreconcilable despite all your attempts to be fair and empathetic, you may wish to put them aside. Sometimes, long-standing differences really cannot be resolved. To try to do so may raise more anxiety and conflict than you had before. You can always choose not to deal with something, especially when you've tried with genuine sincerity to figure out what's going on.

Sometimes conflicts can't be resolved because what they seem to be about isn't really what they are about at all. In that case you might be using sex to act out conflicts in the relationship which really have more to do with power, independence, or a lack of interest than they do with sex. The next chapter is about conflicts that aren't what they seem.

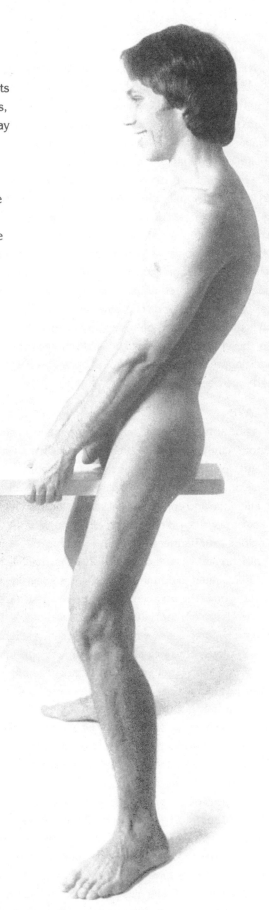

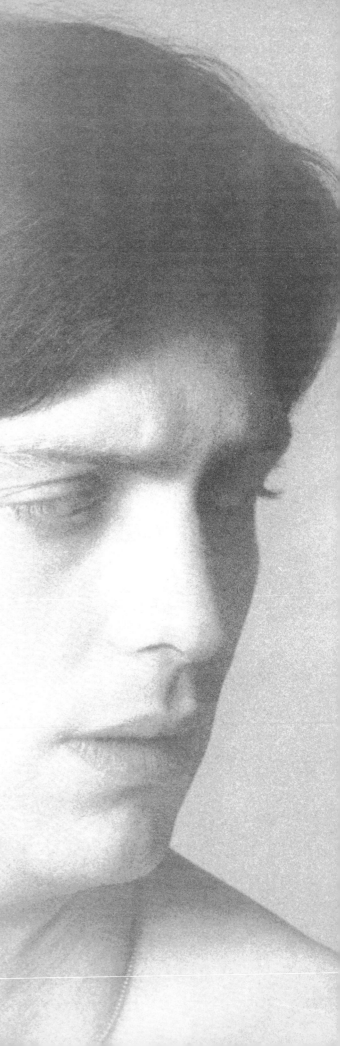

Running Battles

INTRODUCTION

If your sexual concerns and problems don't seem to be responding to your best efforts to follow the suggestions in this book, maybe sex isn't the central issue. It is perfectly natural to refer other problems to your sex life, but when these get mislabeled as sexual problems it is hard to improve the sex or the underlying issues.

Some examples of this mislabeling are using sex to act out power plays in relationships, using sex as a weapon against your partner or yourself, using your sex life as a dumping ground for all the other things that may be bothering you, or using sex to make up for things that are missing in the rest of your life. In order to see how this can be done, you have to look at your whole life and the non-sexual needs that you bring to sexual relationships.

In this chapter we'll look at why communicating and negotiating about sex won't always lessen conflicts between sexual partners. The self-questioning and testing techniques of sex therapy can often be successfully applied to other kinds of problems, especially in terms of identifying just what those problems are. Since this book can't cover everything, this chapter is limited to possible sources of trouble beyond sex, recognizing what else could be going on, and seeking outside help if you decide you need it.

POWER PLAYS

Domination and submission are natural components of sexual behavior. Although they supposedly break along sex lines, with men being dominant and women submissive, in fact a balance is evident in any successful sexual relationship. Each partner needs to feel that he or she has some influence and control sexually over what happens in the relationship. Power plays do go on through all relationships. You get your boss, your child, your partner to do what's best for you by overwhelming them with threats, wit, authority, reason, tears, guilt, disapproval, or approval. When a need to dominate or submit is so strong that there is rigidity and tension in the sexual relationship, you may have to examine how power needs are not met in your life.

One of the most obvious power issues in a sexual relationship is who initiates sex. Is it always the same person? Some people think that they just sort of fall into each other's arms or that sex just happens. But when does it "just happen" and where? Couples fall into routines without recalling how they got started. Sometimes there are subtle clues in how you look at each other, what you are wearing or talking about, that say sex is on the way. In trying to look at your own pattern, pay particular attention to who makes the first move and what kind of a move it is.

Just as there are many styles of initiation, so are there many interpretations of that style. The style may be straightforward, unconflicted. But it could represent something else. For instance, if you always initiate sex when there isn't time for it, you're assured of being one up on your partner. He or she has to turn you down despite guilt feelings about it. If you slip into something comfortable when you know your partner isn't interested in sex, you can make him or her feel bad or inadequate. If you say, "Let's fuck," to a partner who prefers a more romantic opener, you could be setting yourself up to be refused. If your approach is very vague and indirect, you can decide later what you meant, depending on what makes you look good.

Any approach can be perverted by a drive for power or a desire to be put down. Think about how you react to rejection, for example. You might sulk, withdraw, turn the other cheek, get scared. If there are some rewards for you in acting this way, you might have set yourself up for it. By pouting, you get sympathy or attention from your partner. Being able to get angry at your partner for turning you down sexually may make up for being angry about something else. If you get strength from martyrdom, being rejected may help satisfy that need.

A need to be dominant or submissive sexually may echo a need from another part of your life. If everyone at school or in the office has more status than you, you may only get some sense of power from lording it over your partner. If you have to take care of people all day at work or in the home, you might need to be taken care of by your partner. Now this could work out fine if your sex life is rewarding and your partner content to be your slave or master.

But if you feel all is not well, try examining just what does go on between you and your partner around the initiation of sex. If you would like to initiate more, talk to your partner about what prevents you. You may be afraid of imposing on your partner, but is that the whole story? Maybe you prefer being imposed upon. That could be the only way you feel free to really respond sexually. Guilt about sexual feelings in yourself may be negated only when someone else takes the responsibility for your arousal, when someone else overpowers you.

If you often feel put upon but are afraid to reject, you could want to hurt your partner and fear it'll get out of hand if you take to rejecting sexual advances. You could have a great fear of being left alone if you don't accept your partner. Your right to refuse if you don't feel interested in sex, or if you feel that your partner is using you, may be mixed up with issues that aren't really sexual.

Power struggles around initiation exist in casual as well as long-standing relationships. A frantic need to accept every sexual overture could represent a fear of loss in your life that is much more general than sexual. An irrational need to deny sex to a potential partner may symbolize a fear of not having control should you accept. If you don't have control elsewhere in your life, this could be your only power. If the rest of your life is unpredictable or too much in flux, you may hold onto power-seeking in your sex life because that's all you have.

People who feel compelled to overpower others sexually may be expressing powerlessness in general. Rape is an accurate, if extreme, example of using sex to make up for the anger and fear felt toward the world. For both men and women, aggression is a part of sexuality; but when that aggression is turned violently outward, as in rape or sadism, or inward, as in masochism, it may be an expression of rage, helplessness, or hostility toward society as a whole.

Sexual behavior in prison is often an example of the power struggle between men or women and the world that has incarcerated them. Homosexual rape in prison is not an expression of sexual need, even though homosexuality may be. The power implicit in rape is necessary for establishing the pecking order. If there weren't more to rape than sex, masturbation might suffice.

We all have in us the potential to hurt others or ourselves on many different levels. Squeezes, scratches, moans, and groans are evidence that it is possible to enjoy pain in the heat of a passionate exchange. Hurting another psychologically can range from the very serious to a minor kind of acting out that is easily absorbed in the relationship. But if you are hurting someone who doesn't want to be hurt, something could be seriously wrong.

Sometimes recognizing what you are doing is enough to get you started on new ways of acting. If you feel incapable of giving up your power struggle, you may wish to seek the help of an outside person such as a psychiatrist, a marriage counselor, or a minister. Certainly if you, or someone you know, is causing others physical pain, professional help is called for. We'll talk later in this chapter about how to find it.

SCAPEGOATING

When you start finding fault with your sex life or your partner even though they haven't changed lately, you may be dumping some garbage from other parts of your life into your sex life. Manifestations of this scapegoating might be that you aren't interested in sex any more, you're bored by your husband or wife, you're no longer thrilled by your lover. You might be doing this for legitimate reasons—you are bored. But it's possible that you are feeling upset about your work or family life and projecting that into your sex life. You could be worried about getting older, or poorer, or fatter, and your sex life suffers because you can't face those issues directly.

Scapegoating is bad for two reasons. It hurts your sex life and it keeps you from examining the more serious or real issues that are troubling you. A pattern of scapegoating may keep you from establishing a good sexual relationship because you'll always think sex, not something else, is what's wrong.

Excessively high expectations for your sex life may also encourage scapegoating. If you feel that sex is the answer to all your needs or that perfection can be achieved sexually, you'll blame sex for not living up to what you had in mind. The problem then is the high expectations and your reasons for them, rather than what is actually going on sexually.

Well, if you are scapegoating your sex life, how are you to know it? How can you distinguish between real sexual problems and those that are masking something else? For one thing, real sexual concerns will respond to the suggestions outlined throughout this book. If you still feel things aren't right with you sexually, despite your devoted attention to all the exercises presented here, perhaps you aren't getting at something else in your relationship or your life that is bothering you.

Think about when you feel least interested in, most bored by, or impatient with sex. See if there are parallels to other things that are going on. Maybe you've had a lousy day, lost at poker, made a mistake of some kind. Perhaps you've recently discovered that you don't really like your work or your children. You might feel that you aren't getting anywhere in areas that would fulfill you professionally or personally. Your sense of emptiness or uselessness is carried over into your sex life.

It is certainly possible to be obsessed with a project that allows you no time or energy to think about sex. That may be all right for brief stretches but if it becomes your pattern to the detriment or deterioration of your sex life, maybe it isn't all right.

If you suspect that there is more to a loss of interest in sex than sex, you may want to ask someone for help in breaking a pattern of scapegoating sex. Sex therapy on your own or with a partner can make you more confident all around, but if that still leaves something uncovered, you may need more. Professional help from any good counseling service can be your guide to dealing directly with relationship or personal issues that are being unfairly relegated to sex.

WARFARE

Sometimes the same dilemmas that bring you to scapegoat sex will bring you to use sex as a weapon against yourself or a partner. In scapegoating you mask your true feelings. In warfare you lash out. Any one person may use both techniques. All these categories of the running battles you have with yourself or your partners overlap and collide in the same person.

In warfare, instead of losing interest in a partner, you might start picking on him or her. You decide that you don't like the way they kiss, how they approach you sexually, the way they smell, how they look. You natter away about their physical attributes or lack of same, their sexual interests and preferences. You complain about how often or how seldom they want sex, how they make love, and so on. These might be legitimate complaints, but not the way you deliver them.

All sexual dysfunctions can be used as weapons against a partner. Although most sexual dysfunctions are the result of misinformation, lack of self-knowledge, and bad habits, it is possible to use them to hurt another. You make your partner feel that he or she is inept so that their inability to erase your problem is their problem. Or you use dysfunctions to get a partner to feel sorry for you to the point of wanting to take care of you or be responsible for you. Dysfunctions also distance you. If you can't "perform" with someone, you may feel safe from getting involved with them or being vulnerable to them.

Unusual sexual practices such as voyeurism, exhibitionism, necrophilia, pedophilia, incest, sadomasochism, and bestiality may be examples of using sex as a weapon to frighten, hurt, or really harm another or yourself. Anyone who feels a compulsion to commit these acts, especially those involving unwilling victims, obviously needs professional help.

Other unusual, but not harmful, practices are homosexuality, transvestism, promiscuity, group sex, and fetishism. These may be used to shock others, especially parents or partners, but they can also be turned against the self, if needed. You might use your homosexuality, for example, as an excuse for not becoming involved with others sexually, whether heterosexual or homosexual.

Any use of sex as a weapon against yourself can be destructive to establishing good sex as well as good relationships. The person who complains that he or she can never get laid because they can't find the right person may not want to find a right person. Making sure that you aren't successful sexually may indicate a need to feel unsuccessful. Comfort with discomfort may be something learned at your mother's knee or it may be something that covers up the guilt or fear you feel about sex. Punishing yourself is an escape from that involvement, guilt, fear, whatever.

But discomfort isn't the only tactic. Take comfort, for example. The

super stud, the sexpert, the touchy-feeler all use superior comfort to put others at a distance. By appearing to be sexier-than-thou, they may avoid sex altogether. If you seem very at ease with sexual topics, you can inhibit others and make them feel uncomfortable. If you are always touching others suggestively or touching yourself to draw attention to your body, you may be manipulating a situation in order to make others feel self-conscious and impotent. Of course you can also use these formulas for seduction. It's all a matter of motivation.

Many people don't recognize that they are making others uncomfortable by being "open," "affectionate," "experienced," "knowledgeable," or even consciously flirtatious. You might think you were making others feel warm and cozy when actually what you are doing is making sure that you'll be warm and cozy.

Many of these routines aren't particularly bad. They are natural ways of defending yourself in unfamiliar circumstances. But if you do them over and over again, you may be trapped in a running battle with yourself. Naturally you want to protect yourself at times, but if this is at the expense of your sex life, you could give it up. If you feel you need help changing that pattern, you may wish to seek outside help from a sexually uninvolved friend or professional counselor.

SEXUAL SURROGATES

When things aren't going too well for you it may be very tempting to fill in your empty places with sex. Sex can be a good escape or substitute. It can restore your confidence and offer a breather. But it can also be a way of sidestepping confrontation. Take fights between partners which end in sex—the "kiss-and-make-up syndrome." This may be just what was needed to forgive and be forgiven. But it could be using passion and sexuality to avoid whatever you were fighting about.

A similar sexual surrogating pattern is that of turning to sex when all else fails. You try to talk to your spouse, to explain your feelings, ask for help, or complain, and you find that it is easier just to turn your partner on. You may go around feeling full of internal monologues and unspoken resentments, but that may be better for you than trying to figure out what else could be wrong. It's not that uncommon for couples to tell counselors that the sex is just fine—it's everything else between them that is bad. Sex is seemingly their refuge.

Affairs may also be a refuge, a good way to eclipse every other thing going on. Affairs sometimes grow out of the realization that no one person can be all things to another. Other times you don't stop to think that what is missing in your primary relationship isn't just sex.

The trouble with affairs as substitutes for what is lacking in a marriage or relationship is that they can be complicated. It's not usually a simple matter of deciding that you can get such-and-such from that one, something else from another, and still more from a third. There is too much invested in sexual relationships—possession, dependency, love, and desire—not to experience some overlapping and confusion. Even if you are perfectly clear about what you want and what you are doing, you can't count on your lover or spouse finding it all as acceptable as you do. Perfection is for your regular partner to have an affair at the same time you do and even that could be a very fragile arrangement.

The need to have other people make up for what is missing in a marriage or long-term relationship may be an inability to find in yourself the resources not to need surrogates. A certain amount of playing around and reestablishing your desirability may be totally acceptable; but if it is a continual pattern, you may be missing something else that is happening to you. A string of affairs may mean that your search for the "right" person is a way of avoiding finding any right person. Always messing around and longing for more may symbolize a longing inside you to fill in empty places sex can't touch. The restlessness of always thinking the grass will be greener may have something to do with your inability to look at yourself and your situation with any honesty.

In order to think about where sex and other values fit into your life, think about friends and lovers you have or have had, what you get from them, and what you don't get from anyone. Make checks on the chart below or on a piece of paper inserted in that space. There is room for you to add "values" and you can fill in the people slots over and over.

VALUES	Friend No. 1	Friend No. 2	Friend No. 3
Empathy			
Thrills			
Conversation			
Sex			
Intellectual stimulation			
Looks			
Food			
Money			
Spirituality			
Kids and family			
Professional stimulation			
Fun			

Of course friendships, let alone love affairs, cannot be reduced to a chart. But when you look over what you get from friends and lovers, you may be able to see whether or not your sexual relationships correlate with other values for you. If they don't, are you content with having things that way? Is your partner? Are you willing not to find everything in the same person?

Sex isn't the only determinant in any relationship. It isn't any more important than anything else, but if it becomes more important, you may find that you are using sex to make up for a lack of adventure and excitement, a paucity of status and prestige, or a need for warmth and security. And when psychic longings are translated into sexual needs, you may never find sex very satisfying.

Sexual substitutions can be valuable and no risk for some people. But if you think you are using sex to make up for something you don't have elsewhere, you may be being unfair to yourself and to your partners. If seeing that makes you able and willing to change, you may find you can break the pattern on your own. If seeing it only reminds you that you are in a rut, perhaps you need to think about a kind of therapy in which you could examine your need for seeking surrogates.

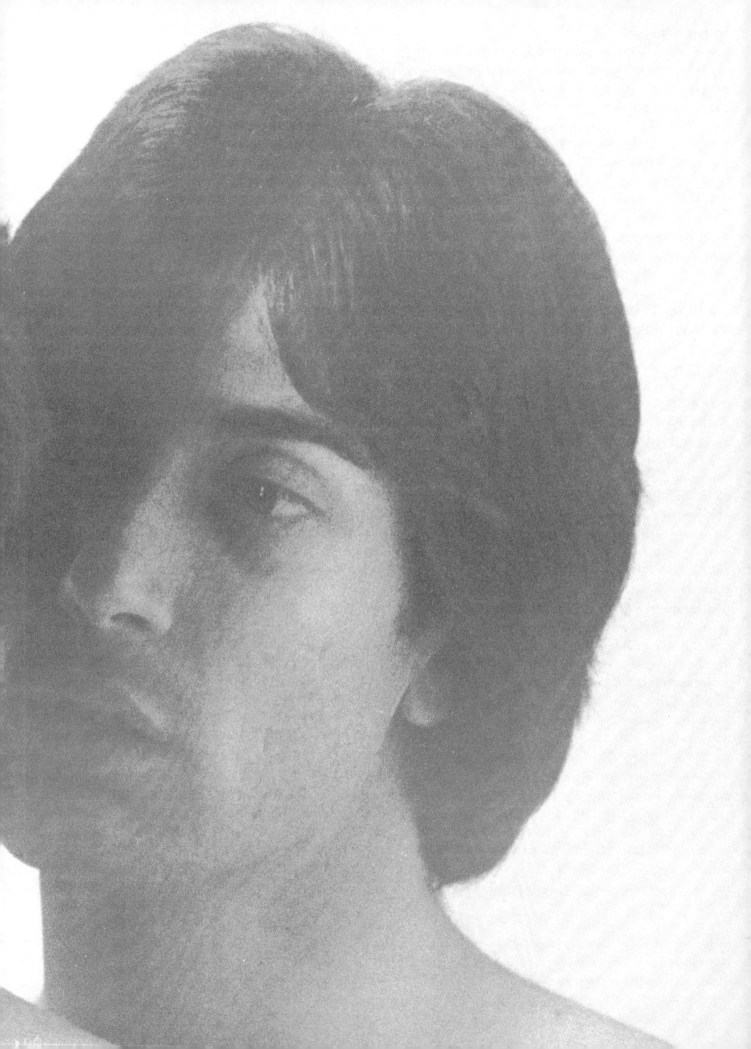

TO THE RESCUE

How do you go about getting extra help if you feel you need it? Many people are reluctant to seek professional help because they hear (1) that it means something is terribly wrong, (2) that it's expensive, (3) that it augurs years of therapy. Actually, if you have an idea of what you need from your work here and what your limits are in terms of time and money, you can find the kind of help you need. For example, most cities have clinics that offer low-fee psychotherapy. You may not find low-fee sex therapy, but then sex therapy doesn't usually take as long as other kinds of therapy.

The first thing you should try to find is a clinic or an individual who will give you what is called an in-take interview. Sometimes there is no charge for this service, sometimes a standard or sliding fee is charged. You can find out before you go. The purpose of an in-take interview is for you to talk about what is troubling you and for the interviewer to explain how that need may be met. You also talk about fees, insurance coverage, number of sessions, and so on. If the interviewer is reluctant to go into these things or does not offer the kind of service that appeals to you, you should look further.

To find the place or person where you can have an in-take interview, you have three options. First of all, ask your friends for the names of psychologists, social workers, sex therapists, marriage counselors, ministers or psychiatrists. If someone you know has a recommendation for you, you may feel safer and more comfortable following that lead than going out on your own. If you feel self-conscious going to someone a friend goes to, ask that professional for a reference.

Secondly, try your local phone book. Check in the yellow pages under counseling centers and mental health clinics. Look under local, state, and federal listings for public health services and social welfare organizations. Call local colleges and universities to see if they offer outpatient counseling or psychological services. Check to see if there is a Family Service Agency, a Mental Health Association or a branch of the National Association of Social Workers in your area.

Next, try your local library and newspapers. Look for announcements from free clinics and hot lines in the papers. Ask your librarian to check local members of the American Association of Marriage and Family Counselors, the American Psychological Association, the American Psychiatric Association, the American Association of Sex Educators and Counselors, and other organizations, such as the American Association of Pastoral Counselors or Planned Parenthood.

There is no guarantee that the first person you go to will be the right person, and you can't know if you'll decide this right away or after a few sessions. Some people fall into a pattern of never being able to find the "best" or "right" therapist. It's sort of like looking for the "right" partner. You may not want to find them. But give yourself leeway so that you don't feel stuck with a counselor who really doesn't help you at all. You need someone who can speak to your problem, someone toward whom you feel open.

There is a saying that most people get better whether they are in therapy or not. Although that is probably true, just because crises and depression seem to be somewhat cyclical in most of us, that doesn't mean that therapy can't help you come out of a crisis with a better purchase on your life than you'd have without it.

Certainly anyone who feels compulsive about their sex life or obsessive about sexual acts that bring harm to others should seek therapy. If you feel rewarded by hurting others, if it is something you cannot stop doing, you must tell someone who can either help you or find help for you.

CONCLUSION

The purpose of this chapter is to have you reflect a little on how you might be using sex for non-sexual ends. Everyone does this to some extent, possibly to the enhancement of the sexual life. But if it becomes a destructive pattern and you realize that other things are involved, you may need something other than sex therapy to set you straight. Everything else in this book to the contrary, sex is not the most important thing in the world. Even though being a conscientious self-therapist of any kind can help you recognize what is going on, you shouldn't feel that you have to do everything for yourself. Sometimes just a few sessions with an outside person will help you break through those running battles you have with yourself or with a partner.

An Erotic Life

INTRODUCTION

There are some underlying currents we haven't talked about yet in this book, even though they've been here all along. These currents are the everyday erotic experiences that don't lead to sex, are not genitally arousing, and may not be shared with or by anyone else. They exist in situations that give you a sexual charge even though they aren't necessarily sexual in themselves. To be aware of these currents, to be able to respond to them, is to have an erotic life.

You become aware of the erotic life in much the same way you become aware of your sexual attitudes and feelings. You try to be open and honest with yourself, you question what might be going on, and you experiment with different ideas and suggestions until you find out what is right for you. Being alert and responsive to the sexual energy in daily life calls for getting off the couch and into the world. Rather than concentrating on image, orgasm, and introspection, you open yourself to all the absurd and delightful ways to eroticize the outside world.

You might prefer to call this the sensual life, the sensuous life, or the sexy life; but whatever name you use, an erotic life is made up of finding sex in non-sexual settings. You can be turned on by a fleshy, fuzzy perfect peach or an unexpected glimpse of bare skin. You can be excited by the acting out of sexual roles in groups that are all the same sex. You find a painting, an idea, a motorcycle ride thrilling in a way that is akin to, if not exactly like, a sexual experience. Sexual energy is not just in your body or your head but in the world.

In the descriptions which follow, try to project yourself into the situation to see if there is anything in it for you. These are just suggestions and you may have some much better ones of your own. That which you find erotic is really whatever you wish to label erotic. You might try role-playing some of the examples here to see what, if anything, they do for you. If you have a partner, you can compare feelings. Sometimes knowing what others find erotic is in itself erotic.

Now you are under no obligation to become senselessly sensual over this. There is no need to adopt this erotic life style. Your assignment here is to find your own erotic life and to become aware of when and how you use it. There are no specific guidelines or standards for what or how much you eroticize.

THE EROTIC LIFE

Society allows us certain erotic symbols, such as rock stars, nudes, and cars. But to get an erotic shiver from a piece of raw meat or someone else's partner is not as widely accepted. Because you may feel embarrassed or guilty about these attractions, you may repress an awareness that an erotic life of any kind exists for you.

Yet it is possible to have a secret erotic life. There is no reason to be guilty about the erotic potential in your own observations and experiences. In fact, if you cut off this awareness you may be compartmentalizing your sex life and limiting it to mere genital pleasures.

Voyeurism

You are crossing a street or passing through a crowd where everyone seems to be looking at you. You find yourself focusing on certain bodies, parts of those bodies . . .

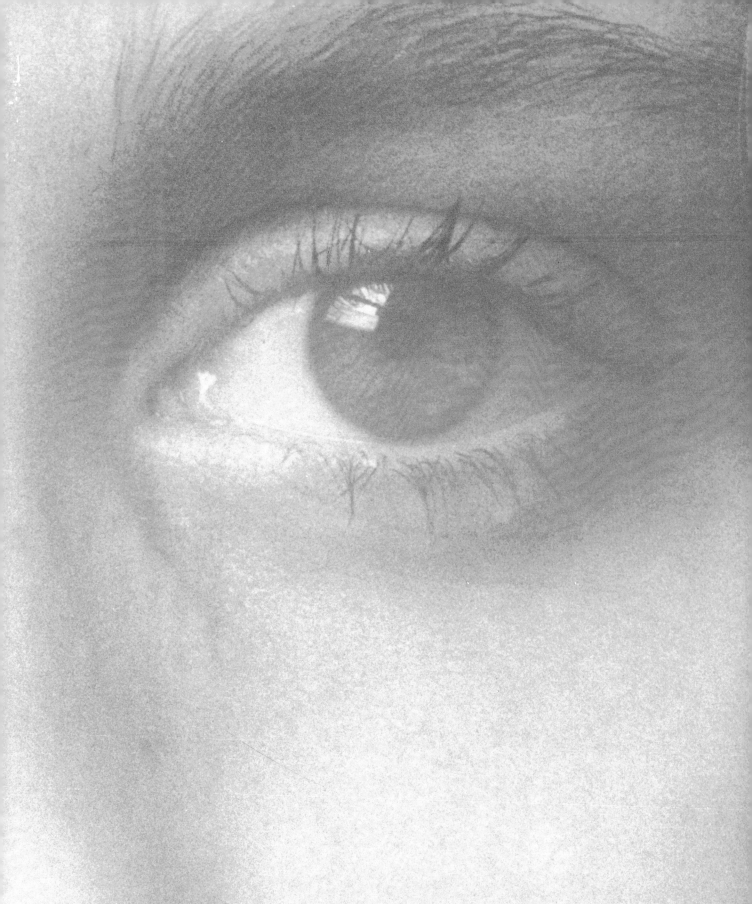

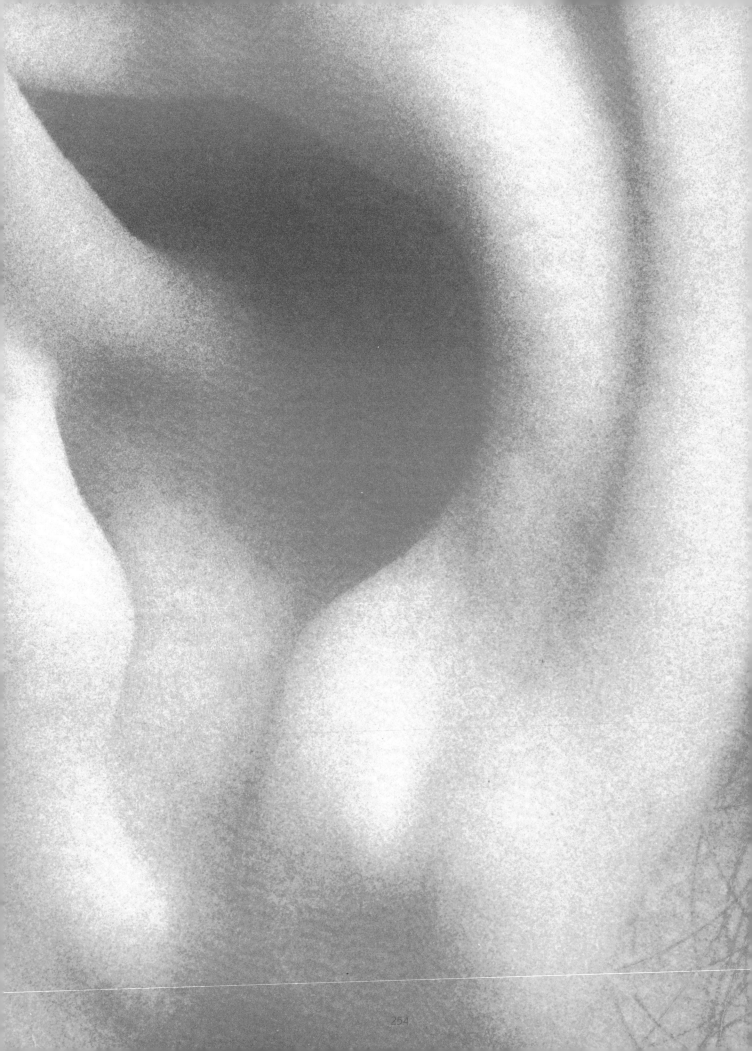

You're at a party and you find yourself feeling quite attracted to someone there. This person has a partner present, as do you. But you manage to touch casually during conversation, to watch the way he or she moves and talks . . .

You are in a locker room or steam bath. Everyone is in varying stages of undress. You find yourself consciously keeping your eyes straight ahead, although you have an overwhelming desire to look at those other bodies between towels, showers, changes . . .

Observations Although many people think of voyeurism as being a little peculiar or perverse, we all have bouts of it. There is a lot to see from any public observation post. You can concentrate on nipples, asses, thighs, crotches, arms, legs, midriffs, and skin. You can check to see how underwear shows through clothes, how people move, and how they touch each other. You can speculate about their sex lives and think about how long it's been since they've had sex.

People-watching gives you an exciting kind of freedom to check out who is attractive to you or why they are attractive to the person they are with. Since you aren't going to talk to these people or even see them again, you can be bolder, more self-indulgent than you might be in more circumscribed surroundings.

At a private party you might be a little more careful. The twenty-second affair you have on the street might get extended in another setting. If you get scared or frustrated by such an attraction, you might not want anyone else to know about it. Still, those attractions do occur and it is possible to enjoy them for the duration of the evening even if they don't go anywhere. All sex doesn't end, and doesn't have to end, in sex.

In the baths you'd think that the sensual pleasures of exercising, steaming, and relaxing might extend to the viewing of other bodies. However, it isn't considered polite to express curiosity about the way the hair grows on others' bodies, to be thrilled about a bare breast or ass that isn't your own, to stare at another's genitals. Unless you belong to a group that espouses nudity, it is hard to be comfortable with your curiosity about other bodies.

Lest you think you are the only one who doesn't feel blasé in the showers, observe how people hold their towels, how some people are modest and some go through an exhibitionistic show. See if anyone drops their glance or seems curious about you. Consider how much this might have to do with people's fear about the homosexuality in themselves. Look for people who seem to be at ease. There is something erotic in the awareness of your own and others' self-consciousness.

An aspect of voyeurism which might be called aurism is the overheard conversation. There is something very exciting about the act of listening in. Part of it is the expectation that you might hear something particularly salacious and part of it is the idea that you are hearing something you shouldn't. There may be conversations you don't want to overhear, especially between people you know; but listening in in restaurants and bars, on trains and park benches, through walls and corridors can be very stimulating. Many people find that gossip has a similar erotic flavor. There's nothing like a peep into someone else's private world to appeal to your prurient interests.

Gamesmanship

It's poker night and a group of men is around your dining table. It's hot, you're all drinking beer, and most of the fellows have their shirts off. You're winning and so is Tom who sits across from you. It's the first time you've seen him shirtless and you're fascinated by the hairlessness of his chest and the smoothness of quite well-developed muscles. You'd like very much to bluff him this hand.

You are in a business meeting of an all-female office staff. You are very aware of the hierarchy here, based on positions in the company. You notice a kind of matronizing going on where women you find strong seem to be playing weak in this meeting. You also notice what everyone is wearing and you find your eyes resting on legs and hands and hair . . .

You like to take classes. There is something exciting to you about listening to someone who has a handle on Hegel or a pipeline to the occult. You find that you experience an almost sexual thrill out of acquiring knowledge and making certain abstract intellectual connections.

Observations In any "game" where there is something to be gained, be it money, influence, or knowledge, something similar to sexual energy may be present. There is a sense of challenge, the possibility for seduction and aggression, for dominance and submission. There is often an element of flirting between people who are in competition for some kind of power, which goes on in same sex groups much as it happens in mixed groups.

You can also be sensitive to the interplay between the players in this game. There is the type of joking that goes on, the sexual references perhaps, the demonstration of skill. Some participants may act out particularly masculine or feminine roles, based on who is winning and losing, who is most dominant or submissive in the group, and so on.

Office politics bring out similar erotic elements in that people play almost sexual roles in relation to who has and who wants power. Then there is proximity—you spend several hours a day in close contact with people whose bodies, clothes, habits you know almost as intimately as you know a partner's. You may not choose to find this knowledge sexual in any way, but there is nothing odd about a little idle speculation even in same sex groups. Sexual tension can exist without sex.

People may play up or play down their capabilities in a group, depending on who they are trying to seduce. One boss may be susceptible to sycophants, another to go-getters. People in charge get others to work by seduction or threats, by fraternization or authoritarianism, by challenge or flattery. There are multitudinous relationships that are not sexual at all in which you may experience an exchange of sexual energy. Whether you find these erotic or not depends on you.

That excitement of seeking answers and making connections in or out of the classroom has an extra dimension for some people. The searching that goes on in intellectual, religious, mystical pursuits can represent a desire to know, a longing to be involved, a hunger to learn, a need to be with like-minded people. The energy that brings people together, for P.T.A. or therapy, may have some erotic overtones.

256

Consumption

You are driving along daydreaming when a beautiful, long black sports car pulls up beside you. The driver is wearing some heavy jewelry, shades, and he holds the wheel as if it were a woman.

There is a woman ahead of you on the street who just reeks of money and Norell. There is something well taken care of about her, an aura of luxury and of having plenty of time.

You love to shop. You really can't stop buying little outfits and cosmetics and exercisers and vacations that you think will improve your looks or your life.

Observations There is a strong assumption in this country that if you have money you can afford the erotic life. Fast cars, fine restaurants, Miracle Mornings at Elizabeth Arden's, yachts, designer clothes, and many, many other trappings are all seen as conducive to a sexier, more exciting existence. This is a fact not lost on Madison Avenue. Thanks to the sexual images in advertising, consumerism is advanced as a sexual necessity.

The trouble with making this assumption is that you may ignore the erotic life all around you, the things in your own real environment that are or can be erotic to you. Although looking at the man in the beautiful car or the woman who smells of money may give you a little boost, waiting to be in their Guccis may mean you'll miss what's happening right under your nose.

It's not uncommon to be the victim of advertising that promises a new look or a new you. Almost anyone can be manipulated by such hopes, at least occasionally. Spend some time thinking about what products you use throughout the day and what your association is to them from advertising. Think about when you feel "like a million bucks."

Another kind of consumerism you may eroticize, perhaps to your own detriment, is a life style that is different from yours. Just as people want to buy into the rich life style, they "buy" into the counter-culture. Many people go around thinking that those who are black, hip, young, or homosexual live more fulfilling sex lives than others do. Others have images of the suburbs, the beach, or co-ed dorms as being hotbeds of swinging sensuality. It's a mistake to think that erotic is exotic, expensive, or remote. It's wherever you are.

Contact sports

You are visiting friends who have a new baby. You become aware while holding it that a little tingle goes up your spine as the tiny thing makes sucking motions against your arm and chest.

Although the person cutting your hair is perfectly impersonal, you get a little palpitation every time your ears and neck are touched by his fingers. Even that fleet comb seems suggestive.

Your girlfriend's cat has a beautiful, shiny coat and loves to be stroked. There is something about petting him that really pleases you.

Observations There is an amazing amount of incidental touching that goes on in everyday life which would be considered erotic if there weren't some barriers to thinking it so. For instance, real contact sports do give you opportunities for holding onto others in intimate ways. You may not allow yourself to think about the pleasure in that. If the game is with your own sex, too much touching might imply that you were "unnatural," and that certainly wouldn't do. In a mixed group you can get by with a little touching, but groping isn't polite.

There are many non-sporty situations, however, where you come into contact with another body or bodies. Most of us have learned to depersonalize the touching that goes on in a crowded bus or elevator, but every so often something about that serried flesh gets to you, or to someone near you. Then there are the accidental bumpings into others, the slaps on the back or bottom, the hello or goodbye kiss, the casual physicality of children.

A baby is a totally erotic creature, unable to separate itself from its environment. When you hold it, you become part of its world in a way you never do when touching an older child or an adult. A baby doesn't respect boundaries about what is "safe" to nuzzle in public and what isn't. It will reach for a breast or a penis with the same simplicity that it reaches for a finger. You are reduced to being an object for a baby, often an erotic object of some sensual gratification. You may be able to turn this around and enjoy the baby as much as it enjoys you.

The man or woman who cuts your hair probably isn't thinking about the downy film on your neck or cheek, but what if they were? It could be a very exciting job to be required to massage scalps, explore ears, run fingers through hair. The same is true of the shoe salesman who likes feet and the seamstress who likes measuring. The important thing is not so much what they think as what you think they think. In eroticizing their lives unbeknownst to them, you eroticize your own.

Having yourself taken care of, from a simple haircut to an elaborate massage, is often a sensual experience. Just the idea that you are being improved, relaxed, or served may be exciting. There is also the sensation of having someone touch a part of your body purposefully and not sexually. Even feeling uncomfortable in these situations could be erotic.

Cats are pretty standard erotic symbols but other animals may be more suggestive to you. You may be among those who report being excited by animals in zoos. Some people are thrilled by huge birds, slippery seals, powerful lions. Then there is always the chance of catching some animals mating, which is a more straightforward sexual experience. Just think about how you react or would react seeing dogs, birds, monkeys copulating.

You may see something erotic in how other people react to such scenes, or to other unsolicited experiences. Check out how other people hold babies, watch animals, touch each other. Some people will turn away, some will hold their breath in hopes or fear it will continue, some don't seem to notice. Any of these responses may seem or be erotic for you when you see it. Like all the kinds of erotic we are discussing here, you can't make these things happen, but you can be aware of how you feel when they do happen.

Inanimate eros
There is something about a particular freeway interchange that thrills you every time you go through it. You can't explain it, but it turns you on.

You're watering your plants and all of a sudden you are seized by an overwhelming desire to press your thumbnail into your jade tree's succulent petals.

There is nothing quite so exciting to you as a good electrical storm. That charged air, the danger and expectations of rain are all like a sexual analogy for you.

Observations You really can eroticize about anything you want to. It doesn't have to be other people, social relationships, nude ladies, or peculiar experiences. There are many objects in art and in nature which you may find erotic, whether you have any direct sexual associations to them or not. Even though you may not want to and never have made love to a cantaloupe, it is possible to project your own sexual energy into that round, mellow, delicate, juicy fruit in a way that may surprise or arouse you.

Now freeways, as well as skyscrapers, sculpture, any building or objet, can be sexually interesting to you, whether the creator of that monument ever had eros on his or her mind or not. Some music and painting seems terribly sensual and arousing and is intended to be so. Other works may have a particular erotic appeal just to you. For some people an abstract composition, an Italian chair, or a perfectly tuned engine is erotic. Others like their inanimate eros to be a bit more explicitly sexual.

Speaking of engines and freeways, there are any number of moving vehicles that might seem somewhat exciting to you. Just think about taking off in an airplane, sailing, riding a roller coaster. And for the more everyday, there are cars, bikes, buses, and trains. Anything with a vibration, a lift off, a sense of motion is a re-creation of the sexual experience, at least for some people.

The jade tree and the cantaloupe are examples of objects that appeal to the senses. Many, many kinds of food, from the vine-ripened naturally plump tomato to the man-or-woman-made lemon meringue pie, can be seen or felt or tasted erotically. Just think about the things you take pleasure in eating, smelling, preparing, and so on. Some of that enjoyment, that incorporation, that oral gratification, must be sexual.

If you think of cooking or grocery shopping or gardening as a grind with no erotic potential beyond the box boy or the neighbor's gardener, you may find you can perk up those chores by regarding foods and plants as sexual objects. Pay attention to them. Touch them, smell them, rub them against your body.

Weather can set a mood, appeal to a sense of excitement or well-being, that permeates a whole day. Even if an electrical storm doesn't have much eros for you, perhaps waking up in a hot, steamy room does. Weather is connected to memories and if these are sexual for you, the weather may carry that message for you. If dry desert air makes you feel thin and sexy, don't fight it. If rain makes you more aware of your body or other wet bodies around you, use it. Whatever your associations, acknowledge and enjoy them. Being aware of what is happening around you means being aware of as many sense impressions as possible.

All kinds of things that you touch, sit on, pass through, eat, do, and

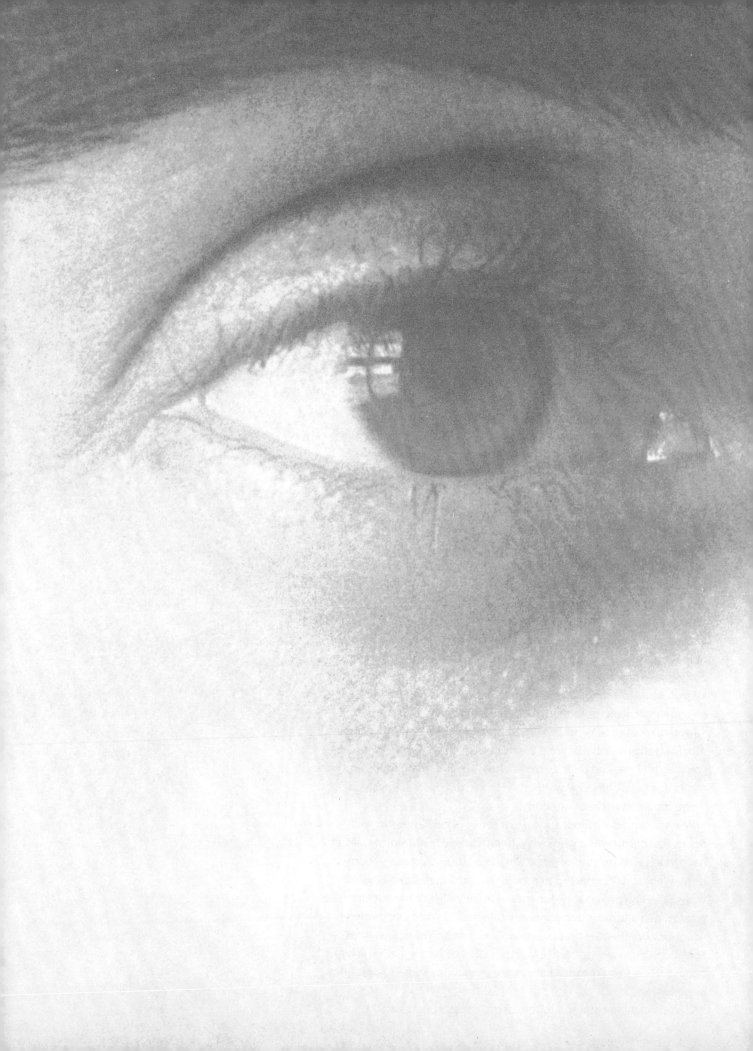

see daily may qualify as a little touch of eros. All around you are lines, shapes, movements, aromas, colors, auras, tastes, and things that might interest you in some special way. When you become aware of them, stop to think about why they appeal to you, what your associations to them are. Think about why their juxtaposition or timing seemed arresting to you. And stop long enough to enjoy them, not just become aware of them.

CONCLUSION

Although there is no need to find everything in your world erotic, you can train yourself to become more alert to the erotic around you just by paying attention. You have hundreds of chances daily to enhance your life with the perception of this extra dimension to ordinary experience. If you cut off or ignore these small thrills it may be because you have cut sex itself off from everyday life. To do that may be to make sex detached and forced rather than natural and lively.

One reason you haven't been asked to write anything down in this chapter is that there is no systematic way to find the erotic life. If you wrote down what you think you react to, you might not react spontaneously to the other things that you saw going on. So, what you must do is keep your eyes open, stay alert, and start noticing what you responded to after you do so. You can certainly wind up your journal with some reflections about your erotic life, but don't do so until you've lived it a little.

Conclusion

If you just read this book and haven't yet tried any of the suggestions, you shouldn't expect to know yourself much better than you did when you started. You will know more about the book and what's in store for you. But now you have to back up, try some of the suggestions, question your feelings and motivations. This is actually a workbook, with opportunities for really exploring your sexual concerns either alone or with a partner.

If you "did" the book, you do know more about yourself and about sex. You shouldn't worry if you couldn't cover all of the topics raised. This is a book that will last you a lifetime. Some of the things you are curious about or interested in you can return to later. You can also keep using this book as a resource when new situations or problems arise. Even the same old concerns may reoccur when you change your life or your partner. You can always review sections you need or run through sections you enjoyed.

Not only can you keep using the book, you can keep referring to your journal, if you made one. That journal could get to be a habit. You don't have to end it just because the book is ending. After all, your sex life is going to continue.

Besides returning to parts of the book that you liked because they were fun, interesting, or helpful to you, you could try returning to parts you didn't like too. If you didn't like them because they weren't interesting or relevant to you, fine. But if they discouraged you or made you feel inadequate in some way, don't give up. Maybe you were expecting too much of yourself or of the book. Maybe you haven't been able to work on or think about some particular subject that is bogging you down. Give yourself plenty of time and lots of tries when you come to something that you feel is essential but you just can't seem to deal with. Maybe you are rushing or becoming too compulsive. It is all right to feel frustrated, anxious, and unhappy in the process of working some hard things through.

Some people find it impossible to continue reading or doing a book like this. They get stopped somewhere and can't pick it up again. If you are one to which this happened and you are just reading the last pages to see how it turns out, consider this: You may have become bored or unable to continue due to some anxiety about actually getting rid of your concerns. That isn't unusual in any kind of therapy. It is hard to face changes sometimes. You may not even be aware of why you had to put the book aside. But you still have time to go back. Think about where you stopped and why. Perhaps that problem was about to go away. You could, of course, have been legitimately bored. Not "getting better," not liking the exercises, not wanting to involve your partner, could all be signs that you felt threatened by the imminent loss of your symptoms.

There is a phenomenon in sex therapy known as the ripple effect. This means that improvement or more enjoyment in your sex life ripples out to improve some other parts of your life as well. Now, although sex therapy won't make you a different person, give your life meaning, or change you in any basic way, there is plenty of evidence that feeling better about yourself sexually can extend to other areas of your life. Certainly the fact that you did something for yourself should give you

confidence. If you taught yourself to face your sexual concerns more openly and unself-consciously, you may very well be able to use the methods of sex therapy to look at other issues as well.

The ripple effect may not be something that works automatically, but you can encourage its development. Use the same approach as you've learned in sex therapy. Look beyond the immediate manifestations of the problem or concern to when you first noticed it, what other things were going on at the time, how it progressed. Then look to see if for some reason you have a particular investment in a specific problem that would make you want to keep it, unreasonable as that seems. Check to see if you are bored or unhappy with your life because you are not putting any effort into changing it. See how scary or threatening a change would be. Seek information and help to clear up gaps in your knowledge or understanding. And try to articulate your concerns to yourself, a partner, or others, if appropriate. You can act in your own be-half.

One thing is certain. You do know more about sex than you did. This information can help you in handling future sexual issues. The more you communicate about sex to a partner or with friends, the easier it will be to communicate about anything. Sex, from the erotic life to body image to specific dysfunctions, is hard to learn to talk about. That down, you can now go on to other things.

Remember that being observant, aware, honest, and patient will work in your favor. When you can see through yourself a little, you can start seeing other people. You can appreciate that everyone, including you, has likes and dislikes, strengths and weaknesses about sex. Being your own sex therapist doesn't stop with this book. Refer back to it, show it to a friend or partner, use your journal. More than anything else, though, use yourself. You are now your own best resource. Your reactions and observations are what count and they are what you should rely on.

Index

Abortion, 104, 106
Abstinence, 106
Adolescence, experiences during, 27-28, 31-32
Affairs: attitudes about, 64; first, 34; negotiating with partner about, 235-238; as sexual surrogate, 247-248
Afterglow, 131, 133
Age: arousal and, 45; attitudes about, 48; impotency and, 176; orgasm and, 202
Aggression, 241-242
Alcohol, 169-170
Allergic reactions, 148, 177
Amniocentesis, 104
Anal sex: attitudes about, 52-53; negotiating with partner about, 233-235
Anatomy. See Sexual anatomy and physiology
Animal sex, attitudes about, 66
Anus: self-examination of, 84, 86-87. See also Anal sex
Anxiety, 160, 162
Arousal, 110-123; age and, 45; barriers to, 110, 113; changes in patterns of, 115-116; impotency and, 165-166, 169; losing, 116; masturbation and (see Masturbation); nonorgasmic women and, 145, 147; recognition of, 113-115, 121; sensate focus exercises, 181-187; sex fantasy and, 16, 18, 118-119, 121
Attitude survey, 46-49; age, 48; anal sex, 52-53; animal sex, 66; breast size, 47; children and sex, 58-59; group sex, 67-68; homosexuality, 54-55; incest, 61-62; initiating relationships, 50; intercourse, 48, 59-60; love, 66-67; marriage, 51, 64; masturbation, 49; menstruation, 53; nursing, 60-61; oral sex, 57-58; penis size, 46-47; pornography, 62-63; rape, 56
Aurism, 255
Autoeroticism. See Masturbation

Bartholin's gland, 98
Bestiality, 245
Birth control, 101-109
Bisexuality, 154-155
Bladder infections, 37-38
Body image, 71-83; body scents and, 78; comparisons and, 80-81; mental picture of body parts, 71-76; self-image and, 81-83;

sensory examination of body, 76-80
Breasts: attitudes about size of, 47; childhood concerns about, 28, 31; self-examination of, 78, 97; stimulation of nonorgasmic women and, 147; surgery to, 44

Castration, 100
Cervix, 93, 98
Childbirth, 37-38
Childhood experiences, 23-32
Children: attitudes about sex and, 58-59; parental relationship with, 39, 41-42
Circumcision, 93, 95
Clitoris: self-examination of, 91, 93; stimulation of, 93, 119, 141, 147, 199-200
Clothing, 82-83
Coitus. See Intercourse
Coitus interruptus, 106
Communication, 208-219; conversation initiation, 212-213; during aftermath of orgasm, 133; importance of, 208; impotency and, 170-171; overcoming fear of, 208; practicing, 213-217; vocabulary, finding, 209-210, 212
Conception, 101-104
Condoms, 104-105
Conflict: during aftermath of orgasm, 133; power plays, 240-242; professional help and, 245, 250-251; scapegoating, 242, 245; sexual surrogates, 247-248; warfare, 245, 247. See also Communication; Negotiation
Consumption, 259
Contact sports, 259-260
Contraception, 101, 104-109, 148, 149-150, 177
Control problems: sensate focus exercises, 181-187. See also Orgasm timing
Conversation initiation, 212-213
Corona, 95
Cowper's glands, 99
Cunnilingus. See Oral sex

Detumescence, 131, 133
Diaphragm, 104, 105
Domination, 34, 240, 241
Douching, 106, 177

Eggs, 97-98, 103
Ejaculation: childhood reactions to, 28; in fifty to sixty-five year olds, 44; premature, 170, 189-195; retarded, 175; retrograde, 99; stages of, 122. See also Impotence; Orgasm; Orgasm timing

Ejaculatory ducts, 99
Endometriosis, 148
Enema, 87
Epididymis, 98, 99
Erection, 44, 95, 122. See also
  Impotence
Erotic life, 252-265; consumption,
  259; contact sports, 259-260;
  gamesmanship, 256; inanimate
  eros, 260, 263; voyeurism, 252,
  255
Estrogen, 100
Exhibitionism, 245

Fallopian tubes, 98, 106
Fantasy, 9-20; common examples of,
  9-10; versus dreams, 10; sex
  (see Sex fantasy)
Fellatio. See Oral sex
Fetishism, 245
Fidelity. See Affairs
Foreskin, 93, 95
Frenulum, 95
Freud, Sigmund, 10, 155

Gamesmanship, 256
Genitalia, self-examination of,
  84-97
Glans, 95
Gonad, 97
Group sex, 67-68, 245
Guilt, 117, 153, 173, 241

Homosexuality: affairs and, 235;
  anal sex and, 52; attitudes
  about, 54-55; fear of, 225;
  impotence and, 173; nonorgasmic
  women and, 154-155; rape and,
  241; used as sexual weapon, 245
Hormones, 44, 99-100, 130, 135,
  177
Hymen, 91

Impotence, 160-179; anxiety and,
  160, 162; defined, 160; in
  forty year olds, 42-43; physical
  problems and, 176-179; practical
  suggestions for treating, 162-169;
  psychological problems and,
  169-176
In-take interview, 250
Inanimate eros, 260, 263
Incest, 61-62, 154, 245
Inexperience, 34
Infections, 37-38, 148, 177
Infidelity. See Affairs
Initiation: of sex, 50, 240-241;
  of sexual conversation, 212-213
Intercourse: anal (see Anal sex);
  anatomical abnormalities and,
  152; attitudes about, 48, 59-60;
  first experience with, 32, 34;

frequency of, 221-224; increasing
  stimulation during, 200-201;
  negotiating with partner about,
  221-224; nonorgasmic women and,
  144-145, 147; painful, 148, 177;
  positions, 192, 194, 196, 200-201,
  203
IUDs, 104, 105

Johnson, Virginia E., 2, 98, 131,
  135, 143, 170, 181, 194

Kinsey, Alfred E., 12, 55, 224

Labia majora, 89
Labia minora, 89
Lateral position, 200-201, 203
Lexicon, sexual, 209-210
Love, attitudes about, 66-67
Lubrication, 87, 184

Marriage, attitudes about, 51, 64
Masters, William H., 2, 98, 131,
  135, 143, 170, 181, 194
Masturbation: attitudes about,
  49, 116-117; in childhood, 24,
  28; clitoral, 119; fantasy and,
  12; guide for men, 121-123;
  guide for women, 181-121; guilt
  and, 117; mutual, 149; negotiating
  with partner about, 228-229;
  nonorgasmic women and, 141
Mechanical stimulation, 118, 136
Medical problems. See Physical
  problems
Medication, impotence and, 177
Menarche, 98
Menopause, 43
Menstruation: attitudes about,
  53; childhood reactions to, 28;
  first, 98; hormone levels and,
  100, 135; orgasm and, 135;
  ovulation and, 102
Missionary postion, 194, 196
Moment of inevitability, 122, 192
Mons publis, 93

Necrophilia, 245
Negotiations: affairs, 235-238;
  anal sex, 233-235; frequency of
  intercourse, 221-224; masturbation,
  228-229; oral sex, 224-227,
  229-232; petty problems, 232-233
Nipples, 97
Nondemand position, 143-144
Nonorgasmic women, 138-159; physical
  problems and, 147-153; psychological
  problems and, 153-158; sexual
  troubles and, 140-147
Nudity, 76-77
Nursing, 60-61

Oedipus complex, 24, 154
Oral sex: attitudes about, 57-58;
  negotiating with partner about,
  224-227, 229-232; nonorgasmic
  women and, 143-144
Orgasm, 124-137; aftermath of,
  131, 133; analyzing, 129-131;
  anatomical abnormalities and,
  152; clitoral, 93; expectations
  about, 124-131; faking, 188-189;
  in fifty to sixty-five year
  olds, 43-44; first experience
  with, 32, 34; multiple, 131;
  myths about, 133, 135-136;
  painful, 148; timing of (see
  Orgasm timing); vaginal, 135;
  vaginal alkalinity and, 103-104.
  See also Impotence; Nonorgasmic
  women
Orgasm timing: before or after
  partner, 205; not fast enough,
  188, 197-203; simultaneous, 188,
  203-205; too fast, men, 189-195;
  too fast, women, 195-197
Ovaries, 97, 98
Ovulation, calculating, 102-103, 104

Pap tests, 93
Pedophilia, 245
Penile squeeze, 194-195
Penis: attitudes about, 46-47;
  childhood concerns about, 28,
  31; contraction of, in orgasm,
  127; erection of, 44, 95, 122;
  masturbation techniques, 122-123;
  self-examination of, 78, 93, 95;
  size of, 46-47, 95. See also
  Oral sex
Perineum, 84, 86
Physical problems, 37-38; impotent
  men and, 176-179; nonorgasmic
  women and, 147-153
Physiology. See Sexual anatomy
  and physiology
Pill, contraceptive, 104, 105
Pituitary gland, 99-100
Planned Parenthood, 150, 250
Pornography, 62-63
Power plays, 240-242
Pregnancy: fear of, and impotence,
  175; orgasm during, 136;
  unwanted, 101-102, 149-150
Premature ejaculation, 170,
  189-195
Priapism, 177
Privacy, 34, 45, 69, 215
Professional help, 245, 250-251
Progesterone, 100
Promiscuity, 245
Prostate gland: infection of,
  177; self-examination of, 86,

87; surgery to, 44, 99
Psychological problems: impotent
  men and, 169-176; nonorgasmic
  women and, 153-158
Puberty, experiences during, 27-28,
  31-32

Rape, 16, 18, 56, 241
Rectum, 86-87
Rhythm method, 104
Run-down condition, 148-149, 179

Sadomasochism, 245
Scapegoating, 242, 245
Scents, body, 78, 97
Scrotal sac, 89
Seduction fantasies, 16
Self-consciousness, 158, 166
Self-examination, 76-80, 84-87
Self-image, 81-83
Self-respect, 37
Semans, James, 194
Semen, 58, 99, 225
Seminal fluid, 99
Seminal vesicles, 99
Seminiferous tubules, 98
Sensate focus exercises, 181-187
Sex fantasy, 10-20; arousal and,
  16, 18, 118-119, 121; categories
  of, 10, 12; completion exercises,
  12, 14, 16; in early adolescence,
  32; experimentation with, 18, 20;
  explicit, 32; fear of, 18;
  learning about sexual attitudes
  from, 16, 18
Sex history, 22-45; defined, 22;
  earliest memories, 22-24; early
  adolescence, 27-28, 31-32;
  eighty year olds and beyond,
  45; fifty to sixty-five year
  olds, 43-44; first long affair
  or marriage, 34; first sexual
  encounter, 32, 34; forty year
  olds, 41-43; midchildhood, 24,
  27; puberty, 27-28, 31-32;
  sixty-six year olds and beyond,
  44-45; thirty year olds, 38-41;
  twenty year olds, 37-38
Sex hormones, 99-100, 135
Sex therapy, defined, 2, 5
Sexual anatomy and physiology,
  84-104; conception, 101-104;
  contraception, 101, 104-109;
  external genitalia, 84-97;
  internal genitalia, 97-99; sex
  hormones, 99-100, 135
Sexual aversion, 147
Sexual drive, differences in. See
  Negotiations
Sexual surrogates, 247-248
Sexual problems, nonorgasmic women
  and, 140-147

Sounds of the body, 79-80
Sperm, 98-99, 103, 104
Spermicides, 104, 105
Sterilization, 104, 106, 150
Submission, 240, 241
Surgery, 44, 99, 177
Surrogates, sexual, 247-248
Sweat glands, 89
Systemic diseases, 149

Taste, sense of, 78
Testes, 89, 97, 98
Testosterone, 99-100, 135, 177
Touch, sense of, 77-78
Transvestism, 245
Tubal ligation, 150

Urethra, 91, 95, 99, 127, 177
Uterus, 44, 93, 98, 127

Vacuum aspiration, 106
Vagina: contraction of, in
  orgasm, 127; increasing
  alkalinity of, 103-104;
  infections of, 37-38; muscular
  control of, 91-92, 121, 145;
  reproductive function of, 98;
  self-examination of, 91-93.
  See also Oral sex
Vaginal orgasm, 135
Vaginismus, 150-152, 176
Vas deferens, 99
Vasectomy, 150
Veneral diseases, 37-38, 177
Vibrators, 118, 136
Visual examination of body, 76-77
Vocabulary, sexual, 209-210, 212
Voyeurism, 245, 252, 255

Warfare, 245, 247
Wet dreams, 28, 135-136
Withdrawal, 106